THE US-MEXICO BORDER IN AMERICAN COLD WAR FILM

SCREENING SPACES

Series editor: Pamela Robertson Wojcik

Screening Spaces is a series dedicated to showcasing interdisciplinary books that explore the multiple and various intersections of space, place, and screen cultures.

Cinema, Gender, and Everyday Space: Comedy, Italian Style
Natalie Fullwood

The US-Mexico Border in American Cold War Film: Romance, Revolution, and Regulation
Stephanie Fuller

Movie Towns and Sitcom Suburbs: Building Hollywood's Ideal Communities
Stephen Rowley

Cinematic Geographies and Multicultural Spectatorship in America
Amy Lynn Corbin

The US-Mexico Border in American Cold War Film

Romance, Revolution, and Regulation

Stephanie Fuller

First published 2015 by
PALGRAVE MACMILLAN

The author has asserted their right to be identified as the author of this work in accordance with the Copyright, Designs and Patents Act 1988.

Palgrave Macmillan in the UK is an imprint of Macmillan Publishers Limited, registered in England, company number 785998, of Houndmills, Basingstoke, Hampshire, RG21 6XS.

Palgrave Macmillan in the US is a division of Nature America, Inc., One New York Plaza, Suite 4500, New York, NY 10004-1562.

Palgrave Macmillan is the global academic imprint of the above companies and has companies and representatives throughout the world.

Hardback ISBN: 978–1–137–53856–7
E-PUB ISBN: 978–1–137–53563–4
E-PDF ISBN: 978–1–137–53560–3
DOI: 10.1057/9781137535603

Distribution in the UK, Europe and the rest of the world is by Palgrave Macmillan®, a division of Macmillan Publishers Limited, registered in England, company number 785998, of Houndmills, Basingstoke, Hampshire RG21 6XS.

Library of Congress Cataloging-in-Publication Data

Fuller, Stephanie, 1983–
    The US-Mexico Border in American Cold War Film : Romance, Revolution, and Regulation / by Stephanie Fuller.
        pages cm.—(Screening spaces)
    Based on the author's thesis (doctoral—University of East Anglia.
    Includes bibliographical references and index.
    Includes filmography.
    ISBN 978–1–137–53856–7 (alk. paper)
    1. Mexican-American Border Region—In motion pictures. 2. Motion pictures—United States—History—20th century. 3. Borderlands in motion pictures. 4. Tourism in motion pictures. 5. Immigrants in motion pictures. 6. Aliens in motion pictures. I. Title. II. Title: United States-Mexico border in American Cold War film.

PN1995.9.M48F85 2015
791.43′658721—dc23   2015015275

A catalogue record of the book is available from the British Library.

Contents

Part III   Regulation

Figures

Figures

Acknowledgments

This book is based on research undertaken for my PhD at the University of East Anglia (UEA), which was funded by the Arts and Humanities Research Council, studentship award reference AH/I009582/1. I would like to thank the Screening Spaces series editor, Pam Wojcik, for her valuable feedback and guidance on the process of turning my thesis into this book as well as Shaun Vigil, Erica Buchman, and the Palgrave Macmillan team for all their assistance. Many thanks also to my PhD supervisor Mark Jancovich for advice and guidance throughout my time at UEA and to my examiners Peter Stanfield and Tim Snelson for their useful feedback on the thesis. Thanks are also due to Jann Matlock for support with the initial project proposal. I am grateful to the helpful staff at the British Film Institute library and the British Library for all their assistance. I am extremely grateful to Nina Mickwitz and Sophie Halliday for proofreading and providing comments on my thesis in its final stages, and especially for our Thursday night drinks in Norwich.

I must also extend heartfelt thanks to a great many friends and family who have given me their support throughout this process. Special thanks to Rachel Eddy, Sarah Ross, and Jo Phillips for regularly hosting me in London, visiting Norwich, and for some brilliant and much-needed holidays! I am also hugely grateful to Maria Thomas for her encouragement and generous advice on all aspects of academic life. Thanks as well to Mat Croft, Tamar Nissin, Eleri Lloyd, and Anthony Lloyd for their friendship and support.

Special thanks are due to Matthew Woody for his continuous support and interest in my project, helpful ideas, and moving to Norwich with me. To Sally, Graham, Carrie and Ellie Fuller, and Val and Roy Muscutt, I will always be grateful for your love and encouragement throughout my university career and for all the wonderful visits to Long Buckby, Lincoln, Heacham, and San Felieu.

Introduction

Screening the Spaces of the US-Mexico Border

The US-Mexico border has been an iconic space in American cinema ever since movies were invented. As the Ringo Kid and Dallas head across the border into Mexico to start a new life at the end of *Stagecoach* (Ford, 1939) (see figure 0.1), the border becomes a space of renewal and hope where their romance can flourish. For *South of the Border* (Sherman, 1939) starring Gene Autry's singing cowboy, the border similarly offers the promise of romance; but while Autry serenades a beautiful señorita one moment, he is captured by Mexican revolutionaries the next. Mexico also becomes synonymous with ideas of revolution in films such as *Vera Cruz* (Aldrich, 1954) and *The Professionals* (Brooks, 1966) as American heroes head south of the border to join the revolution and test their political ambitions against those of the Mexican radicals. In these and other movies, crossing the US-Mexico border has served as an escape from the regulations of American law. As Bart and Laurie tear south through the United States in *Gun Crazy* (Lewis, 1950), the international line harbors an elusive promise of escape from the police on their tail. But cinematic border crossings are also policed and regulated, particularly for those seeking to head north into the United States, and films such as *Border Incident* (Mann, 1949) dramatize the exploitation and hardships faced by Mexican workers in the American south. Marked variously by barbed-wire fences, border posts, rivers, immigration checkpoints, or by nothing at all, the US-Mexico border inhabits different forms in keeping with the different stories of romance, revolution, and regulation that these films tell. The 1950s saw perhaps the largest number of American films set on and around the US-Mexico border of any period of the twentieth century.[1] This book investigates

Figure 0.1   The closing scenes of *Stagecoach* see an early and iconic border crossing into Mexico depicting new horizons and a new start for the characters.

why this concentration of films appeared at this time. Its central aim is to explore what the analysis of this cinematic location might reveal about the culture and politics of this period in American history.[2]

While much existing scholarship has examined the relationship of particular genres such as science fiction and film noir to American culture in the 1950s, this book moves away from generic constraints to bring together a collection of films that are all set on and around the US-Mexico border and undertakes a spatially focused analysis of these movies.[3] It contends that through their explorations of the changes in policy and practice taking place along the borderline, the films also engage with cold war politics. The book focuses on eight central case study films that cover the period from 1949 to 1958: *Border Incident* (Mann, 1949), *Borderline* (Seiter, 1950), *Where Danger Lives* (Farrow, 1950), *Vera Cruz* (Aldrich, 1954), *Border River* (Sherman, 1954), *Wetbacks* (McCune, 1956), *The Tijuana Story* (Kardos, 1957), and *Touch of Evil* (Welles, 1958). These central case studies are supplemented with additional examples from the wider series of border films and are arranged thematically into chapters. The films were chosen to reflect a variety of genres and include both lesser- and well-known titles that were selected on the basis of the border's appearance as a physical location within the films' diegeses.

This book centers around a specific location and undertakes a spatial analysis influenced by the work of many cultural geographers who argue for the importance of employing analytical frameworks that focus on space. Yi-Fu Tuan's groundbreaking work *Topophilia* is a geographically centered study of history, culture, and society in which he undertakes a "survey of environmental attitudes and values."[4] In considering a dazzling array of places, cultures, beliefs, and environments, his spatially focused analysis brings new understandings to broad philosophical questions about "perception, attitude and value."[5] Michel Foucault has also argued that the study of space is a vital way of understanding the "tactics and strategies of power" within historical studies.[6] For Foucault, "space itself has a history in Western experience, and it is not possible to disregard the fatal intersection of time with space."[7] This book seeks to explore precisely the history of the spaces of the US-Mexico border, and for this reason, film, arguably the most spatially conscious media form, provides the central vehicle for this excursion. The book also joins recent developments in work on space in cinema, but hopes to offer a different perspective to studies that focus on filmic space in relation to specific genres.[8] Following the work of critics such as Giuliana Bruno, Tom Conley and Pamela Robertson Wojcik, I rather seek to engage cinematic space to interrogate existing generic criticism and structures, and, in Wojcik's words, to "attend to the spatial dynamics of...films and consider whether and how space sets the parameters for the plot, themes and ideology of not only individual films but also genres."[9]

In beginning from the border, the book seeks to explore how the cinematic boundary was produced during the cold war period, as well as to question the ways in which cold war culture has been defined by critics through generic frameworks. In his study of this era, Booker argues that "the science fiction of the long 1950s, in both novel and film, closely parallels the social criticism of the decade in the terms of its critique of American society."[10] Other generic forms of cultural texts are not considered in the study. Similarly, Peter Lev claims that at this time "critical social commentary was largely limited to indirect expressions in adventure genres such as the western and science fiction."[11] This book's focus upon mapping and cinematic spaces across a range of genres and industrial strategies offers a new way of thinking about the relationships between film, politics, and society that moves beyond canonical texts and questions of quality to consider a broad, inclusive range of films that engage with the border. As Franco Moretti advocates in his highly spatial approach to literature in *Graphs, Maps, Trees*, charting cycles of texts becomes a democratic act, enabling a shift in the study of culture "from the extraordinary to the everyday, from exceptional events to the large mass of facts."[12] Taking border crossings as its starting point, the book is methodologically informed by Homi K. Bhabha's assertion that "it is the 'inter'—the cutting edge of translation and negotiation, the *in-between* space—that carries the burden of the meaning of culture. It makes it possible to begin envisaging national, antinationalist histories of the 'people.'"[13] For Bhabha it is thus only possible to escape the reproduction of existing power structures in discussions of cultural difference through working from in-between spaces and borderlines, a path this book hopes to follow. By interrogating the value judgments behind studies of this period that are centered in genre, working from the boundary becomes a methodology that aims not to reproduce dominant power relations but to productively trouble them and open up wider possibilities.

The Cold War Border

The 1950s was a highly turbulent period in terms of border policy.[14] It saw temporary labor programs recruit tens of thousands of Mexican workers in the southern US, huge rises in undocumented migration, and mass deportation exercises.[15] Public opinion on the increased presence of Mexicans in the United States was sharply divided, with business leaders keen for labor programs to extend and expand, while American workers often saw the lowering of wages in the south as a direct result of the presence of documented and undocumented Mexican migrants.[16] Against this rising public objection, the year 1954 saw the deployment of "Operation Wetback." It was the largest deportation operation the country had seen and sought to remove Mexicans present in the United States without proper documentation and send them back beyond the border. The operation resulted in the deportation of around two million Mexicans, but in reality this also included many legally resident Mexican-Americans and Americans who were caught in the sweep.[17] In addition, the US government embarked on programs to increase the physical fortification of the boundary, to bolster Border Patrol presence, and to tighten regulations at border checkpoints.[18]

Given today's crises of migration, drugs, and violence on the US-Mexico border, it is crucially important to understand the boundary's history. Because this book contends that cinema is one of the key spaces in which the United States imagines itself, the history of cinematic engagement with the borderline becomes vital to understanding the way in which the border operates in American culture today. Despite continued efforts by US and Mexican governments to control the international boundary, it continues to see undocumented migrant traffic, drugs and arms trade, femicide in Ciudad Juarez, the rise of lethal cartel warfare, and the killing of unarmed migrants by American border police.[19] This book argues that representations of the border in American cold war culture served not just to engage with, debate, or raise awareness of border policies but also as an arena where the United States' place in the cold war world was negotiated. This implies that today too, cultural understandings of the border in American culture may be more closely related to the United States' global positioning than to addressing the critical situation on the borderline itself. In order to understand the problems with migration, drugs, and security that exist along the borderline today, we need to investigate how the meanings of the border are produced by and through culture, historically and up to the present day.

A range of books and articles have previously been published that specifically address the representation of the US-Mexico border in American cinema. These studies tend to view the cinematic border and Mexico as devices used to promote particular "American" ideals such as expansion and individualism. For David Maciel, the cinematic border represents "the lawless, primitive and rugged last frontier of the United States."[20] Maciel invokes the history of America's conquest of the continent, suggesting that films featuring the boundary represent the spirit of manifest destiny, or the God-given right to conquer any land, even Mexico. In contrast, Camilla Fojas argues that border films "do important social work: they offer a cinematic space through which viewers can manage traumatic and undesirable histories and ultimately reaffirm core 'American' values."[21] Carlos E. Cortés offers another view, suggesting that Hollywood's border serves simply as "a backdrop for American activity, a foil for displays of American superiority."[22] Although these scholars take different approaches, common to all of their arguments is the idea that Hollywood's cinematic border functions chiefly to champion or reaffirm American culture and identity—an assertion that this book seeks to challenge.

By the time of the Cold War, the United States had long seen itself as opposite and antidote to old world empires. The 1823 Monroe Doctrine had established the policy of preventing European interference and intervention in the Americas.[23] Through this foreign policy, the United States sought to prevent Latin America from becoming subject to colonization by Europe again. In the 1950s, the language of colonialism was enlisted in cold war debates and formed a key component of cold war rhetoric. The spirit of the Monroe Doctrine pervaded policy statements that declared the country fully in support of the "principles of self-determination for all peoples who desire it and are able and willing to undertake its burdens."[24] The US government framed the Soviet Union's encroachment into Eastern Europe as a colonial phenomenon and maintained a staunchly anticolonialist position itself, calling Russia the "largest existing colonial power" and condemning the "menace" of the "Soviet brand of colonialism."[25] However, as Mark Philip Bradley has suggested, this was a form of anticolonialism "in which racialized perceptions of backward non-Western peoples undercut support for immediate independence."[26] The US government regularly interfered and interceded in other countries and in Latin America in particular as part of its efforts to combat global communism. Intervention in countries such as Guatemala was sold to the American public as "a great act of Guatemalan self-determination, a popular uprising against Communist tyranny" rather than the quasi-colonial actions of a new global power.[27] Ostensibly aimed at combating communism, these actions directly undercut the Monroe Doctrine and government arguments about the colonial menace of the Soviet Union. Under Republican president Eisenhower, the US government also sought to build alliances with newly decolonized countries before Russia could move in. Richard Slotkin has argued that in order to build these connections, the United States employed tactics such as financial investment, political and military intervention, as well as the practice of "nation-building," which equated to actively creating an American friendly environment.[28] These actions and many others constituted a policy of what historian John Britton has described as "informal imperialism" across the globe.[29]

Colonialism was thus central to critical debate and discourse during the Cold War. William Pietz has asserted that cold war rhetoric stood precisely as a "substitute for the language of colonialism."[30] In particular, he argues that the work of George Kennan, George Orwell, Arthur Koestler, and Hannah Arendt and their debates about totalitarianism are articulated through colonialism.[31] For Pietz, one of the most significant elements of this totalitarianist discourse was its declaration of the "end of ideology."[32] Daniel Bell's 1960 treatise of the same name contended that the 1950s saw a "disconcerting caesura" in critical thinking that rejected political ideologies and saw an absence of clear distinctions between the political Left and Right.[33] Pietz finds this position analogous to Orwell's "doublethink" that served as "an updated version of British empiricist argumentation," directly linking the conclusions of Bell and other scholars writing in the period to the larger framework of colonial discourse that pervaded the Cold War.[34] The conclusions of cold war scholars such as Bell are engaged with and debated in the cycle of border films produced at this time. The same terms of debate are indeed shared throughout these films as they engage ideas of colonialism to explore the US-Mexico border. However, contrary to Bell's claims, which echo US government ambitions to eradicate dissent during this period, there remains a diverse and politically multifarious output of American films that reach into Mexico in order to interrogate the United States' relationship with the wider world.

Cinematic Border Crossings

One of the most prevalent narrative structures in cold war border films sees Americans traveling south into Mexico to pursue romance. The formation of romantic relationships through travel to Mexico lies at the heart of the narratives of *Where Danger Lives, Borderline, Wetbacks, Gun Crazy, Out of the Past* (Tourneur, 1947), *His Kind of Woman* (Farrow, 1951), and more. Part I of the book explores the confluence of these romance narratives with romanticized imaginings of Mexican locations. Histories of romantic tourism are used to explore the connections between tourism and romanticism, and close analysis of romantic images of Mexico is used to interrogate representation and mapping as colonial practices. The romance of exotic locations, which contrast with everyday sights and sites, is a crucial element of what John Urry has theorized as the "tourist gaze." For Urry, "such practices involve the notion of 'departure,' of a limited breaking with established routines and practices of everyday life and allowing one's senses to engage with a set of stimuli that contrast with the everyday and the mundane."[35] Implicit in Urry's search for contrast and breaks from the mundane is the need for an other to be maintained and kept fixed in place; an other which is often more traditional than modern US society. Rather than using Urry's terminology of the "tourist gaze," which as Bronwyn Morkham and Russell Staiff argue is reductive and collapses the relationship between different cultures, the book develops a conception of the touristic encounter through space and movement, and sites rather than sights.[36] Taking inspiration from Bruno's move away from visual conceptions of practices of viewing to one that is geographic, inhabited, and mobile, tourism will be understood as a physical, spatial practice rather than a vision-based one.[37]

Following this spatial approach to tourism, colonial discourses will be interrogated through ideas of space and cartography in the case study films. As Edward Said has argued, colonialism is always a necessarily geographic phenomenon. He attests, "To think about distant places, to colonize them, to populate or depopulate them: all of this occurs on, about, or because of land. The actual geographical possession of land is what empire in the final analysis is all about."[38] More precisely, and as other scholars such as Cole Harris suggest, it is the act of mapping that is one of the most powerful tools of colonization.[39] In questioning colonialism, the book also draws on Bhabha's work on colonial discourses and his understanding of mobilities in relation to power dynamics. Questions of motion and fixity are crucial to Bhabha's analysis, particularly in terms of the overwriting of others through stereotypes.[40] In its investigation of American travels in Mexico, the first part of the book will therefore examine the ways in which cinema participates in and illuminates these geographic colonial practices. In line with Said's approach, "colonialism" is used to refer to the physical settling and occupation of another state and "imperialism" to denote the processes and policies that accompany the domination of another state.[41] I understand both colonialism and imperialism to be "supported and perhaps even impelled by impressive ideological formations that include notions that certain territories and people *require* and beseech domination."[42] As the book will argue, many of the case study texts exert imperialist ideologies that construct Mexico as a state requiring intercession, and at a broader level, these ideologies will also be investigated in terms of US cold war policies of intervention in Latin America.

Although the films selected as case studies here fall within a variety of different genres, much work on the presence of Mexican cinematic locations to date has been undertaken within the field of Western genre scholarship.[43] Echoing the views of the critics writing on the border discussed above, Stanley Corkin and Christopher Frayling claim that Western genre films make use of Mexican locations and scenery principally in order to foreground the United States' greatness.[44] For these scholars, Mexico is used either as fodder for the expansion of the American nation or as an inconsequential backdrop to the adventures of American characters.[45] Corkin posits that Westerns made during the Cold War reflect the "inevitability of U.S. expansion" at this time.[46] Taking a similar position to Maciel, he argues that these films draw on the idea that America's history is imbued with manifest destiny and the right to control the entire North American continent. In contrast, Frayling contests that in many films

"Mexico simply provided colourful exteriors, cheap extras and a fashionably 'Third World' atmosphere."[47] While Frayling rightly moves away from the idea that Mexico is used as an indicator of American expansionism, like Cortés, his argument still understands the role of Mexico as one that serves to foreground and celebrate the United States in Western films.

Part II of the book examines films that use revolutionary Mexican backdrops, focusing on the central case studies of *Vera Cruz* and *Border River*, films that were generally classified as Westerns upon their release. In the past, much critical work on the Western has drawn on the premise, taken originally from Frederick Jackson Turner's "frontier thesis," that frontier mythology pervades cultural representations of the American west.[48] Slotkin's three-volume investigation into the frontier and American culture, *Regeneration through Violence, The Fatal Environment*, and *Gunfighter Nation*, is one of the most accomplished and influential of these works.[49] Peter Stanfield has highlighted this trend, and writes of work on post–Second World War Westerns that "there is a consensus that westerns do 'speak' to contemporary concerns, and that this is best translated through the myth of the frontier."[50] While Slotkin's study of frontier mythology is hugely important, it, and the works of others that follow from it, reduces the many complexities and contradictions within the Western genre to a singular mythology. Stanfield challenges the frontier mythology approach, arguing that Slotkin's formula cannot account for the diversity of Westerns produced in the 1930s.[51] Following Stanfield, Part II of the book will contend that frontier mythology is an equally inadequate account of the Western genre in the cold war period. Rather than responding to the frontier, Western films which are set on the border engage with their contemporary cultural contexts through questions of colonialism. Considering the films through the cinematic space of the US-Mexico border, the book suggests that existing accounts of the Western genre in the cold war period are thus too restrictive and too narrowly focused on frontier mythology.

This book joins a growing body of scholarship concerned with cold war culture that seeks to understand the connections between American film and politics in the 1950s. As such it engages closely with works such as Lary May's *The Big Tomorrow*, Alan Nadel's *Containment Culture*, and Michael Denning's *The Cultural Front*.[52] Looking beyond the politics and policies that directly relate to the US-Mexico border, the wider political situation in the United States in the 1950s was a highly complex one. With the onset of the Cold War, concerns about both external and internal communist threats were growing, culminating in the hunt for communist party members led by Senator Joseph McCarthy and the House Un-American Activities Committee (HUAC). A great deal of attention was focused on Hollywood during this process, as HUAC called on liberal, left-wing, and communist Hollywood personnel to admit to membership of the Communist Party or to name the names of those who were members. This resulted in an atmosphere of high pressure on industry personnel, with many blacklisted and left unable to secure work, and tight regulation of film productions by censorship bodies and studios. The prevailing culture of the 1950s has been described by film historians Ronald and Allis Radosh as "a dark period" for Hollywood, and by May as "intolerant and monolithic."[53] It resulted, according to Drew Casper, in the "fear, hatred, and eradication not only of the card-carrying, the fallen-away or, as in most cases, the suspected commie, but the foreigner, the intellectual, the radical and...the liberal as well."[54]

Much scholarly attention has been paid to left-wing groups and individuals operating within the Hollywood system during the 1930s and 1940s.[55] However, when it comes to the 1950s, much of this work argues that this vibrant left-wing culture was quashed as Hollywood came under the spotlight of communist investigations, leading studios to ensure that their movies were at least banal if not virulently anticommunist in stance. For example, while Paul Buhle and Dave Wagner argue persuasively that film was a crucial vehicle for the communication of leftist politics from the Depression onward, they also assert that this politicized period of Hollywood's history ended in the early 1950s.[56] At this time, they claim, "the gatekeepers slammed the gates shut," apparently precluding the production of any leftwing or liberal films after this period.[57]

Similarly, both Nadel and Casper contend that the 1950s saw the production of movies that were largely apolitical and simply reflected the position of the US government. Both critics emphasize that leftist movements fell away during the Cold War as society coalesced behind a new, more homogenous, political consensus. Casper contends that "any deviation from Cold War orthodoxy" during this period was "highly problematic."[58] Similarly, for Nadel's model of containment culture, the 1950s bore witness to cultural texts that served simply to "repeat or modify the narrative that unifies the sexual, political, and economic aspects of containment" before the emergence of more subversive forms in the 1960s.[59] Historian John Fousek also supports the notion that during the 1950s political consensus reigned in the United States. Fousek argues that cold war rhetoric pitted the United

States against the communist threat from Russia and championed capitalist society in expressly American terms. He claims that it was therefore through a specifically "American nationalist ideology" that the Left and Right came together in this period.[60]

Conversely, other scholars have begun to identify moments of radical politics that persevere into the 1950s. May finds potentially subversive challenges to the political consensus within film noir and teen rebellion movies, which, he argues, grew into the more outspokenly countercultural filmmaking of the 1960s.[61] Denning too charts fractures in the supposed political consensus, arguing that the broad left-wing movement known as the popular front remained a divided entity into the mid-century period with many different elements working outside and against the political consensus. Denning asserts that "the communisms of the depression triggered a deep and lasting transformation of American modernism and mass culture," which, rather than simply evaporating during the Cold War, persisted through the 1950s and beyond.[62] As a counterpoint to Fousek's claims that political consensus was framed in American nationalist terms, Denning argues that the popular front actively celebrated connections between the United States and the rest of the world and between different ethnicities within the country.[63] This resistance to the consensus was thus a multicultural one, which looked both inside and outside of the United States to build an inclusive, heterogeneous identity. For the Left, Denning claims,

> the romance of revolution was manifested not only in the popularity of the Soviet films of Eisenstein and Pudovkin, but also in the romance of the Mexican revolution, embodied in the grand murals of Diego Rivera and José Clemente Orozco, the novels of B. Traven, and the films *Juarez* and *Viva Zapata*. The success of the Popular Front politics of international solidarity lay in the ability of these narratives to displace the imperial fantasies of race war that dominated American popular culture.[64]

Mexico thus began to play an important role within the leftist movement's notion of international solidarity and multicultural identity. The images of Mexican revolutionaries popularized by Rivera, Orozco, and other muralists were echoed in Hollywood movies, creating an indelible link between left-wing politics and Mexican revolution that would persist within American cinema throughout the twentieth century. Additionally, as Rebecca Schreiber has argued, Mexico provided an important safe haven for many communist and left-wing artists and filmmakers fleeing persecution in the United

States during the HUAC investigations.[65] Therefore Mexico played a vitally important role in the cultural imaginary of the American Left during this period and occupied a central position in the country's political imagination more broadly.

Cinematic images of the US-Mexico border enact a diverse range of positions across the political spectrum. While some films depicting this location present noble Mexican revolutionaries and exploited migrant laborers, others show despotic rebellion leaders and usurping invaders. Rather than viewing the 1950s as a period of benign, "escapist and sentimental" films, through close analysis of the ways in which images of the border and Mexico are used, this book argues that the 1950s did indeed see a body of political films that use the US-Mexico border to articulate questions about the United States' position in the cold war world.[66] Part III of the book explores the political relationship between filmmakers and the content of these border films, both through the theme of regulation that runs throughout the texts, and by exploring the forms of political and cultural regulation that the productions were subject to. Connections between regulation and mobility are of central importance to the analysis of the way the films present power and politics. Centering on the case studies *Border Incident*, *The Tijuana Story* and *Touch of Evil*, ideas of regulation and mobility also inform the political movements that are central to their narratives and play important roles in their production contexts.[67]

Mapping Methodologies

In line with a research project that is focused on the representation of a particular space, my close textual work on these films has a literal, spatial, and geographic focus in both visual and narrative analysis. Drawing on the scholarship of cultural geographers such as Peter Jackson, the book begins from the premise that analyzing a particular space can reveal information about a culture; in Jackson's words, it understands that "culture is *spatially constituted*."[68] The close textual analysis of the cinematic space of the films is interested in features such as the appearance and layout of buildings within a scene, the positioning of structures in the background of a shot, or the movement of the camera within and around a space. In this way the book owes a clear methodological debt to film scholars Bruno and Conley and their explicitly physical and geographic approach to textual analysis of film.[69] Bruno's filmic "voyageur," as a challenge to the traditional voyeur of film studies, has guided me through the places and spaces of the cinematic border, where this book explores (in a physical, spatial sense) the cinematic sites within the frame.[70]

Conley's assertion that "maps appear in most of the movies we see" also informs my analysis of the cartography of the cinematic border.[71] His claim that "a map in a film is an element at once foreign to the film but also, paradoxically, of the same essence as film" is a position that echoes through the book as it investigates the ways in which cinema works to map out the border.[72] In this approach, I am also inspired by Edward Soja's notion of "Thirdspace" and hope to contribute to the broader project of investigating the "simultaneity and interwoven complexity of the social, the historical, and the spatial, their inseparability and interdependence."[73] Soja's *Thirdspace* also speaks to marginality and the process of "*restructuring* that draws selectively and strategically from . . . two opposing categories to open new alternatives."[74] In focusing specifically on the borderline between the United States and Mexico, here, I too hope to open new alternatives and approaches from a space in-between.

This spatially focused textual analysis is combined with postcolonial approaches to discourse analysis, drawing in particular on Said's work on "Orientalism" in order to comprehend the ways in which American images of Mexico operate.[75] Notwithstanding criticism leveled against *Orientalism* for oversimplifying and reinforcing the binary oppositions his text seeks to identify and question, key elements of Said's argument remain of use in examining the relationship between different cultures.[76] Said argues that Orientalism, the process by which Western countries distinguished between the Orient and Occident, "responded more to the culture that produced it than to its putative object, which was also produced by the West."[77] Building on this premise, the book understands the cinematic images of Mexico and the border as a response to the culture that produced them rather than bearing a direct relation to any "real" border or Mexico. These films are active participants in the production of the spaces and cultures they represent. Conceptualizing the United States and Mexico as "imagined communities," I am therefore concerned with the ways in which the United States imagines itself through images of the border and Mexico.[78] I assert that film is one of the key forms in which this cultural imagining takes place and that in order to understand what the border means, both today and historically, we must interrogate the history and legacy of the cinematic border.

Alongside textual analysis, the book will attempt to resituate the films within some of their original cultural, political, and historical contexts in order to better appreciate the significance they may have held within their contemporary cultures. Primary research into newspapers, magazines, and other commentary is undertaken in publications including the *New York Times*, the *LA Mirror*, and *Life* magazine. This research is combined with a range of secondary historical sources to build a picture of the environment in which these films were produced.[79] Of course, when undertaking historical research the lens of the present can never be fully escaped, and this contextual approach will inevitably construct just one of many possible arguments about what the role and function of the US-Mexico border was in cinema at this time. Research into the contemporary critical reception of films is conducted in newspapers, trade press, and fan publications such as *Variety, The Hollywood Reporter*, and the *Motion Picture Herald*, and is focused on commentary around the representation of Mexico.[80] The personal politics of key members of cast and crew are also investigated through magazine and newspaper interviews, biographies, and autobiographies in order to examine the impact that individual filmmakers may have had on the movies. In terms of authorship, films are understood as cultural artifacts, produced through a collaborative process in which contemporary society at large leaves as significant an imprint on movies as any individual filmmaker involved in them. Therefore, special attention is paid to attempting to contextualize the movies through an understanding of that contemporary culture, which complements and counterpoints research into individual filmmakers' personal and political positions.

Combining textual and contextual work, this two-strand method of analysis looks to the borderline and marginal zones of films in order to destabilize their narratives and explore the political implications therein. This deconstructive approach understands that all texts are inherently contradictory and, following Jacques Derrida, that small, marginal details always already present within the text can unhinge the whole at any moment.[81] For instance, the book considers the implications of signs and billboards in the background of the filmic space for representations of American tourism. It also questions, for example, the impact that Ricardo Montalban's involvement in the Chicano civil rights movement may have had on the construction of his star persona both within films and in the press. Although small details in the background of shots and fragments of biographical information may appear to be marginal concerns, they can offer new perspectives and entirely reframe our understanding of films.

The borderline is referred to throughout the book as the "US-Mexico border." Of course, this is incorrect as the boundary is just as much the "Mexico-US border," but because this project focuses on American images of the border, it uses the name given to the dividing line in these American films. Borrowing Jeffrey Geiger's approach, I avoid using "America" as a noun because it seems to casually appropriate the whole continent, instead referring to the country as the "United States." But I make use of the adjective "American" precisely because, as Geiger argues, it "indicat[es] a powerful idea—and hegemonic construct...—of national identity."[82]

The Route Ahead

The book is divided into three parts, which focus on the themes of romance, revolution, and regulation, while issues of colonialism, genre, and cold war politics thread through and across these thematic divides. Part I centers on the representation of Mexico as a romanticized and romantic site. Close textual analysis of the ways in which border crossings physically manifest in cinematic space is used to argue that these representations of Mexico engage explicitly with questions of the United States' imperial relationship with the country. Chapter 1 centers on *Where Danger Lives* and a number of other films that dramatize escapes across the border from the United States into Mexico. Through exploring the history of romantic travel, this chapter investigates the practice of tourism, positing a mobile and moving tourist encounter. Chapter 2 focuses on *Borderline*. It argues that while crossing the border into Mexico enables the film's American protagonists to playfully perform different identities as they travel the country, it also calls into question the practice of ethnic passing in Hollywood and the film industry's flexible approach to ethnicity at this time. The third chapter takes *Wetbacks* as its starting point in order to examine the depiction of Mexico as an exotic location. It argues that in overwriting Mexican terrain with American exoticism, *Wetbacks*, alongside other border films, foregrounds the imperial processes at the heart of the romanticization of Mexico.

Part II of the book considers the importance of revolution in American visions of the US-Mexico border. Taking as its focus two films most often classified as Westerns, this part challenges accounts of cold war cinema that focus on genre by resituating these films outside of Western genre frameworks. Chapter 4 examines *Vera Cruz* and its representation of individualism and collectivism to argue that it responds not to a Western frontier mythology but rather to ideas of revolution and radical politics. The chapter explores the connections between the film's cinematic Mexican spaces, its political positioning, and its understanding of the US-Mexico relationship. Chapter 5 continues with this theme and engages *Border River* to interrogate existing academic work on the frontier and cold war culture, arguing that questions of space and territory are linked directly to colonialism in the film. The positioning of gender in frontier studies and Western genre criticism is also analyzed, and the chapter argues that the politicization of female Mexican characters in *Border River* and other revolution films lends them a centrality not often recognized in films of this style and period.

The final part of the book focuses on the theme of regulation and is particularly interested in the regulation of movements, both physical and political. In coupling brief production and industrial histories with textual analysis, this part investigates the politics of films as well as the industry regulation that they may have faced. It argues that despite the ostensible political consensus of the Cold War, the involvement of key left-wing Hollywood personnel in many of the case study films suggests that the US-Mexico border served as a space that enabled the articulation of dissenting politics and a broad spectrum of heterogeneous ideologies. Chapter 6 centers on *Border Incident* and its dramatization of the policing of the border and Mexican migrants, arguing that it is through the theme of regulation that the film challenges labor practices in the United States. The migrants are controlled and dominated through their lack of freedom of movement, and the chapter considers the connections between political and physical mobility. Chapter 7 examines *The Tijuana Story*'s depiction of the border city of Tijuana and argues that the film challenges prevailing cinematic visions of the city through deliberately fragmenting and fragmented perspectives. The chapter thus contends that the cinematic city can form a vital space of postcolonial resistance. The final chapter focuses on *Touch of Evil*, arguing that it must be seen in the context of this entire series of border films rather than as a standalone Wellesian masterpiece. Focusing on the representation of stasis and movement, the chapter asks what space and mobility might reveal about the film's production of identity, its politics, and its construction of the United States as an imperial influence in Mexico.

Two further major fields of study with which this investigation intersects are Chicano studies, the area of scholarship arising out of the Mexican-American civil rights movement that emerged during the 1950s and 1960s, and Chicana/o studies, borne out of

Gloria Anzaldúa's groundbreaking *Borderlands/La Frontera: The New Mestiza*, which was published in 1987.[83] While these areas of scholarship are drawn upon and engaged with throughout the book, the historical nature of this project means that it is largely focused on the hegemonic social, cultural, and critical approaches of the cold war period. Some of the many complex themes and debates of Chicana/o studies will therefore be considered in more detail in the conclusion to the book, which explores the implications of this study for cultural understandings of the border today within both the United States and Mexico.

Part I

Romance

Chapter 1

The Romance of Mexico: Tourists, Fugitives, and Escaping the United States

M argo Lannington's plan to escape across the border into Mexico forms the central narrative thrust of John Farrow's 1950 film, *Where Danger Lives*. The film takes the protagonists motoring across the United States, dramatizing Lannington's fall "from Penthouse...to Bordertown Dives!" as promised by the movie's trailer. Played by Faith Domergue, Lannington's romantic dream of Mexico pervades the whole film. This dream motivates her to pursue the charming Dr. Jeff Cameron (Robert Mitchum) and persuade him to start a new life with her south of the border. However, she is not drawn to Mexico solely for touristic reasons. Lannington is also on the run from American police and Cameron becomes entwined in her criminal plot. As they drive south toward the border the couple take on different disguises, pretending to be runaway lovers on their way to be married secretly in Mexico. The 1950s saw the production of a proliferation of American films that feature journeys to Mexico like this one, combining romance and escape from the strictures of American society in some form. Journeys to Mexico and the formation of romantic relationships are central to the narratives of films including *Where Danger Lives*, *Out of the Past* (Tourneur, 1947), *Borderline* (Seiter, 1950), *Gun Crazy* (Lewis, 1950), *His Kind of Woman* (Farrow, 1951), *Wetbacks* (McCune, 1956), *The Fast and the Furious* (Ireland, 1954), and *The River's Edge* (Dwan, 1957). In each of these films, US protagonists wanted by the police decide to flee to the Mexican border and their journeys take on both romantic and fugitive imperatives.

Romance has always been an integral element of tourism and travel, and it was during the Romantic period that tourism first became a popular pursuit in the West. Although many critics draw clear lines of influence between romanticism and tourism, the particular characteristics of romantic tourism have been debated widely. Patricia Jasen attests that "romanticism's association between images, commodities, feelings, and personal fulfilment was a vital contributing factor to the development of...the tourist industry."[1] For Amanda Gilroy, romantic tourism was characterized by a "fascination with...exotic topography and racial others" and offered "access to imaginary spaces of personal liberation and medicine for the troubled mind."[2] George Dekker asserts that touristic romanticism was inextricably linked to the literary form, claiming, "Romantic tourists and novelists shared an aesthetic that effectively defined both tour and novel as privileged spaces exempt from the boring routines and hampering contingencies of ordinary life and rich with opportunities for imaginative transport."[3] As in these notions of romantic tourism, in border-crossing films of the Cold War, the romance of traveling to Mexico is connected to the expansion of consumer culture and commodification. Exoticism and primitivism are also important features, as is the potential for imaginary liberation and "imaginative transport." This search for freedom and a contrast from everyday sights and sites is an important element of John Urry's "tourist gaze."[4] Also connected to ideas of primitivism, in an earlier study Dean MacCannell found that his data consistently pointed to the idea that "tourist attractions are precisely analogous to the religious symbolism of primitive peoples."[5] These conceptions of tourism require a more traditional and more primitive other to be kept fixed in place, positioning modern spectators in opposition to primitive sights. However, this chapter instead develops an understanding of the touristic encounter through space and movement, and sites rather than sights.

The border films' preoccupation with escapes to Mexico is deeply connected to American cultural mythologies of the romance of Mexico. These romantic understandings of the country play out the relationship between tourists and the sites they encounter as spatial and mobile in nature. Newly available to ordinary American families in the 1950s, automobiles played a crucial role in this new notion of romantic travel. In particular, the opening of the Pan-American Highway meant that the lure of Mexico was entirely caught up with the romance of the road. In *Where Danger Lives*, *Gun Crazy*, and *Out of the Past*, Mexico becomes a romantic dream where characters can begin life anew, offering escape from the American law and criminal interests that pursue them. It is this dual role as both touristic ideal and fugitive escape that Mexico inhabits in these films and in the wider US cultural imaginary at this time.

Escaping the United States: Fugitives, Tourists, and Politics

Since its establishment in the nineteenth century, the US-Mexico border has functioned as a symbol of escape from American rules and laws.[6] It is estimated that by the 1850s over four thousand American slaves had crossed the border into Mexico where slavery was outlawed and no extradition treaty was in place.[7] Later, the Civil War saw many Confederates escape into Mexico to avoid imprisonment. Perhaps the most famous border escapee was the Mexican revolutionary leader Pancho Villa, who fled south into Mexico after an incursion into Columbus, New Mexico, managing to evade capture by US cavalry under the command of General John Pershing.[8] As Steven Bender has argued, the US-Mexico border has served as a route of escape as much for US citizens as for Mexicans and people of other nationalities, contrary to the depictions in today's media, which tend only to show Mexican wrongdoers fleeing across the border to safety.[9] In film too, the boundary has been presented as a route of escape for Mexicans and Americans alike. Early pictures such as *Mixed Blood* (Swickard, 1916) show both US and Mexican characters fleeing to the border to escape retribution and the movie *Bordertown* (Mayo, 1935) tells the story of Mexican-American Juan/Johnny Ramírez who has no option but to head across the border into Mexico when pursued on charges of murder.[10]

While early border films often featured tales of fugitives trying to escape law and order south of the boundary, by the 1950s the United States had also become increasingly obsessed with traveling to Mexico on vacation. This period saw a huge rise in American travel to Mexico. Newspapers describe an "amazing tourist boom" beginning in 1950, with more than half a million tourists crossing the border a year.[11] This explosion in journeys south across the international divide coincided directly with the advertisement of Mexican holiday resorts to the general public for the first time. Newspaper articles such as "Pesos Go Farther at Story-Book Acapulco" and "Acapulco—Resort City for Budgeteers, Too" emphasized that exotic resorts "no longer should be considered exclusively the playground for those with unlimited funds."[12] The inauguration of the Pan-American Highway also played a key role in drawing ordinary Americans into Mexico. The then 748-mile highway was hailed as "the only paved road reaching deep into Mexico," which enabled the holiday to start "the moment the border is crossed."[13]

Alongside the huge numbers of American tourists heading south, the many US artists, writers, and filmmakers who sought political refuge in Mexico formed another significant group of border crossers during this period. Mexico City was the destination of choice for many communists, liberals, and left-wingers avoiding prosecution in the United States, and newspapers often featured headlines about the need to close the border to fleeing radicals.[14] As Rebecca Schreiber reports, early cold war exiles included many African American artists who sought freedom from "racial discrimination and political persecution" in the United States.[15] They were followed by Hollywood workers who had been blacklisted by the film industry, such as screenwriters Hugo Butler, Dalton Trumbo, Gordon Kahn, Albert Maltz, and John Bright.[16] These cultural producers chose to leave the United States in light of "government harassment" under Senator McCarthy's communist hunt and fled the policies that could see them subpoenaed by committees or detained under the Internal Security Act.[17] Mexico was the country of choice for a number of reasons alongside its proximity. The lack of an extradition treaty, the fact that American citizens did not need a passport to cross the border (and anyone suspected of connections to the Communist Party would not have been issued a passport), and the cheaper cost of living were all important draws.[18]

While American tourism to Mexico functioned as a symbol and symptom of the type of "informal imperialism" that John Britton argues characterized the relationship between the countries during this period, it also provided these exiles a way to articulate concerns about the United States' connections with Mexico.[19] Writing of Willard Motley's work, Schreiber argues, "Tourism...functioned as a literary trope for discussing US racism and imperialism."[20] In his writing, "Motley's experimentations in point of view, specifically refracted across lines of race, class, and nation, contributed to...an expressly anti-imperialist mode of representation that, by staging indigenous perspectives that frame and challenge tourism, undermines the unilateral point of view that shapes traditional travel narratives."[21] For Schreiber, American imperialism is thrown into focus through the questioning and breaking down of traditional tourist perspectives. In the texts she analyses, the use of US tourism as a means of questioning the country's position in the world begins to destabilize the position of the United States as protector of the American continent and opponent of old world colonialism. Similarly, in the films this part of the book examines, the depiction of the United States' influence and intervention south of the border is questioned through tourism, travel narratives, and colonialism.

The Romance of the Road

The romantic draw of Mexico for Lannington and Cameron in *Where Danger Lives* is so strong that it structures the entire narrative of the film. Following the movie's exposition set in San Francisco, the characters drive steadily south from San Francisco through the changing American landscape until they arrive in the border town of Nogales. Once this journey begins, the film's locations are constantly changing and the narrative pace is fast. The story features various incidents that impede the journey, building tension as the protagonists get closer to reaching the borderline. A car crash in a small town almost exposes their true identities to the police and a strange encounter with a "Wild West Whiskers Week" festival in another frontier town detains them overnight. Police roadblocks and patrols force the couple to change their route, and they are eventually led into the dark backstreets and cabaret theaters of Nogales. These delays and holdups disrupt the journey to the border and serve to highlight the importance of the boundary in demarcating the limits of the narrative. The film's early dialogue prefigures the explicitly spatial story that follows. Before they leave, Lannington's husband (Claude Rains) warns Cameron, "If you take her, it's a long road and there's no turning back…time passes and then there's the end of the road." Cameron and Lannington's romance plays out spatially through their journey and the border functions as the "end of the road" for the narrative, which finally sees Lannington shot by American border police as she clings to the boundary fence.

Similarly, in *Gun Crazy*, the film's protagonists head steadily south throughout the film, eventually planning to cross the border, set up a ranch, and start a family together. As they travel through the country in a variety of stolen vehicles, their romance is played out on the road and their increasingly criminal endeavors are visualized through the cars' interaction with the landscape. The sale of automobiles rose sharply in the post–Second World War period in the United States, and at this time, traveling and exploring the country by car became an important part of what it meant to be American. Mark Osteen has argued that in the late 1940s and 1950s, "Americans internalized their identification with cars, commodifying themselves via automotive self-extension."[22] Osteen describes how this form of auto-mobility was marketed as a solution to all forms of personal problems. It also enabled ordinary families to travel and brought a new degree of freedom to American life. In his study of the production of free roadmaps by oil companies in this period, James Akerman has claimed that automobile travel and exploration of the United States became "the quintessential expression of American identity."[23] Drawing on themes of frontier mythology, Akerman argues that this new mobile construction of American identity emphasized moving, exploring, and mapping territory.[24] Traveling by car became an intrinsic part of what it meant to be an American at this time; the free maps were significant in that they often promoted routes away from major high-ways and pointed out sites of national interest, for example, national parks. For Akerman, this large body of free maps demonstrates the "industry-wide promotional argument that discretionary automobile travel was not merely a pleasant diversion, but was in fact an essential act of American citizenship in the twentieth century."[25]

The natural landscape and national parks play an important role in *Gun Crazy*'s journey across the United States. After deciding to get married, Annie Starr (Peggy Cummins) and Barton Tare (John Dall) spend their honeymoon in an idyllic natural paradise surrounded by tropical plants and waterfalls. As they drive through the countryside in this section of the film, automobility becomes a way of appreciating the great outdoors and the US natural landscape. Parts of the film were shot on location at the Angeles Crest Highway, a 66-mile stretch of road through the Angeles National Forest and its tight mountain passes. Driving against these dramatic natural scenes in an open-top car, the characters trace a route across the country, exploring and discovering the natural environment. At points, the camera hovers just in front of the vehicle looking through the windscreen at the characters as both camera and motor move through the countryside, shaking with every bump and shudder of the road. These shots literally transport viewers along with the car, creating haptic sensations of motion and automobile travel, and enacting the kind of mobile American identity Akerman describes. However, the characters' participation in this idealized American automobility lapses when they turn to crime in order to pay for their new life together. When they go on the run, the couple frequently change vehicles and disguises, finally deciding to head across the border to escape the police. In the film's final showdown, as the characters try to outrun the cops, the camera pauses on a sign indicating that they have headed into the Madera National Park. This time, however, their car tears through the landscape, not concerned with exploring or appreciating its natural beauty but with escaping the police, whatever the cost to the natural world around them. Driving too fast with dust filling the screen behind them, Starr and Tare run the car off the road into the forest. The characters are soon dispatched by officers, demonstrating that there are also unacceptable forms of American automobility.

In *Where Danger Lives*, the protagonists' automobile journey is also connected with ideas of national identity and American citizenship. In this film, emphasis is placed on the planning and mapping of the journey as the characters are regularly shown using maps in the car. While Lannington is at the wheel, Cameron traces their route with his finger along a folded road map, which may well be an example of the free gas station maps that Akerman describes. As the characters drive further south, shots of the vehicle amidst the landscape are shown, tracing its progress through the changing terrain. This emphasis on tourism and touring in *Where Danger Lives* and *Gun Crazy* also implicates cinema in the production of a mobile, traveling American identity. Examining the connections between cinema and earlier practices of spectatorship, Giuliana Bruno has argued that "the art of viewing followed the older touristic drive to survey and embrace a particular terrain: the compulsion to map a territory and position oneself within it."[26] Thus for Bruno, cinema derives from the very same genealogy as traveling and mapping, and shares with them an important spatial and geographic lineage. For these films the explicit emphasis on cartography and landscape brings this connection to the fore, and the film itself is positioned as a touristic act—one that is constitutive of American identity.

Touristic and Romantic Encounters

The acts of mapping in *Where Danger Lives* are closely linked to the positioning of the protagonists, and the film's audience, as tourists. Through their journey to the border, Cameron and Lannington are constructed as traveling subjects, and their identities become entwined with the journey itself. As the police follow their trail, Cameron and Lannington are constantly identified and defined by their vehicle. The convertible they set off in is swapped for a rusty van in order to throw off their pursuers. As they traverse the parched, empty desert, the action cuts between the incessant spinning of the vehicle's wheels and close-ups of the faces of the characters. A tracking shot moves along the side of the van from the front wheel to the back, with the blurred road filling the rest of the screen behind the vehicle. A close-up of a spinning tire fades into a shot of Lannington's face, and later another shot of a wheel turning relentlessly on the hot tarmac is faded across an extreme close-up of Cameron's eyes and forehead (see figure 1.1). This intercutting between the wheels and the characters' faces evokes not only their tense and whirling state of mind at this point in the journey but also constructs Lannington and Cameron as traveling subjects whose identities are inextricably bound with movement, touring, and travel.

These traveling protagonists participate in touristic encounters on their journey as they pass through two towns, pretending to be a couple on their way to wed in Mexico. In both places they are addressed as tourists, and the differences between the modern, vibrant city of San Francisco, where the movie began, and these old-fashioned, backwater towns become extant. The film's opening in San Francisco highlights American modernity, as skyscrapers glimmer and car headlights move steadily through the streets. Scenes of city buildings at night fade into one another, shimmering with the glamour and modernity of this metropolitan space. In sharp contrast, as the film approaches the border, the landscape becomes increasingly empty, dull, and deserted. The characters stop in two small towns, one called Postville and the other unnamed, which are home to bilingual populations of both Americans and Mexicans. The only Mexican speaking role in the

Figure 1.1 *Where Danger Lives* puts its protagonists on the road, merging images of spinning tires with close-ups of the characters.

movie is that of Pablo (Julian Rivero), an aging drunk driver who is helped out of trouble with the US sheriff by his Spanish-speaking friend Dr. Maynard (Harry Shannon). Pablo is unable to operate his decrepit car correctly, and is dressed in dirty, shabby clothing. He accidentally crashes into Lannington and Cameron, and this encounter cannot help but create contrasts between the modern Americans with their technology, smart clothes, and mobility, and the borderlands that are filled with broken vehicles and backward inhabitants who seem to be stuck in the past.[27]

Touristic encounters also take place in a bar in San Francisco early on in the movie. The set here features an explicitly tropical decor, with lush vegetation and palm trees filling the screen, creating the effect of an exotic untouched landscape. Cocktails are served in coconut shells, and seating is constructed of bamboo and foliage. As Cameron enters the bar, a long tracking shot follows him through the smoky atmosphere as he searches for Lannington, the physical movement of the camera recalling the exploring, tracking, and mapping qualities of American identity proposed by Akerman.[28] The tropical bar constructs the two lovers as tourists as they sample exotic drinks and food and dance the night away in a place outside of the space and time of their ordinary everyday lives. The bar prefigures their escape to Mexico as their romance is tied to the tropical space; this is the only place where they meet, and the lovers' language emphasizes this sense of spatial specificity as Cameron declares he wants Lannington "here, like this." The fact that they go on to encounter only barren, dusty landscapes and dark, dangerous towns on their journey is significant. Their dream of romantic Mexico is attainable only in the simulated space of the tropical bar, and likewise their relationship cannot survive the realities of their decidedly unexotic journey to Mexico. Through the difference between the reality of the characters' borderlands encounters and the romanticized vision of Mexico evoked in the bar, the film seems to call attention to its own exoticizing of the country.

Throughout *Where Danger Lives*, the modern traveling Americans are clearly contrasted with the backward borderlands dwellings and inhabitants that they encounter. Cameron and Lannington enact mobile, modern identities, which fix into place the undeveloped locations around them. Produced as the US tourists' others, these primitive towns are presented as artifacts and are fixed in time and place. Thus the film adds an extra dimension to Akerman's understanding of the connections between traveling and American national identity. While the depiction of tourism as an essentially American pastime produces an idea of the nation as mobile and explorational, it also constructs Mexico for the United States as a fixed, static space. In mapping out the mobility of traveling Americans, *Where Danger Lives* also demarcates and fixes Mexico into place. The romance of Mexico produces mobile, traveling American subjects but simultaneously takes away possibilities of movement for Mexico and Mexicans. This spatial manifestation of the difference between the two countries suggests that rather than Urry's tourist gaze, what is at stake is a matter of mobility and movement.

This is echoed in the way in which tourism and cinema are connected through Mexican landscapes in *Out of the Past*. In this film, ex-crook Jeff Bailey (Robert Mitchum) is sent to Mexico to trace Kathy Moffat (Jane Greer), the runaway girlfriend of a mobster. Bailey follows her across Mexico, finally catching up with her in Acapulco. Set against the resort's romantic Mexican backdrops, romance grows between the characters and they make plans to run away together. All of the Mexican scenes in the film take place as flashbacks and the country comes to function as a dreamy, unattainable past which cannot be reclaimed. As it depicts Bailey's initial journey south, *Out of the Past* clearly locates audiences as it travels through Mexico City, Taxco, and on to Acapulco through Mitchum's narration. The camera tracks high across the streets of Mexico City as if looking down from a plane and then hitches a ride on the side of a bus as the church and central plaza of Taxco are revealed. Picture-postcard scenes in Acapulco present the sparkling coastline, a rustic well, and a church before showing Bailey walking down a bustling street. Here, the pavements are lined with typical Mexican fare and the Spanish signs covering the walls of shops and bars clearly signal the Mexican location. When Markham enters the Café Mar Azul, the music that spills out from the movie house on the opposite side of the street is also distinctively Mexican with violin, trumpet, and marimba.

This sequence explicitly positions the camera as a tourist traveling through the country and is indicative of the way in which Bailey and Moffat are identified as American tourists throughout their stay in Mexico. Their romance is conducted on the beaches of the resort and in tourist bars and hotel rooms, and does not survive outside of this romantic, tropical location. Although they have both traveled to Mexico for illicit reasons—Moffat to escape persecution for stealing money from her ex, Whit Sterling (Kirk Douglas), and Bailey under duress to return her to the gangster—the freedom and apparent lack of law and order in the country allows them both to temporarily forget their criminal pasts. As in *Where Danger Lives*, the highly exoticized spaces of their romance seem to call into question *Out of the Past*'s exotic Mexican landscapes.

Conclusion

This chapter has argued that one of the key ways in which Mexico is represented in American cold war cinema is as a romanticized site. In *Where Danger Lives*, *Gun Crazy*, and *Out of the Past*, the romance of Mexico pervades the films' narratives, drawing characters toward the border in order to escape their pasts and start new lives together. The Mexico border has served as an escape route from the United States ever since its establishment, and has been depicted as such in cinema since the beginning of the twentieth century. In these films the protagonists plan to head south of the border not only to escape US jurisdiction but also to enjoy the romantic, tropical sites on offer. It is through the representation of Mexico as primitive that its romance takes on both touristic and fugitive imperatives, offering both an exotic escape from everyday life, as well as refuge from the modern law and order of the United States. Mexico's role as sanctuary in the films also recalls the left-wing political refugees who traveled to Mexico to escape persecution and prosecution under American cold war policies. It is perhaps no coincidence then that one of the screenwriters who fled to Mexico during this period, Trumbo, would later claim credit for the script of *Gun Crazy*, where Mexico represents an unachievable escape from the relentless police hunt the characters face. Mexico continues to draw Americans across the border to this day, and in a provocative recent study that "reverses the lens," Sheila Croucher argues that increasing numbers of American immigrants in Mexico are having "as great, or greater" impact as that of Mexicans in the United States.[29]

Although the characters only reach the border in the final scenes of *Where Danger Lives*, the international boundary is present throughout the film as a romantic ideal. Not concerned with the realities of the US-Mexico border in the 1950s, it is the dream of reaching Mexico that drives the film's narrative, and it is through the process of traveling that the American characters' identities are constituted. At the very end of the film, as Lannington dies, the sign "dreamland" flashes unreachable through the border fence. Her romantic Mexican dream is literally shot down by the American border police and the film knowingly suggests it has been unattainable all along.

Chapter 2

Mapping Borders and Identity: Representation, Transformation, and Ethnicity

As a car approaches a checkpoint along the US-Mexico border in the film *Borderline* (Seiter, 1950), its American passengers prepare to have their identity checked. The two protagonists of the film have been sent undercover into Mexico to bust a cross-border smuggling ring, and in the course of their investigations they assume different layers of disguise. As they complete their investigations and head to the American border, both characters are performing three separate identities concurrently: US police officers, criminals, and honeymooners. The audience is aware of these shifting personas but neither character knows the real identity of the other. They cross back into the United States with their various layers of disguise intact, despite undergoing interrogation by an immigration official. This emphasis on disguise and identity is typical of several of the border-crossing films from this period. Alongside *Borderline*, for *Border Incident* (Mann, 1949), *His Kind of Woman* (Farrow, 1951), and *Wetbacks* (McCune, 1956) too, crossing the border initiates a process of identity transformation. These movies display a focus on undercover agents, disguise, and identity alongside their central thematic concern with journeys across the border.

One of the central themes of romantic travel writing was that tourism provided an opportunity for personal imaginary exploration and transformational experiences. Amanda Gilroy argues that tourism was conceptualized through the construction of "imaginary spaces of personal liberation," and that imaginative personal discovery was equally important as the physical journeys undertaken.[1] For the lead characters in *Borderline*, traveling to Mexico involves precisely this form of physical and imaginative journey as its protagonists explore different disguises and identities while they travel, and ultimately discover that they have fallen in love. The romance of Mexico precipitates the characters' own romance, and crossing the border begins a process in which identities undergo change and transformation in *Borderline* and in other movies including *His Kind of Woman*. Curiously, the physical borderline neither appears within the cinematic space of *Borderline* nor within other films set in the borderlands from this period such as *The River's Edge* (Dwan, 1957). Instead, the crossing of the boundary is represented through its absence and via the presence of symbolic objects. This inability to clearly and directly represent the border is something seen throughout different attempts to define its route since the boundary's inception. The seemingly indefinable border seems connected to the flexibility of identity that the protagonists in *Borderline* enjoy. However, this playful crossing of different borders, boundaries, and identities is only open to Americans in the movie, leaving the Mexicans they encounter fixed in place. Through its central focus on identity transformation, *Borderline* also raises important questions about ethnicity and ethnic passing in Hollywood at this time.

Mapping a Symbolic Boundary

In *Borderline*, the US-Mexico border becomes a place of transformation and escape from everyday life for its American characters. Before closely examining how border crossings are visually and spatially depicted in the film, it is useful to consider the representational problems faced by historical attempts to define and pin down the border. The following excerpt from the Treaty of Guadalupe Hidalgo, which was written to map out the line of the US-Mexico border in 1848, demonstrates just how problematic the task of defining this international boundary is:

> The Boundary line between the two Republics shall commence in the Gulf of Mexico, three leagues from land, opposite the mouth of the Rio Grande, otherwise called Rio Bravo del Norte, opposite the mouth of it's [*sic*] deepest branch, if it should have more than one branch emptying directly into the sea; from thence, up the middle of that river, following the deepest channel, where it has more than one to the point where it strikes the Southern boundary of New Mexico; thence, westwardly along the whole Southern Boundary of New Mexico (which runs north of the town called *Paso*) to it's [*sic*] western termination;

thence, northward, along the western line of New Mexico, until it
intersects the first branch of the river Gila; (or if it should not intersect
any branch of that river, then, to the point on the said line nearest to
such branch, and thence in a direct line to the same;) thence down the
middle of the said branch and of the said river, until it empties into the
Rio Colorado; thence, across the Rio Colorado, following the division
line between Upper and Lower California, to the Pacific Ocean.[2]

Through this treaty, which was drawn up following the US-Mexican
war, Mexico was forced to sell around a third of its territory to the
United States; the lengthy sentence above is just part of a larger text
with accompanying map, which seeks to pin down the borderline. The
text is filled with clarifying statements and sub-clauses that attempt
to fix meaning and remove any ambiguity around the border's route.[3]
But rather than establishing a clear borderline, the superfluous language seems to overwrite the border. Through its attempts to provide
a clear delineation of the boundary, the treaty text demonstrates the
very impossibility of representing it.

The representation of the border is so difficult in the treaty because
the text must compensate for the possibility of physical movements
and changes in the boundary line. Although it defines the border
through physical referents, these are subject to change and movement. The borderline cannot ultimately be fixed because it has under-
gone, and continues to undergo, almost constant physical change.
Alongside large-scale changes in the boundary that preceded and
followed this treaty through international negotiations, the fact that
rivers determine parts of its course reveals a boundary in constant
flux. David Lorey reports that in the 1860s a 600-acre strip of land
that was originally part of Mexico suddenly found itself north of the
river and part of US territory after flooding had changed the river's
course, resulting in an international dispute over the land which was
not resolved until 1963.[4]

Maps play an important role within *Borderline* and the presence
of maps of the border region in the background of certain scenes
forms another key way in which the representation of the boundary is negotiated in the film. The relationship between mapping and
space is a complex one. Jean Baudrillard has posited that it is "the
map that precedes the territory," positioning cartographic representation as the forerunner to the landscape itself.[5] Similarly, John Pickles
argues that "mapping, even as it claimed to represent the world, produced it."[6] For Pickles, the difference between the map and the world
disappears as the mapped representations become the borders and

boundaries themselves. From the example of the textual mapping of the US-Mexico border in the Treaty of Guadalupe Hidalgo, it is clear that in many ways the map does precede the territory. The text of the treaty literally maps out a border that did not previously exist. However, the process of mapping does not always recognize itself as "representing the real," as Pickles asserts. The Treaty of Guadalupe Hidalgo's representation of the border overwrites and overloads its own definition, calling attention to itself and the fact that there is no real line on the ground that it depicts. Even the title of the map accompanying the text reveals the textuality of its cartography. Called "Map of the United Mexican States, as Organized and Defined by Various Acts of the Congress of Said Republic, and Constructed According to the Best Authorities," the map is positioned as a representation that is contingent on other representations (the various acts of Congress) rather than any physical terrain.[7] Jeffrey Peters is more accurate when he asserts that a map "denotes place while simultaneously connoting its own discursive authority."[8] Peters argues that maps foreground their own constructedness in the very process of depiction, recognizing that, contrary to Pickles's claims, cartography acknowledges its own status as a representation. In this process, the "authority" of maps is also highlighted, recalling that these self-consciously constructed borderlines and other mapped features exert significant power and effects on the world.

This understanding of maps and the self-conscious construction of boundaries is useful for examining the way border crossings operate in *Borderline*. In the film, the initial border crossing from the United States into Mexico takes place off-camera as an invisible locational shift. The film cuts from opening scenes set in the US customs offices and lands viewers straight into Mexico with no use of signs, fences, or maps to indicate the change in national terrain. Unlike many other critics writing about the US-Mexico border in cultural texts, Claire Fox has productively focused on the physical, visible, and spatial aspects of mediations of the border. She argues that "the fence and the river" are the key visual modes in which the border is signified.[9] But in *Borderline* the border crossing is unrepresentable and appears only as a cut—a break and gap in the filmic space—and a representative strategy that falls outside of Fox's analysis. In contrast to the physicality of the border fence in *Where Danger Lives* (Farrow, 1950), which is emphasized as Lannington clings to its wires, *Borderline*'s border is present only through its absence and seems to undermine attempts to visually represent the border directly.

In order to signify that a locational change has taken place, the film instead deploys signs and symbols of Mexico (see figure 2.1). Following the cut, the new scene opens with the camera situated underneath an archway in the shade, peering out onto a bright, dusty road. In the foreground of the image a woman prepares tacos on a hot plate and a man in a sombrero rests on a stool. The scene is bustling with street vendors selling food, people having their shoes shined, and donkeys loaded with goods. Buildings are run down and mismatched, their adobe fronts scattered with signs in both English and Spanish, which crowd the screen. The music here is also instantly recognizable as Mexican in style with trumpets, guitar, and Latin rhythms. This locational shift moves the film's action straight from the American customs office to the archway, and the lack of a border or a physical divide within the cinematic landscape seems to provoke the need for the overuse of signs and symbols that situate the action in Mexico. As Fox has argued with reference to postcards of the border produced during the early twentieth century, "national differentiation was a process of training spectators by means of symbolic codes."[10] Just as was the case with these metaphoric postcards, *Borderline*'s border crossing is purely symbolic; it does not take place on-screen, and is depicted only through its absence, followed by the signs and symbols indicating that the national terrain of the film has shifted.

Figure 2.1 Signs and symbols explicitly locate audiences in Mexico following an invisible change in national territory in *Borderline*.

The River's Edge is also concerned with an unidentifiable border crossing. This movie sees a fugitive couple flee for Mexico from Texas, planning to start a life together with stolen money; the narrative centers on the fact that the borderline itself is impossible to identify. Fearing that her criminal ex will harm her new husband, Meg Cameron (Debra Paget) pretends that they have almost reached the border. She fools crook Nardo (Ray Milland) into thinking they have crossed into Mexico, instead leading them to an Indian reservation to try and get help. Finally, the three characters are led across the border by the husband (Anthony Quinn), but the film gives no indication when the moment of border crossing takes place. Driving the narrative, as in other border films, here it is specifically the unknowable nature of the borderline that forms the key to the plot. Amid the inhospitable mountainous terrain of the Texas borderlands, the only signal that the border has been crossed is when Nardo arrives at a dirt road that bears a wooden sign pointing toward the village of Santa Isabel.

The second and final border-crossing scene in *Borderline* negotiates the representation of the boundary in yet another way. Here, the divide between the two countries is depicted as an administrative one and an immigration checkpoint becomes the crossing signifier. This border-crossing scene is set up with a series of two establishing shots showing checkpoints laid out across a wide road, while the borderline itself remains unmarked. US flags are situated on the nearside of the checkpoint, indicating that viewers are watching from the American side. Giuliana Bruno has argued that an establishing shot like this

> makes manifest a particular form of mapping: it exerts the pressure of a regulatory measure against the practice of border crossing. The drawing of place established by the establishing shot reveals a geographic phenomenon at work in film that we can recognize as cartographic anxiety and its release.[11]

For Bruno, the establishing shot literally maps film viewers into place, clearly situating them in space before cutting to the next piece of action. "Cartographic anxiety" is caused by the dislocating effects of film, which, without the establishing shots, would leave viewers ungrounded and destabilized.

The cartographic anxiety induced by *Borderline*'s border crossing reveals a flux and flow between the territories of the two countries in the film. Unable to draw a firm line between them, the filmic space overcompensates through embedding overt signs of nationality, such as the flag, within the landscape that highlight the unstable nature of national terrain and identity. Camilla Fojas argues that many Westerns from this period set on and around the border "show the difference between nations in makeshift signs indicating the limits of the United States."[12] For Fojas, these signs demonstrate "how effectively the United States has institutionalized control of the border."[13] Although neither *Borderline* nor *The River's Edge* has been categorized as a Western, the undetermined and symbolic boundaries of the films are the same as those found in many Westerns from this period. The absent or indeterminate cinematic border is just as important as the fences, rivers, and signs that serve to symbolize its presence in other texts. These shifting cinematic landscapes bring important geographic and political concerns to the fore, whatever the particular form the symbolic border takes. Through its absence and over-determination in cinematic signs and symbols, the filmic borders in *Borderline* and *The River's Edge* recall the problems of representation encountered in the Treaty of Guadalupe Hidalgo's attempts to define the international boundary.

Maps feature within *Borderline* as attempts to fix and control the unruly borderlands space, just as they served in *Where Danger Lives* to give the fleeing couple the mobility to navigate their way across the country. Maps appear on the wall behind the desks of two key authority figures in the film, Mr. Peterson (Charles Lane) at the US customs office, and Harvey Gumbin (Roy Roberts), head of a cross-border drug ring. The maps signify their competing wishes to control the border and to hold absolute knowledge of the area. Peterson's map shows Mexico, the southern United States, and the border between them. He is presented as master of this map of the borderlands as he issues instructions in front of and over it; the map and the authority it represents speaks of control of the area and emphasizes the power of the US authorities. Similarly, in Gumbin's office, the map is situated behind his desk. He is shown standing next to the map, illustrating his attempts to master the territory through his smuggling racket. The maps' impossible terrains play out the desire to control and map out the border by both police and criminals alike. They enable the drug ring to run its trade through the region, and subsequently, help the police to map out their movements and pin them down. As representations of the borderline, these cinematic maps create a boundary that is unfixable and symbolic, produced and determined only through documentation and signs.

Identity Transformations

Borderline's plot sees a female US police officer, Madeleine Haley (Claire Trevor), sent undercover into Mexico to bust a cross-border drug-smuggling gang. In the course of her investigations she meets a US gangster, Jonny McEvoy (Fred MacMurray), who is later revealed to be another undercover police officer. The two protagonists head to Mexico, fall in love, travel back across the border together, and proceed to catch the criminals. Opening in a US customs office, the film's action begins as Haley is quickly appointed to the job south of the border. From her arrival in Mexico, the locations are constantly shifting as the movie travels around the country and this traveling drives the narrative forward. After meeting McEvoy and being coerced (while undercover) to transport drugs into the United States for the narcotics boss Gumbin, a deadline north of the border steers the narrative direction back toward the United States. The countdown until the border is reached builds tension because crossing back over will mean that Haley's and McEvoy's layers of disguises will be exposed. As in *Where Danger Lives*, it is the presence of the border that controls the space and time of the narrative and directs the levels of tension and suspense throughout the film.

In addition to serving this explicit narrative function in the film, the border becomes a romantic space of escape. In order to cross over, the characters must take on new personas, and they revel in this break from their everyday lives and normal identities. Indeed, both Haley and McEvoy playfully inhabit a whole series of different disguises as they travel throughout Mexico. In their initial undercover roles, Officer Haley becomes Gladys Laroue, floozy showgirl, and McEvoy becomes Johnny Macklin, a tough-talking mobster. When they are ordered to smuggle drugs across the border, they subsequently assume another layer of masquerade as a couple, Mr. and Mrs. Macklin, on their honeymoon. Further layers of disguise are added near the end of the journey as the pair try to forget the impending end of their romantic encounter by becoming Señor and Señora Jackson. After they arrive back in the United States, these different personas fall away as the characters are revealed to be undercover police officers. The film's press kit highlights the characters' performative layers of identity, stating that "at the border...they are unmasked to each other."[14]

The continued playful performance of different personas in the film recalls the ways in which travel in the romantic period was figured as an imaginary, self-constitutive process as well as a geographic journey. As Paul Smethurst argues of romantic travel writing, "The motifs of empirical exploration and discovery are transformed and internalised such that the sensation of new horizons (*horizontality*) becomes the impetus for inner journeys."[15] In *Borderline*'s romanticized encounters with Mexico, too, the purpose of the physical journey becomes one of "self-discovery," in which the characters explicitly engage in the invention of other selves.[16] The different personas they inhabit through their travels in Mexico show their identities to be unstable and performative, guaranteed only through external signs.

At the end of the film as the characters return to the United States, the border between the two countries is represented as an administrative one, and is depicted through the characters' interactions with immigration and customs officers. Admission into the United States is contingent on the extremely brief exchange between the immigration officer and the characters. The checkpoint officer observes them, looking for signs of nationality, and apparently because he considers the couple sufficiently American, they are ushered across the boundary without having to produce any identity papers. The officer also inquires about their places of birth and clearly listens with interest to their accents but the audience is given no indication that these are truthful answers. The protagonists pass through the immigration checkpoint with their double-disguises intact, not only raising questions around the issue of proof of identity but also highlighting the potential for discrimination when interrogations of identity are based on appearance.

Historian John Torpey has argued that "boundaries between persons that are rooted in the legal category of nationality can only be maintained, it turns out, by documents indicating a person's nationality, for there simply is no other way to know this fact about someone."[17] For Torpey, legal nationality cannot be fully determined by anything other than possession of the correct documents, in other words, through signs external to the person. At *Borderline*'s border, identity is similarly contingent on external signs. Once back in the United States, the protagonists protest their true identities as US citizens and police officers, yet neither character will believe the other until another officer provides confirmation. Here, at the border checkpoint, the supreme site of identity checking and confirmation, identities are revealed to be unstable constructions that can only be determined externally.

During the film, Trevor's character undergoes the most identity transformations on-screen, and the play between her different layers of disguise is constantly foregrounded. In a scene where Haley (as Laroue) is searching for information about the narcotics boss in his empty room, he suddenly returns. She is able to escape discovery as an undercover cop by applying a different identity in the mirror; putting on makeup and appropriating a drunken act enables her to avoid arousing suspicion. A further transformative moment occurs when the couple spends the night at a hotel. This time, we see Haley (as Laroue disguised as Mrs. Macklin) apply a face masque in the bathroom mirror before returning to the bedroom and resisting McEvoy's attempts at uncovering her identity. He asks her, "What's your name, your real name?" and "where are you from?" Her cover remains intact as she retorts, "What on earth difference could that make" and "here and there." The literal face masque adds another layer of disguise, highlighting the multiple identities that Haley embodies at this moment.

The layers of identities and masks inhabited by the characters in the film recalls Annette Kuhn's conception of performance and identity. Kuhn argues,

> An actor's role is assumed like a mask, the mask concealing the performer's "true self."…In effecting a distance between assumed persona and real self, the practice of performance constructs a subject which is both fixed in the distinction between role and self and the same time, paradoxically, called into question in the very act of performance. For over against the "real self," a performance poses the possibility of a mutable self, of a fluidity of subjectivity.[18]

The fact that the characters take on further roles and performances in *Borderline* multiplies Kuhn's formulation, complicating the relationship between personas and self through the many different roles inhabited. The actors' star personas are also implicated in the film as further layers of meaning, which, as Kuhn contends, functions to call ideas of performance and identity into question. The multifarious identities of the film's characters work precisely to suggest "the possibility of a mutable self, of a fluidity of subjectivity" that, for *Borderline*, is only open to the traveling Americans.

An early exchange in the movie emphasizes the extent of the transformations Haley undergoes. While she is briefed on the criminal gang ahead of her assignment in Mexico, the male officer heading the case is skeptical that she will be successful because of the drug boss's preference for "tawdry, cheap-looking dames." But other men in the room reassure him, "She could pass." As the chief is convinced Haley can transform herself into the kind of dame that will tempt the criminal, the movie makes an extratextual nod to Trevor's previous roles, as well as an explicit reference to the practice of ethnic passing, which will be discussed below. Ray Hagen argues that Trevor was best known at this time for playing "the hard-boiled Western saloon keeper-madam with a feather boa and a heart of gold," and most notably for her role as the prostitute Dallas in *Stagecoach* (Ford, 1939).[19] Therefore, *Borderline*'s contemporary audience would have been well aware that Trevor could "pass" as the kind of woman required for the job. Haley's transformation into Gladys Laroue here is a clear reprise of the Dallas role, seeing her clad in similar attire as she dances and tries to lure the gangster with her performance. This slippage between Haley and Trevor adds yet another layer to the identities inscribed on the character.[20] Trevor gets equal billing with MacMurray in the film's publicity but it is really her character that takes the lead and steals the show. However, it is of course significant that in order undertake the investigation in Mexico, Trevor's character must play a whore. It is only through taking on this heavily gendered role, one that it seems the actor could not escape, that Trevor can become the lead.

Identity is equally malleable for John Farrow's *His Kind of Woman*, released just a year after *Borderline*. This movie follows Dan Milner (Robert Mitchum) to a remote Mexican resort in Baja California where all appearances are deceptive. A penniless barroom singer poses as a wealthy heiress to try and snag a husband, an undercover immigration officer plays a drunken pilot, and the hotel owner and staff provide a front for gangster Nick Ferraro's (Raymond Burr) operations. The constant revelations throughout the film mean that neither Milner nor audiences can ever be truly sure of anyone. The Shakespearean theatrics of Hollywood actor Mark Cardigan (Vincent Price) add yet another layer of role playing to the movie. But this flexible playing of different identities is carried to the extreme through the exiled Ferraro's plans to reenter the United States by stealing Milner's identity. When Ferraro's gruesome plans are revealed, it transpires that Milner was chosen because his height and weight match the gangster's profile and that a Nazi plastic surgeon has been hired to transplant Milner's face onto Ferraro. The Italian gangster needs to take on the identity of the gullible American gambler in order to return to the United States and continue his criminal business. Previously deported from the United States, the Mexico border becomes his chosen route of return. However, thanks to Cardigan's help, the bumbling Mexican authorities foil the plot and the American border is protected from this criminal migrant infiltration. But the film depicts a world where not even the physical materiality of a face can reliably determine identity. There is no way for identity to be definitively known, and the film leaves audiences with the lingering possibility that ethnic others could be surgically remodeling themselves as Americans in order to enter the country. This highly malleable understanding of ethnicity is echoed in Hollywood's casting and character practice during this period.

Hollywood Ethnicities

In *Borderline*, the explicit reference to "passing" in the characters' discussion of Haley's undercover role is particularly relevant in terms of the regular practice of racial passing in the movie industry. During the 1950s, Mexican and Chicano actors regularly played a variety of nationalities on screen, something that was prevalent among actors of many different backgrounds.[21] For example, as Victoria Sturtevant has shown, in only her first few years in Hollywood, Mexican actor Lupe Vélez performed Native American, Cuban, Greek, Chinese, Indochinese, French Canadian, Russian, Portuguese, and Mexican roles.[22] *The River's Edge* stars Mexican actor Anthony Quinn, who famously played a wide range of different ethnicities on-screen in addition to his many highly acclaimed Mexican roles.[23] His parts ranged from that of an Italian strongman in *La Strada* (Fellini, 1954) to French painter Paul Gauguin in *Lust for Life* (Minelli, 1956), the titular Mongol warrior in *Attila* (Francisci, 1958), and an Eskimo in *The Savage Innocents* (Ray, 1961). *Borderline* too features Italian American character actor Grazia Narciso as Mrs. Porfirio, wife of the local sheriff encountered by Madeleine and Johnny. Narciso not only regularly played Italians in Hollywood movies but also played various other nationalities, including Mexican here.

Of course, white actors also passed as ethnic and Mexican characters in Hollywood. Charlton Heston's performance as Mexican narcotics officer Miguel/Mike Vargas in *Touch of Evil* (Welles, 1958) will be explored in detail in the final chapter of the book. Other notable examples include Burt Lancaster's performance as Native American Massai in *Apache* (Aldrich, 1954), John Wayne as Genghis Khan in *The Conqueror* (Powell, 1956), and Marlon Brando as Emiliano Zapata in *Viva Zapata!* (Kazan, 1952). For *His Kind of Woman*, Canadian Raymond Burr is employed as an Italian gangster while he plays an American crook in *Borderline*. As one of Hollywood's leading bad guys, Burr's roles covered a wide spectrum of different nationalities such as Boreg, an Arabian vizier in *The Magic Carpet*

(Landers, 1951), Corsican villain Baron Cesare Jonatto in *Bandits of Corsica* (Nazarro, 1953), and Lars Thorwald, the killer of apparent Scandinavian descent, in *Rear Window* (Hitchcock, 1954). Almost the entire range of Hollywood nationalities was open to white actors; this mobility of roles contrasts sharply with the fact that nonwhite or ethnic actors were seldom able to play white American characters. Despite the apparent fluidity within the "ethnic" grouping, Hollywood's practices kept these ethnic others fixed in place without granting them individualized identities.

Scholarly debate around the construction of race and ethnicity in Hollywood and the United States at large is broad and complex. Here I am referring only to "ethnicity" as this term appears most in writing from the Cold War period and was also commonly used and differentiated from the more scientifically determinist concept of "race" by scientists, sociologists, and ethnographers.[24] The interchangeability of ethnicity in Hollywood has been described by Lester Friedman as a "melting-pot mentality, one that ignores crucial differences in ethnic identities and blends cultural oppositions into a bland conception of Americanness."[25] Friedman claims that for Hollywood, "a Hispanic, a Jew, a black or an Asian" could be classified together in Hollywood's "mix and match" approach to ethnicity but in a category that remained distinct from white Americans.[26] In contrast, Matthew Frye Jacobson contends that ethnicity was historically bound up with forms of "probationary whiteness" through which "one might be both white *and* racially distinct from other whites."[27] Diane Negra differentiates between "white ethnic" and other ethnic identities, such as Mexican, arguing that many European immigrants chose to capitalize on this separation as they "retained, exaggerated or invented altogether a profitable ethnic persona."[28] However, speaking specifically of Latin Americans in Hollywood, Clara Rodriguez argues that by the 1950s, actors either had to "'Europeanize' their images" and attempt to make their ethnic origins invisible, as in Rita Hayworth's case, or alternatively "play up the stereotypes."[29] For example, Dolores del Río's star persona emphasized her ethnicity and otherness, and she played a whole variety of ethnic roles that were not specifically Mexican and were more defined through her association with upper-class sophistication.[30]

There is much critical debate on the historical position of Mexicans, Chicanas/os, and Latin Americans within this discussion of ethnicity in US society. For example, Mary Beltrán and Fojas argue that Latin Americans have historically held "shifting, uncertain positions" along a "black-white binary" in the United States, which positions them as "nonwhite."[31] However, it is clear that in the 1950s Hollywood's understanding of ethnicity explicitly differentiated between black Americans and other ethnic groupings; although Latin Americans were certainly considered nonwhite, they were also not black and enjoyed far greater visibility on Hollywood screens than African Americans during this period. The apparent separation between white and other actors in Hollywood appears to be central to the film industry's construction of ethnicity. Yet the categories begin to collapse almost immediately upon closer inspection, as the supposedly all-American white Hollywood star could also be a recent European immigrant. Amidst these constantly fluctuating categories, the key issue seems to be one of assimilation. Members of those ethnic groups that were considered assimilated into the US nation were granted greater mobility in terms of roles available to them. These groups fit into what Gary Gerstle calls the country's tradition of "civic nationalism."[32] This ideology centered on beliefs in "the fundamental equality of all human beings, in every individual's inalienable rights to life, liberty, and the pursuit of happiness, and in a democratic government."[33] This civic nationalism was however accompanied and qualified by a "racial nationalism" that understood the United States as "a people held together by common blood and skin color," an ideology also endorsed in the constitution that persisted in American law until 1952.[34] Assimilated or invisible immigrants with the correct origins and skin color thus had greater mobility in terms of roles available to them in the movies, including leading white American roles. There are examples of invisibly ethnic Mexican stars, such as Hayworth and Raquel Welch who actively performed idealized white American identities and were able to break out of the restricted range of roles initially on offer to them as their careers progressed.[35] Of course for Hayworth (formerly Marguerita Cansino), this performance infamously involved months of painful electrolysis to shift her hairline to a position more appropriate for an "American Hollywood star."[36]

However, these assimilated groups did not include a significant proportion of Mexicans or Chicanos during the 1950s, with access to "Mexican Americanism" and self-identification as "white Americans of Mexican ancestry" determined by language, individual appearance, and skin color.[37] Although, unlike African Americans, Mexican or Chicano actors were often incorporated within the melting pot of ethnic roles, they were rarely granted access to white American leading roles.[38] This, combined with the sheer variety of different parts played by Latin American stars like Vélez leads me to contend that at this time, Mexicans and other Latin Americans were most often cast within Hollywood's ethnic category. However, as with all attempts to define matters of identity, this categorical distinction remains blurred, artificial, and ultimately indefinable. In discussing ethnicity I seek not to establish any definitive classification but rather to retain a sense of the impossibility of making clear divisions, while at the same time emphasizing that the lived experiences and on-screen representations of people occupying different ethnic spaces were (and remain) radically different as a direct result of ethnicity.

The Mexican characters in *Borderline* are portrayed in terms of immobility, which is set in contrast to the excessive movement of the American protagonists. *Borderline*'s traveling narrative fixes Mexico and Mexicans into place, requiring them to remain primitive and backward. For example, a Mexican sheriff who assists Haley and McEvoy as they try to make it back to the United States is left stuck in the undeveloped Mexican wilderness by the film. Outwitted by Haley and McEvoy, he unknowingly aids their escape to Ensenada, a town near the border, while he remains trapped at a tiny airstrip in the countryside. The Mexican police too are physically immobile in the film. Although they are presented as efficient and professional, they are forced to await McEvoy's instructions in order to catch one of the gangsters, despite the fact that the investigation has taken place in Mexico. As McEvoy leaves Ensenada in order to finish the job by pursuing the American side of the smuggling ring, these Mexican officers must remain in Mexico, even though the US police officers have traveled back and forth across the border and all through Mexico in the course of the investigation.

These characters, along with the Mexican landscape, are depicted as historical artifacts, trapped in a less modern, more traditional way of life than that of the United States. In the Mexican countryside, the roads are small, dusty tracks, where donkeys compete with rusty motorcars for space. The landscape is undeveloped, and is dotted with primitive villages of small huts and farm animals. Technological infrastructure is limited to single telephone wires on precarious poles and ramshackle buildings of wood and corrugated sheeting serve as houses. The towns are not bustling metropolitan centers but sleepy backwaters, where the Americans' car is the only traffic. Mexico is shown through the language of fixity, as a country and people stuck in place and time, in sharp contrast with the modern technologies of the American travelers who move around Mexico and back and forth across the border with easy mobility. Unlike the Americans who have the freedom to transform themselves and to change identities as they wish, the Mexicans are rooted in their stock roles and cannot engage in the same performance and masquerade.

Hollywood studios were highly attuned to issues around the representation of different national identities at the time *Borderline* was produced, and were working closely with the Motion Picture Export Association and Hollywood's self-regulatory body the Production Code Administration (PCA), organizations which policed movies' adherence to the Motion Picture Production Code and ensured products were suitable for export to foreign markets. Alongside its remit to monitor images of sex, violence, and amorality, at this time the PCA was engaged with "equal fervour," according to Dale Adams, in improving images of Latin Americans in Hollywood films.[39] In the early 1950s, the United States and Mexico were becoming increasingly interconnected, and after the end of the Second World War, the Good Neighbor policy of the Roosevelt administration generally still pervaded relations between the two countries.[40] During the war, the Office of the Co-ordinator for Inter-American Affairs (CIAA) had encouraged positive depictions of Latin America in US films in order to "keep the hemispheres united in common cause."[41] The PCA played a key role in this mission and was tasked with policing offensive images of other nations and nationalities in film.[42] Throughout the first half of the twentieth century, clause 10 of the Production Code "continued to require that neither foreign nationals nor the history of their countries be defamed."[43] Alfred Richard has argued that the PCA was at its most effective between 1935 and 1955 and that during this time, it "affected every [Latin American image] portrayed."[44] The PCA's involvement in screening productions could result in anything from the extension of shooting schedules to the complete rejection of scripts. In addition to the hangover of good neighborly motives, Hollywood also had an economic impetus in ensuring that films would sell in Latin America as it was fast becoming one of the industry's most important foreign markets, and this is perhaps the key reason why the work of the PCA continued with such fervor well beyond the war.

According to Richard, during its production, *Borderline*'s scenario caused "significant problems" for the PCA with its focus on cross-border drug trade.[45] The censors were also concerned about the film "characterizing one of the Mexicans as 'lecherous.'"[46] The movie that made it to screens in the United States and also in Mexico (as *Trafico de Muerte*)[47] is more focused on developing the relationship between the two leads than the drug trafficking and centers on the American criminals' lecherousness rather than leery Mexicans. Ultimately, it is likely the fact that the criminals are a cross-border consortium of both US and Mexican gangsters that persuaded the PCA to approve the film; both countries are implicated equally in criminality in the film, even though it is the US police officers and institutions that crack the case and solve the crime.

Conclusion

This chapter has examined the representation of Mexico as a romanticized space in *Borderline* and argued that traveling across the border enables the American protagonists to playfully transform themselves and perform multiple, shifting identities. It began from the premise that historical efforts to depict the international divide inform understandings of the way in which the border is represented in the film; historically, the border's overwrought textual representations call attention to the fact that there is no real world referent to which the boundary refers. Instead, the border is formed upon other representations, and is ultimately an unfixable entity. Similarly, in *Borderline* and *The River's Edge*, the boundary is presented only through symbols and absence, hinting at the unrepresentable nature of this division. Of course, the borderline is an all too visible, physical presence for migrants attempting to cross it today. The US government's 2006 Secure Fence Act has seen the Department of Homeland Security erect secure fencing along over 650 miles of the border.[48] However, this attempt to create an impenetrable borderline has not succeeded, instead only driving migrant traffic elsewhere, and seems only to draw attention to the impossibility of constructing a sealed boundary. Further, the concern with processes of establishing identity seen in *Borderline* and *His Kind of Woman* echo key questions about racial profiling prevalent at the border today. A 2014 report by the organization People Helping People in the Border Zone found that "agents are engaged in unlawful practices at the Arivaca Road checkpoint, and in particular, the systematic racial profiling of Latino motorists."[49] The movies' emphasis on the malleability of identity highlights the vulnerability of border checkpoints to discrimination when attempts are made to determine nationality through appearances. As the People Helping People report shows, despite Torpey's correct contention that the only determinant of identity is identity documents and the fact that racial profiling is unlawful, people crossing the border are still subject to this kind of discrimination today.

Chapter 3

Danger, Disappearance, and the Exotic: American Travelers and Mexican Migrants

An instruction to exhibitors of Hank McCune's 1956 film *Wetbacks* suggests that the movie be tied into the regular news stories about Mexican migrants to be found in the press at this time.[1] A common technique used by exhibitors, this appeal to the real-life stories of undocumented migrants demonstrates that the filmmakers understood their movie to be one that linked directly to these current events:

> The subject of wetbacks has made front page news stories recently in papers throughout the country. Check your files and make a montage of blowups of wetback news clips from local dailies.[2]

The 1950s saw a great intensification in the number of border crossings into the United States from Mexico. The Bracero Program, established to recruit Mexican laborers to work in the US south during the Second World War, continued to run throughout the 1940s and on into the next decade. The Program marked the formalization of a process that had been ongoing since the late nineteenth century in which Mexican workers would seasonally migrate across the border to work in the United States, creating circular migratory flows.[3] The introduction of the program meant the effective creation of "legal" Mexican workers; but alongside the several hundred thousand official border crossers, undocumented immigration also began to increase, and at a much greater rate. The only reliable figures available for this type of migration are the numbers of undocumented migrants caught and deported by authorities. According to Kitty Calavita,

"In 1949, when there were 107,000 braceros, the [Immigration and Naturalization Service] apprehended more than twice that many undocumented workers."[4]

Undocumented migrants continued to grow in number because it was a faster, easier way for Mexicans to enter the United States instead of waiting for a bracero permit to be granted. Powerful business leaders in southern states began to rely on this undocumented labor as these migrants were even cheaper and easier to control than official braceros. Because of the businesses' influence in local politics, the US Border Patrol regularly turned a blind eye to undocumented migrants during harvest time and other periods of peak production in the farming calendar.[5] Critics of the Bracero Program on both sides of the border claimed it led to the illegal withholding of wages, forced deportation after work was completed, and unsafe working conditions for documented and undocumented workers alike.[6] As David Lorey has argued, while it formalized the historical seasonal migration of Mexican workers, the Bracero Program also encouraged the notion that "Mexican workers could be returned to Mexico when they were no longer needed."[7]

US opinion was divided on the issue of bracero workers at this time. For agricultural and businesses leaders, they were seen as more or less essential to industry in the south. But a restrictionist sentiment opposed to the presence of both undocumented and documented migrants was also growing among other parts of the community local to the border and on a national level. Since the Great Depression, restrictionism had been a major force in the United States, stemming from anti-immigration fears and a belief that Mexican workers were driving down wages and taking jobs from American citizens. In line with this anti-immigrant feeling, Joseph Nevins reports, "US authorities forcibly expelled an estimated 415,000 Mexicans between 1929 and 1935, with another 85,000 leaving 'voluntarily,' usually under intense pressure from local authorities."[8] With ever-increasing numbers of undocumented migrants and growing public pressure, the 1950s saw the organized and militarized mass deportation of Mexicans. Manuel Gonzales argues that the immigration service's "Operation Wetback" was "conducted as a military operation" and made use of "intimidation tactics" resulting in the apprehension and expulsion of over one million people in 1954 alone.[9] John Garcia contends that this understanding of Mexican labor as temporary and wholly disposable is connected to the concept of manifest destiny and the United States' perceived right to expansion. Garcia claims that in the mid-twentieth-century United States, the "role of the Mexican-origin population was that of a reserved labor pool, an elastic labor source."[10]

During the Cold War, the American media regularly covered news of the government's efforts to deport undocumented migrants and press attention tended to focus on reports that stressed the negative impact of Mexican workers on the United States. In response to the suggestions of *Wetbacks*' press pack, the kinds of clippings that theater owners may have put together to promote the film would likely have included stories about Mexican workers driving down wages and taking jobs from US residents. In the year the film was released, newspapers reported that undocumented migration was being tackled fairly effectively and being reduced but the presence of Mexican workers in the country, whether they had work permits or not, was seen as a larger problem.[11] Papers were full of allegations that the Bracero Program was simply "a device for avoiding the paying of adequate wages to citizen workers,"[12] and the *New York Times* ran a five-part series that blamed undocumented migration for lowering wages for US citizens.[13] Similarly, a 1956 journal article titled "A Critical Analysis of the Wetback Problem" puts the presence of Mexican contract workers at the heart of the United States' employment problems.[14] Mexican workers were regularly perceived to be the root cause of American unemployment and low wages, and this was one of the key issues related to Mexican migration that featured in the American national press during the period of *Wetbacks*' production.

Despite this focus on the real-life situation at the border in the film's marketing, *Wetbacks*' cinematic border crossings take place at sea. The film focuses on the smuggling of undocumented Mexican migrants into the United States around the coast; intriguingly, there is very little evidence of this kind of border crossing taking place during this period. Just as the film's border crossings take place in an imagined scenario, the film's vision of Mexico is similarly constructed from American mythologies of an exotic, tropical, yet dangerous space. Through this vision, the movie engages in an explicit overwriting of Mexican spaces, positioning the relationship between the United States and Mexico as a colonial one.

Border Crossing, Migrant Discourses, and Danger

Wetbacks tells the story of Jim Benson (Lloyd Bridges), an American fisherman who is out of work and out of cash. Benson's position is exploited by the US immigration authorities who secretly use him to entrap a gang of criminals smuggling Mexican workers into the

United States. The immigration service undercover officers leave Benson penniless in a small Mexican village, completely unaware of the agency's plot, while Mexican gang members pursue him violently and mercilessly. However, when their plans begin to unravel, the US officials are unable to help Benson; it is his close connections with the local Mexican community that enable him to make his escape by sea. It is not until the film's final showdown that the US coastguard returns to save the day and capture the smugglers while Benson returns home with his financial troubles behind him and undercover officer Sally Parker (Nancy Gates) on his arm. Border crossings play a key symbolic role in the story, structuring the narrative and signifying Benson's entry into a world full of deceit, corruption, and threat.

Wetbacks' producers and marketers were careful to make explicit the connections between the movie's subject matter and contemporary debates around Mexican migration. However, the film does not dwell on the lives or story of the Mexicans who attempt to reach US soil, and they receive very little screen time within the picture. Rather, the perceived threat of invasion by these undocumented Mexican migrants is negotiated through the dangerous journey Benson makes across the border and back again. The somewhat amorphous hazards that Mexican migrants might present to the United States are played out in the dangers Benson faces in his journey to Mexico. From his financial peril at the beginning of the movie to the prospect of physical violence and entrapment in the Mexican coastal village of Delgado, Benson eventually combats these dangers and the criminals are captured by US forces, while prospective migrants are returned to their side of the border.

Wetbacks presents the border between the United States and Mexico as open and permeable directly from the film's opening. Facing mounting debts at his marina, Benson is offered a fee to take an American tourist and his female companion fishing. As they head out to sea, the customers and Benson agree to head south toward rich fishing areas off the coast of Mexico. In contrast to the other movies analyzed in this book, in *Wetbacks*, border crossings take place at sea, a strategy that seems unique among the border films of this period. But much like many of the other movies, such as *Borderline* (Seiter, 1950) and *The River's Edge* (Dwan, 1957), the border is absent and indeterminate for *Wetbacks*, and the point at which the international boundary is traversed is never revealed.

Paralleling the watery sea borders imagined in the film, a striking discourse of water was used to describe Mexican migration in the American popular press and governmental speeches at this time.

Newspapers describe how a "tide of Mexican 'wetback' workers" "illegally streamed" into the United States and detail the immigration service's efforts to "shut off the flow," and "stem the tide."[15] Invoking the raw power of oceans and rivers, these descriptions create an image of the migrants as an unstoppable, destructive force. Through the same language, Mexicans are also figured as slippery and able to sneak through the tiniest breach in US defenses. However, there is little evidence to suggest that any significant numbers of undocumented Mexicans traveled by sea rather than on land at this time. The movie's insistent depiction of the smuggling of migrants by boat around the coast is thus intriguingly inaccurate, suggesting instead a metaphorical concern with the "tides" of migrants entering the country over land, which taps into media and public discourses around migration and immigration.

In the film, the ocean is shown in extended long shots as the characters travel south stopping intermittently to fish; there are no markers or boundary lines on either the vast expanses of water or the coastlines along which they travel. The film's second border crossing also takes place at sea and a significant proportion of the overall action is nautical. After his passengers alight in Delgado, the narrative quickly returns to the waves as Benson is forced to make a "wetback run" by the criminal gang. After dropping his cargo north of the border, he returns to Delgado once again and is pursued around the village by the smugglers before a final seaborne showdown. In this tense sequence, both boats circle around a huge ocean liner, attempting to shoot one another. Benson's plan is to get the criminals to chase him into US waters. However, there is no indication as to where this watery border might lie and the fact that they have arrived in American waters is only finally signaled when the coastguard appears. Emphasizing this indefinable and permeable sea border, *Wetbacks* depicts a United States besieged by the threat from Mexican migration. The immigration officials' warning that the Mexicans can cross the border "by land, by air, and by water, and maybe even underground" highlights the extent of the threat they perceive. Here the US-Mexico border falls on murky and indeterminate lines in the ever-undulating ocean.

Wetbacks' publicity poster presents a significantly different image of border crossings compared to those within the film. The scene that the poster depicts takes place entirely outside of the cinematic narrative and taps into another prevalent contemporary discourse around migration. Speeches by government officials and civil society groups regularly drew on a language of warlike invasion. In 1955, Immigration Commissioner Joseph M. Swing declared the "wetback invasion" under control for "the first time since before World War II."[16] Similarly, articles in the press regularly drew on metaphors of infiltration, describing, for example, an "annual invasion" and "Wetback influx."[17] In a paper written by the Texas GI Forum and farm unions titled "What Price Wetbacks?" the alleged invasive nature of Mexican migrants is underlined as they are described as

> motivated by the desire to get to the urban and industrial areas of the northern, northcentral and western areas of the country where the possibility of detection and apprehension by immigration authorities is slim and where earnings are larger.[18]

Fears that Mexicans would overrun and penetrate deep into the heart of the United States thus construct the migrants as an infiltrating and infecting force attacking the country and its citizens.

Wetbacks' poster features a gunman in official uniform. His barrel is pointed at a figure lurching through water toward him with hands outstretched, apparently having been shot. The man in the water has an ambiguous facial expression that seems contorted with pain. With straw hat and scruffy shirt, he is clearly marked as a Mexican worker, as are the other people in the water and on the boat. The gunman faces away from the viewer but his hat and uniform are an exact match for a smaller inset in the poster that features Bridges. Although Benson never apprehends or shoots any Mexican workers in the film, the poster's scene seems to be modeled on the movie's opening sequence. The first shots of the film are set apart visually through the stylized use of chiaroscuro. *Wetbacks* opens at night on a dark beach as two headlights pull up toward the camera. A man gets out of the car and looks out across the dark sea when from this blackness come figures illuminated by the headlights, swaying and grappling like inhuman monsters. They head straight toward the camera, arms outstretched. Following the arrival of the coastguard, a criminal emerging from the boat shoots at the US officers, killing one. The action then cuts to the title "Wetbacks," which is splashed dramatically across the screen and accompanied by tense and overwrought music reminiscent of horror film scores.

The publicity poster differs from this opening sequence in important ways. Diverging from the narrative of the movie, the poster positions Bridges with the gun, shooting at Mexicans. The border crossing depicted in the poster is that of an invasive threat to the United States, as monstrous migrants reach out threateningly toward the viewer. This threat is met with a military response, and the poster frames the film's narrative with the idea that Bridges's character and the US forces are at war with Mexican migrants. Overwritten with mythology and metaphor, the border becomes a symbolic threshold in both the film and its poster, tapping into discourses of tides and floods on the one hand and invasion and war on the other.

Exotic Tourism, Tropical Mexico, and Imperial Remappings

The 1950s saw a massive boom in US tourism to Mexico. The American press was full of stories about the new tropical resorts opening in Acapulco and across the Yucatán Peninsula and stressed the fact that a tropical break in Mexico was now affordable even for average American families.[19] Through these exotic resorts, Mexico came to be understood as a destination comparable to Caribbean tropical paradises that was cheaper, easier to get to, and just as glamorous.[20] Exoticness is also an important factor in *Wetbacks'* vision of Mexico. The film's publicity materials highlight its tropical theme, describing the movie as a "romance under tropical skies" and championing the fact that it was shot on location on a "magnetic Island paradise."[21] The film's reviewers did not find too much to like about it but they were almost unanimous in their appreciation of the exotic locations and the Eastman Color process, which rendered them "so beautiful" according to *Harrison's Reports*.[22] *Kine Weekly* found that the "magnificent land and seascapes further compensate for its uneven script. You can feel the sun on your back and taste the salt in the air."[23] Similarly, for *Variety*, the film had "excellent scenic footage" that complemented the "tropical mood."[24]

According to trade press reports, the film's producer-director McCune changed the name of his company from Telecraft Productions to Pacific Coast Pictures specifically for the production of *Wetbacks*.[25] With this name change, McCune created a clear connection between the ostensibly Mexican setting of the film and the Pacific Islands. The fact that location filming took place both in Mexico and on Catalina Island in the Pacific, despite the absence of any island in the film, demonstrates the movie's conceptual interchangeability of Mexico and tropical island locations. Hollywood has a long tradition of this kind of tropical conflation, for example, W. S. Van Dyke's 1928 feature, *White Shadows in the South Seas* (Van Dyke, 1928), was set on the Pacific Island of Tahiti, but featured Mexican actress Raquel Torres in the lead Tahitian role.[26]

Wetbacks' positioning of Mexico as a tropical paradise opens it up to US colonization. In the words of Raymond Betts, this process produces an "illusionary" Mexico, an image constructed entirely by the colonizing nation.[27] Jeffrey Geiger has examined the representation of the Pacific Islands in Hollywood film and argues that these depictions are never just concerned with demonstrating exoticness but are also always bound up with colonial discourses. He posits that *White Shadows in the South Seas* "is self-reflexively gesturing toward the historical textualisation of the Pacific as a site of western fantasy: an impossible Eden glimpsed among the colonized tropics."[28] For Geiger, representations of Pacific Island paradises are thus overlaid with the self-conscious construction of Western fantasies. These American fantasies of tropicalism are also inscribed upon the illusionary Mexican landscape of *Wetbacks.*

Wetbacks' reinscribing of Mexican terrain plays out the distinctly spatial and geographic processes by which colonialism operates. As Edward Said has argued, "Imperialism after all is an act of geographical violence through which virtually every space in the world is explored, charted, and finally brought under control."[29] Similarly, Cole Harris claims that the act of mapping is one of the most powerful tools of colonization. When conquering the Americas, Europeans created maps that reorganized space in Eurocentric perspective, renaming, removing, and ignoring "indigenous ways of knowing and recording space."[30] In *Wetbacks'* case, the production company and reviewers alike understood the film's setting as a denationalized exotic space, not a specifically Mexican landscape. The film remaps the surface of the country with a homogenous tropical environment, explicitly highlighting the fact that many of the scenes were filmed on Pacific Islands. Through this illusionary vision of Mexico, *Wetbacks,* like *White Shadows in the South Seas* before it, gestures toward the United States' colonization and construction of Mexico.

This effective overwriting of Mexico is particularly apparent during scenes set in the film's rather drab immigration service offices where two items draw attention to themselves. A large map on the wall shows the United States and northern Mexico (see figure 3.1). The United States is detailed with reliefs of mountains and valleys, creating a complex and visually beautiful cartography. In contrast, Mexico's terrain is entirely blank on the map, colored in a single tone without any distinguishing marks. Although this map is presumably designed to aid the immigration service in patrolling the border, it lacks any identifying features on the Mexican side of the line. Mexico appears vacant and silenced, ready to be overwritten by the Americans with their own fantasies of what lies beyond the borderline. Next to

Figure 3.1   The colonizing power of maps is witnessed in the silencing of Mexican territory in the US immigration service offices in *Wetbacks*.

this map, the second item on the office wall appears to be a calendar featuring an image of a tropical island.

Historian DeSoto Brown has examined the production of tropical imagery through advertising channels such as calendars in his analysis of representations of Hawaii in the early twentieth century.[31] He argues that the island's fantasy image was produced in large part by American industries such as cruise liner companies and hotels trying to sell holidays to Americans. The appearance of the tropical calendar in the US immigration service office not only highlights the all-pervasive nature of these tropical fantasies in American culture but also hints at the action to come in *Wetbacks*. The calendar foreshadows the film's construction of a fantasy paradise and confirms Mexico's position as a space overwritten with American tropicalism.

Wetbacks features exoticized images of Mexico akin to those found in other border films such as *Out of the Past* (Tourneur, 1947), *His Kind of Woman* (Farrow, 1951), and *Where Danger Lives* (Farrow, 1950). As in these movies, the romanticized backdrops are linked directly to romance between characters. The explicitly touristic postcard scenes of *Out of the Past* create an overtly imaginary location, just as the protagonists' dreams of Mexico in *Where Danger Lives* are played out in a tropically themed bar. For *Wetbacks*, the two lead characters Benson and Parker are stranded in the village of Delgado, where most of the action takes place in a bar owned by Alfonso (Nacho Galindo), which has the appearance of a simple shack or beach hut. The tropical atmosphere of the bar is enhanced by the presence of exotic plants and trees seen outside through the open sides of the room. As the couple sits drinking together, the open panels behind them reveal palm trees and the ocean beyond. The tropical scene is fixed behind the couple, framing their romance in exotic terms; later in the evening while the bar staff fall asleep, the Americans talk into the night, accompanied by a guitarist, whose slow, sliding melody reveals a Hawaiian influence.[32] In *Wetbacks*, the illusionary exotic Mexican landscape is inextricably linked to the growing romantic relationship between the protagonists. However, seen through the open panels of the room, the tropical scene through the window appears like a flattened picture or photo on the wall; thus, the film's exoticized spaces of Mexico seem to call attention to their own colonizing illusion.

Colonialism and the Border

Emerging from the context of changing concerns about the presence of Mexican workers in the United States, *Wetbacks* was produced at a time when the broader relationship between the two countries was also undergoing transition. During the Second World War, the United States had sought to bolster relations with the rest of Latin America in order to build allegiances and ensure that the countries did not fall to fascism. President Roosevelt's Good Neighbor Policy acted on diplomatic, political, and cultural fronts. During and immediately following the Second World War, relationships within the hemisphere were strong. Historian Stewart Brewer has argued that at this time, "the United States and Latin America entered a period of cooperation, cordial associations, and mutual goodwill unlike anything in the history of US-Latin American relations."[33] In the aftermath of the war, which saw the emergence of the United States and the Soviet Union as ideologically opposed nuclear superpowers, the United States implemented a further foreign policy program to build alliances. The Truman Doctrine was introduced to ensure that weakened allies would not fall to the growing threat of communism. Brewer attests that with this measure, President Truman claimed, "Any country in the world that was threatened by communist expansion could expect aid from the United States in the form of funding and military support."[34] Through this doctrine, the Marshall Plan delivered $13 billion of funding to help rebuild vulnerable countries hit by the war. But in reality all of this support was given to Europe, and as Brewer contends, Latin American countries became increasingly frustrated that none of the money came their way.[35]

In addition to a burgeoning antipathy toward the United States in Latin America, the 1950s also saw the growth of popular left-wing social movements in many Latin American countries. US policymakers were late to look to the political state of their own continent after the war but when they finally did take stock of the situation, "they were astonished to discover popular movements in rural Latin American communities and among Latin American politicians alike that looked like communism."[36] Latin American countries held long histories of communism and communist sympathies; after intervening to oust the government in Guatemala in 1954, the United States watched over left-wing politics in Latin America with great interest during this period.[37] On the domestic front, 1954 brought an end to Senator McCarthy's strident anticommunism within the United States and as a result, "public hysteria about domestic communism, no longer so openly fuelled by demagogic politicians, died down."[38] Jonathan Auerbach argues that by the mid-1950s, public concern about "an internal red menace" was diminishing as a result of McCarthy's demise, but also because of the increasing prominence of other domestic issues such as race relations: the year 1954 also saw the landmark *Brown vs. Board of Education* ruling, which brought an end to segregated schools and formed a key milestone in the civil rights movement.[39] At this point in time, attention was focused on the rise of communism outside the United States as much as internally.

Connected to the invading tides of migrants found in press stories and public discourse of the time, it is also significant that the Mexican workers in *Wetbacks* are marked as communist characters. They are always shown on-screen as a collective and are utterly unindividualized with blank expressions and bland characterization. The Mexicans' communality is presented as a lack of personal agency as they are shown blindly following each other around and placidly taking orders. As M. Keith Booker has argued of the alien invaders in another film released in 1956, *Invasion of the Body Snatchers* (Siegel), in their collectivity and lack of individual personality or emotion, the Mexican migrants "directly echo the era's most prevalent stereotypes about communists."[40] Radicalism and unionism among Mexican migrants was a pertinent topic at this time, and as Calavita has shown, the concerned US government issued direct instructions to farm owners to "purge the Bracero Program of 'agitators.'"[41] Further evidence of the conflation of migrants with communists is found in a report written by Immigration Commissioner Swing in which he lauds the expulsion of 184 subversives and 266,000 migrants from the country in the very same phrase.[42]

Wetbacks was produced in the context of this changing relationship between the United States and Latin America and against the backdrop of the war on communism. Accompanying these broad political shifts, the forces exerting pressures on Hollywood movies were also undergoing great changes. In line with the earlier government's Good Neighbor policy, since the Second World War, the PCA had been instructed to pay special attention to the representation of Latin America in US films. As a body that previously affected all representations of Latin Americans on screen, by 1956, the PCA had less influence, less authority, and less obligation to censor images of different nations and nationalities.[43] Alfred Richard attributes this change to a number of issues, including the breakdown of the studio system and the growth of independent production companies that did not fall under the Motion Picture Producers and Distributors of America or PCA auspices.[44] However, the changing relationship between the United States and Latin America at a governmental level was likely an additional factor. Richard argues that PCA censorship of depictions of Latin America waned in the latter half of the decade, and it is probable that PCA head Joseph Breen and his office would not have been interested in *Wetbacks*' characterizations of Mexico and Mexicans to the same extent that they were with earlier productions such as *Borderline*.[45] Emilio García Riera notes that unlike many American films made in the 1950s, *Wetbacks* did not have a release in Mexico at all, indicating either that the filmmakers did not want to sell the film overseas, were unable to get distribution, or that the Mexican government censored the picture.[46] Positioned as a tie-in to the topical and typically hostile US news stories about Mexican migration, the filmmakers were clearly not concerned with appealing to the Latin American market with this production. This echoes the wider governmental shift away from good neighborly relations with Mexico and toward the more complex relationship with the country that developed during the Cold War.

Wetbacks was McCune's first film as director and the first production for his company Pacific Coast Pictures. He had previously produced the melodrama *A Life at Stake* (Guilfoyle, 1954) before embarking on this project as producer and director. One incident relating to the film that received detailed trade press attention was the interruption of the production because of a union dispute. McCune was forced to call filming to a halt for several weeks until actors received backdated salaries and advances checks in accordance with their Screen Actors Guild contracts.[47] The activism of the actors and the escalation of the union dispute is perhaps not entirely surprising given star Bridges's political background. Bridges began his acting career on stage and was a member of the radical theater group "The Actors' Lab" in the 1940s.[48] A member of the Communist Party, Bridges was summoned during the HUAC investigations in Hollywood, and agreed to cooperate with the committee by arranging to "testify in secret."[49] Jeremy Byman notes, "Though he named names, he was still 'graylisted' for several years until the *Sea Hunt* television series revived his career."[50] *Wetbacks* falls into this graylisted period of Bridges's career, which perhaps explains his presence in what was a considerably low-budget and low-profile production compared to his prestigious pre-HUAC pictures such as *Unconquered* (DeMille, 1948) and *High Noon* (Zimmerman, 1952).

Conclusion

Mexico is represented as a romanticized site in *Wetbacks* through the visual emphasis on the country's tropicality and the self-proclaimed fact that it was filmed on an exotic island paradise. This cinematic border is not simply a reflection of events or policy changes at the real US-Mexico border at this time; although *Wetbacks* explicitly positions itself in relation to a real-life topical issue in its marketing strategy, its border crossings take place at sea. There is little evidence that Mexicans were crossing the US-Mexico border by sea; therefore, the movie's imagined maritime menace seems instead to be metaphorically connected to contemporary discourses around the perceived threat of Mexican migrants, which draw on analogies of tides, flows, and floods.

The film's overwriting of Mexican spaces with an indeterminate, denationalized exoticism constructs Mexico as the United States' own tropical resort, and in this way, American connections with its southern neighbor are rendered colonial. While it adopted a policy of intervening in Latin America for the purpose of preventing the spread of communism in the Cold War, the US government also framed its opposition to the Soviet Union in terms of colonialism.[51] In an internal policy statement, the US government clearly condemns colonial practices, writing that "in view of our own history and outlook, [the position of the United States] can only be that we support principles of self-determination."[52] However, the statement also urges that the "menace" of the "Soviet brand of colonialism" be condemned and that the United States should urgently consult and engage with countries including the Latin American nations to "deliver effective blows at Soviet colonialism."[53] *Wetbacks*' border crossings thus seem to dramatize the United States' complex cold war relationship with Latin America. The connection between border crossing and disappearance is a key theme in *Wetbacks* and one that returns repeatedly across this book's case study films. This concern seems to chillingly foreshadow the thousands of migrants who have disappeared into the borderlands while attempting to cross the international boundary in recent years. As more of the border becomes fortified, desperate migrants are forced to try and cross through ever-more dangerous terrain. In 2013, the Pima County Medical Examiner's Office in Tucson held 774 sets of unidentified human remains recovered from the borderlands.[54]

Part II

Revolution

Chapter 4

The Revolutionary Politics of Mexico: Individualism, Communitarianism, and Landscape

Mexico's revolutionary history has long held a particular fascination for Hollywood. So much so that during the Mexican Revolution of 1910–20, the Mutual Film Corporation secured an exclusive contract with northern-Mexican leader Pancho Villa to cover his campaign.[1] Villa agreed to fight in daylight where possible, to prevent other crews from filming, and even to restage battles for the cameras if required.[2] The American film industry was beginning to flourish at the same time that the revolution took place, and when Mexico appeared in early cinema, the films almost always featured a revolutionary backdrop.[3] Hollywood has consistently returned to Mexico's radical past since then, with both the Mexican uprising that led to the overthrow of French Emperor Maximilian in 1867 and the 1910–20 Mexican Revolution inspiring a multitude of films over the years. This range of movies—from the 1939 movie *Juarez* (Dieterle) to 1966's *The Professionals* (Brooks), right up to the 2003 release *And Starring Pancho Villa as Himself* (Beresford)—demonstrates the enduring cinematic appeal of revolutionary Mexico.

The 1950s in particular saw a significant preoccupation with Mexico and revolution in Hollywood. A large number of films concerned with Mexico's revolutionary past and present were produced including *Viva Zapata!* (Kazan, 1952), *Salt of the Earth* (Biberman, 1954), *Border River* (Sherman, 1954), *Vera Cruz* (Aldrich, 1954), *The Treasure of Pancho Villa* (Sherman, 1955), *Bandido* (Fleischer, 1956), *Villa!!* (Clark, 1958), and *They Came to Cordura* (Rossen, 1959). Echoing the explicitly political nature of earlier pictures such as Sergei Eisenstein's unfinished *¡Que Viva México!* (1933), all these films use their images of Mexico or Mexicans to tell political narratives and each occupies a different position on the political scale. *Viva Zapata!*'s critique of communism in favor of a liberal democracy produces a very different effect than *Salt of the Earth*'s celebration of unionism, but both films make use of strikingly similar evocations of revolutionary Mexico and Mexicans. Revolution is one of the major themes in films about the US-Mexico border produced during the Cold War. Through two central case studies, *Vera Cruz* and *Border River*, Part II of the book investigates what this focus on revolution might reveal about American cold war culture.

Much critical work that focuses on Westerns and their historical contexts draws on Richard Slotkin's study of frontier mythology in American culture.[4] For example, writing about individualism, one of the central concerns of this chapter, Michael Coyne asserts that Westerns form "a paean to individualism, a consummate fantasy of freedom of movement and limitless horizons, lacking most social constraints," directly connecting individualism to frontier mythology.[5] Peter Stanfield has argued that one thing most scholars of 1950s Westerns agree on is that the films engage with contemporary issues through the idea of the frontier mythology.[6] However, *Vera Cruz* and *Border River* articulate a response to their contemporary cultural, historical, and political environments through debates around the US-Mexico relationship and colonialism, rather than the frontier.

Where *Vera Cruz* has already received critical attention, the film has often been considered simply in terms of its place within the Western canon and Robert Aldrich's oeuvre. However, Camilla Fojas has probed more deeply and has considered the role of border crossing in *Vera Cruz*, arguing that the movie is concerned with issues of "reunification" following the US Civil War.[7] Echoing the claims of other critics who have written about the presence of Mexico in American cinema more generally, Fojas claims that for *Vera Cruz* "the Mexican context" is "neutral ground upon which soldiers from different sides of the civil war might join together against the American enemy, the French empire."[8] But rather than serving simply as a neutral backdrop or blank screen upon which new American identity is negotiated, the Mexican setting is vital in *Vera Cruz* for the film's narrative and politics. The film's Mexican landscapes celebrate the country's mythic heritage, engaging with contemporary debates about Mexico's position in the world and its relationship with the United States. As in many other Westerns from the Cold War period, individualism is a key concern for *Vera Cruz*. But here, individualist American characters are pitted against the collectivism of Mexican revolutionaries and this communal way of life is celebrated in the movie. Revolutionary Mexico's persistent draw as a subject for Hollywood filmmakers echoes the flight of left-wing American cultural producers south of the border, and similarly *Vera Cruz* offers its filmmakers the critical space to question US cold war culture and policies.

Mexican Mythologies

Against its revolutionary Mexican backdrop, *Vera Cruz* tells the story of two American soldiers who travel to Mexico to offer their services to the highest bidder in the late nineteenth-century fight between French emperor Maximilian and the Mexican followers of revolutionary leader Benito Juárez, known as Juaristas. The film opens showing lone figures on horseback traveling across open country as titles explain that many American soldiers traveled to Mexico during the revolution. This opening border-crossing montage sets up the transformational personal journeys that the American characters will undergo. Ben Trane (Gary Cooper), accompanied by Joe Erin (Lancaster) and a band of US mercenaries, is employed to escort a French countess (Denise Darcel) and a substantial quantity of plundered gold from Mexico City to the port of Veracruz for sailing back to France. On the way, Trane is won over by the revolutionary workers' cause whereas Erin becomes obsessed with individual financial gain and is killed by Trane as he attempts to steal the bullion for himself. At the end of the film, Trane helps secure the gold for the Juaristas and joins their fight to free Mexico from its French oppressors.

Westerns produced during the Cold War have often been seen to reflect an expansive frontier mythology. However, *Vera Cruz* is not concerned with the American frontier but rather with a specifically Mexican mythology, developed through the film's focus on Mexican heritage and landscape. Indeed, it was the film's location that was identified as the key to *Vera Cruz*'s success by its contemporary critics. In his review of the film in *The Hollywood Reporter*, Jack Moffitt observed that the fact the film was shot in Mexico on "colorful and authentic locales" made it "good news for the exhibitor."[9] Even the *New York Times*' Bosley Crowther in his vehemently unfavorable review singled out the "wide open country of Mexico" as a potential saving grace.[10] In addition, the location's importance is stressed by the notice in the film's end credits and theatrical trailer, which states that the picture was "filmed entirely in Mexico." According to Fojas, despite its opening border-crossing scenes, *Vera Cruz* was one of the very first Hollywood features to be filmed wholly in Mexico.[11] The Mexican setting was thus seen as crucially important at the time to both the filmmakers and reviewers.

As *Vera Cruz* presents an epic romanticized Mexican landscape through which the country's cultural heritage is celebrated, it is no wonder that so much was made of the film's setting in reviews. Each of the small towns that the traveling party of Americans enters is full of beautiful but dilapidated buildings and architecture. A scene in one of the first Mexican settlements featured in the film opens with two small boys in traditional dress walking down a street lined with ruinous archways, apparently the remains of buildings or the beginnings of ones that were never completed. Yet, rather than appearing backward or undeveloped, these empty archways standing alone appear like sculptures or ancient monuments as the camera slowly glides through them. The decaying plaster and paintwork does not look dirty or scruffy but becomes a beautiful palette of color set off against the blue sky and brown track.

The image of the archway is repeated frequently throughout the film, most prominently in a scene showing a convoy of Maximilian's forces and the group of Americans traveling to Veracruz. The caravan passes an old aqueduct and its archways form the background to the action. The white, sun-bleached structure with its cracked plaster is dotted with plants; the trees situated behind make it appear a part of nature. The arch is a traditional feature of Mexican architecture but here, as in the town shown earlier, the camera's continual focus on the arches paints them with grandeur like a series of standing stones. This careful attention to ruinous architecture presents the Mexican landscape as an ancient relic to be revered and idolized. The mythic and monumental way in which the decaying structures are filmed recalls the epic landscapes of Westerns set in the old American west. But rather than alluding to the mythology of the frontier, *Vera Cruz* evokes a specifically Mexican mythology, one that also historically fixes the country in an ancient past.

Writing of Western landscapes and mythology, Jane Tompkins has argued that the use of monumental backdrops is an act of mythmaking itself:

> In the beginning, say these shots, was the earth, and the earth was desert. It was here first, before anything. And the story you are about to see goes back to the beginning of things, starts, literally, from the ground up. In the instant before the human figure appears we have the sense of being present at a moment before time began. All there is is space, pure and absolute.[12]

Thus for Tompkins, the Western landscape speaks of stories that stretch back to the very dawn of time, of eternal truths and universal narratives. She also notes the distinct "architectural quality" of the "monumental" spaces of Westerns, such as Monument Valley.[13] For Tompkins's argument, the space and setting of the Western confers on its stories the quality of myths and legends, appealing to the ancient landscapes in which the action takes place. The monumental quality of *Vera Cruz*'s architectural spaces means that they are equally implicated in mythmaking, in this case within a Mexican setting. Through the carefully depicted images of ruinous Mexican architecture, the film creates a Mexican mythology that evokes an ancient lineage and epic beauty. This effect is further enhanced by the presence of real Mexican ruins in the film.

The complex of ancient ruins that the party passes through on their journey appears to have been filmed at Teotihuacán, an archaeological site near Mexico City.[14] Teotihuacán is the name given to the ruins of an enormous Mesoamerican city, which was established in the first or second century BC. At its height, the city may have held up to 100,000 inhabitants, and also appears to have had widespread influence across the region.[15] When the ruins are shown in the film, they appear as if from nowhere. One moment characters are shown in discussion in close-up, and then immediately a long shot of a pyramid appears, filling the sky and the screen. The soundtrack also underlines the ruins' imposing majesty as discordant rhythmic chiming evokes the mystery and power of this ancient city. The film's SuperScope format enables an extreme wide shot of the convoy passing one of the long sides of the pyramid, making clear their diminutive size compared to this awesome structure.

Following from the pyramid, the characters move slowly along what appears to be the Avenue of the Dead, the main street of Teotihuacán, which runs for about two and a half kilometers and is lined with low-level pyramids and tiered walls. The presence of these structures in the background speaks of a mythic Mexico, which is mysterious, powerful, and awe-inspiring to the Americans who travel through it. This mythic and monumental backdrop serves to link Mexico and Mexicans to an ancient heritage and celebrates the ancient cultures and history of the country. In so doing, the movie seems to question the legitimacy of the United States' territorial claims on the continent. Repeatedly the history of the US-Mexico border has seen land taken away from Mexico, for example, when the Treaty of Guadalupe Hidalgo was drawn up after the war between the two countries in 1848, Mexico was forced to sell almost one-third of its territory to the United States. Through its emphasis on Mexico's ancient relationship to the land, *Vera Cruz* questions America's colonization of areas such as Arizona, New Mexico, and Texas through evoking the ancient Mexican cultures that previously existed there.

Individualism and Collectivism

Critics have often identified individualism as a key component of the Western genre, drawing on popular ideas about the role of the frontier in American culture dating back to Frederick Jackson Turner.[16] Those writing in the Cold War period were no exception, and many contended that individualism was one of the key themes and ideologies of the American west. In 1950 Frederick Elkin argued that "rugged individualism" was one of the central values of the Western genre, and in the same year, Henry Nash Smith similarly observed heroes of the West to be "symbols of anarchic freedom," "men who ranged the wilderness [and] had fled the restraints of civilization."[17] These critics saw the individualist pursuit of territory as a core component of American identity and linked it directly to the stories of rugged men who tamed the wilderness of the Western frontier.

More recently, Stanley Corkin has contended that cold war Westerns "express the legitimacy and necessity of the American empire" at this time.[18] For Corkin, Westerns produced in this period such as *Red River* (Hawks, 1946) and *My Darling Clementine* (Ford, 1948) laid the ground for American expansion through their narratives that are focused on capitalism and economic concerns. Corkin claims that the repeated emphasis on trade and free markets in cold war Westerns seeks to legitimize individualist capitalism, assertions that close examination of *Vera Cruz*'s vision of individualism and capitalism challenge. Like the movies Corkin cites, *Vera Cruz* is also concerned with money. However, rather than being related to expansionist frontier mythology, the film's economic narrative and extant conflicts between personal gain and societal benefit are used to question individualism in relation to the communitarian goals of revolution.

The main action of *Vera Cruz* centers on a shipment of gold that must be taken to the port at Veracruz for sailing back to France. All of the characters want to get their hands on the bullion, forming the basis for interlocking narratives of double-crossing and cheating. The initial motivation for Trane and Erin to join forces and offer themselves as fighters is to make money by auctioning and awarding their services to the highest bidder. However, when the Mexican revolutionary leader General Ramírez attempts to entice the Americans to join him, more complex issues of monetary and moral values are raised as he declares, "We offer more than money: we offer a cause." When Trane and Erin join forces with the Juaristas to take back the gold from the French, again, it is for a price but by this point in the film, Trane has begun to develop a very different sense of value from Erin. The synopsis in the film's publicity material also emphasizes the transactional nature of the relationships between the characters:

> each from a different motive, they agree to join the Juaristas in storming the garrison: Trane has been convinced by Nina that the gold honestly belongs to the people of Mexico, and moved by the words of Aguilar [Ramírez[19]] that a man must have a cause to give him a reason for living; but Erin seeks the gold purely for profit.[20]

The individualist Americans must choose whether to put aside their capitalist ambitions to join with the Juaristas and fight for a cause or to pursue the stolen money individually. Attempting to steal the gold for himself leads to Erin's downfall, and Trane, the only American figure left standing by the end of the film, chooses the revolutionary cause, deciding that the gold rightly belongs to the Juaristas.

Although it was produced during a period of high capitalism in the United States, *Vera Cruz* does not simply lay the ground for American expansion or endorse individual financial gain. Considering the huge rise of mass-produced goods and consumer spending in the post–Second World War United States, the film's narrative can be said to adopt a highly ambivalent position on the capitalist mores of the time. Writing in 1958, the economist John Galbraith explains the scale of the change in consumer practices during this period:

> In the five years from the end of 1952 to the end of 1956 total consumer debt (not including real estate loans) increased from $27.4 billions to $41.7 billions or by 53 per cent. Installment credit increased by 63 per cent and that for automobiles by nearly a hundred per cent.[21]

The huge increase in spending and the concomitant need for evermore money meant that this new consumer-led society reinforced the capitalist ethos of the time. Demonstrating the pervasiveness of frontier mythology and its relationship to capitalism, Galbraith claims that this consumer society was a direct result of a unique brand of "American economic ideas" that were influenced by the "expansive mood" of "the frontier and the West."[22] However, for *Vera Cruz*, questions of capitalism are brought into conversation with ideas of revolution, and individualism is interrogated in the film. While the American stars are inevitably individualized and celebrated through individualistic performances, the collective cause of the Mexican revolutionaries is lauded over and above personal financial gain.

A very similar narrative arc is followed in the 1955 feature *The Treasure of Pancho Villa*. This movie sees a lone American mercenary head to Mexico to join the revolution and make money in the process. Tom Bryan (Rory Calhoun) insists throughout the film that he is only in it for the money as he helps followers of Pancho Villa to steal gold from banks in order to fund the revolutionary army. However, by the end of the movie Bryan is won over to his friend Colonel Juan Castro's (Gilbert Roland) way of thinking and rather than taking the money and running, or seeing the gold recaptured by government soldiers, he uses dynamite to bury the bullion on a mountainside. In contrast, for Kazan's *Viva Zapata!*, the moral certitude of revolution is left in doubt as the film charts Zapata's rise from revolutionary hero to despotic tyrant. This movie was based on a concept originally conceived by the Office for Co-Ordinator of Commercial and Cultural Relations between the American Republics (later the Office of Inter-American Affairs) and, as Slotkin has argued, can be seen as "an attempt to make a positive political statement that would distinguish the essential values of American liberalism from both Stalinist Marxism and right-wing conservatism and that would claim for those values a 'revolutionary' or liberating world mission."[23] Kazan's involvement in the project was no coincidence; as a HUAC witness who had been greatly criticized for naming names, the film is at pains to make clear that denouncing communism is not at odds with a liberal or left-wing political outlook.

Vera Cruz's narrative is also closely concerned with communitarian and collective ways of life and this is played out through its focus on the Juarista revolutionaries. The Juaristas' point of view is often privileged within the story—and this is enacted literally through cinematic space and perspective. The American soldiers and French countess pass through the complex of ancient ruins midway through the film. While the characters move past a high temple, a shot suddenly changes the camera position and looks down at a vertiginous angle high up from the pyramid. A Juarista is then shown keeping watch atop the structure, before the camera pans back down, giving a high-angle view of the party below. Long shots filmed from high, hidden, places open almost every new location in the film. For example, as the French carriage and escort approaches a monastery, a shot from within the bell tower looks down on them as they enter the square. Likewise, near the start of the film as Trane and Erin begin their journey together, the camera is placed high on what appears to be the top of a cliff or mountain. The Americans are seen far below, as the camera peers out from behind a rock overhanging the desert below.

These images seem at first to be simple establishing shots, which are unmotivated by characters within the filmic diegesis. However, the explicit linking of the Juarista's position looking down with the shot from the pyramid reveals that these extreme high-angle shots are in fact the Juaristas' points of view and the revolutionaries later reveal that they have been following the movements of the Americans throughout the film. In hiding and watching from high places, the Juaristas occupy the traditional position of bandits in the film. But in *Vera Cruz*, viewers share their position through these lookout shots. As Noël Carroll has argued, the use of point of view shots encourages the audience to empathize with these characters as we see the action through their eyes.[24] Through this device the film creates direct empathy with the Juaristas and their cause.

A scene set in the Juarista camp the night before the film's final battle also makes *Vera Cruz*'s alignment with the revolutionaries explicit. Filmed on the most modest set of the film, the guitar music is subtle, the light is low, and the mood is one of reverence as General Ramírez (Morris Ankrum) delivers a stirring speech. The quiet tone of this moment is strikingly different from the rest of the film. This understated scene is devoid of the flamboyance and tension that characterize the performances of Lancaster and Cooper in other parts of the picture, and emphasizes the simple truth of the general's words. Ramírez calmly says to Trane, "Money. Is that worth risking your life for? A man needs more, something to believe in." The quiet force of the general's speech coupled with images of the soldiers communing and sharing demonstrates the film's celebration of this revolutionary and communal way of life. *Vera Cruz* clearly venerates this simple, yet passionate and political way of life that privileges communal actions for the good of society over individualist actions for personal gain. Although Fojas asserts that the film is concerned with bringing together confederates and unionists in the face of the French imperialists, it is only Trane who joins the revolution to help oust the colonial rulers, in direct opposition to the other American characters.[25] The confederate Trane's choice to join the Mexican communitarian cause speaks more to an anticolonialist position than a unificationist agenda, and the fact that in this act he is directly opposed to the other American characters who seek personal gain is strongly indicative of the film's lack of concern with uniting the United States.

For Philip French, the distinctive visual representation of the Juaristas in *Vera Cruz* demonstrates the influence of Mexican muralists Diego Rivera and José Clemente Orozco and their "stylised groupings of peasants and revolutionaries."[26] For example, Rivera's *Peasants* (1947) and Orozco's *Zapatistas* (1931) show peasants and revolutionaries in white dress with wide-brimmed hats, their outlines arresting against the backgrounds of the paintings. These images find clear echoes in *Vera Cruz*'s Juaristas. The influence of Rivera and Orozco, both explicitly political artists committed to socialism and communism, is significant. Rivera was a particularly potent figure of radicalism and revolution, identifying himself as "a loyal revolutionary in the Bolshevik-Leninist tradition."[27] As Jeffrey Belnap explains, although he was criticized by other Mexican artists for taking on commissions from enterprises supported by American capitalists such as Rockefeller and Ford, Rivera argued that these opportunities enabled him to operate "as a guerrilla fighter who worked for the cause of world revolution behind enemy lines."[28] That *Vera Cruz*'s Juaristas might be influenced by these murals depicting the struggles of Mexican revolutionaries, as well as Rivera's revolutionary politics, emphasizes the film's empathy with this cause and makes the figure of the Mexican peasant a politically potent image.

The Mexican characters are also closely connected with Mexican terrain in the movie. The large group of Juarista soldiers is most frequently seen silently appearing from nowhere, lining the horizon in a ring of hats, white suits, and rifles. They are first shown when Trane, Erin, and their band of American mercenaries meet with Mexican and French forces in a small town square. Once inside the walls of the square, General Ramírez announces that the band of Americans has been taken prisoner. As Erin grins in disbelief, the camera begins a slow circular pan around the square's high walls as hundreds of men armed with rifles appear in turn to silently surround the group (see figure 4.1). Trane and Erin are shown in close-up shots from below as the Juarista soldiers fill the screen behind them, not only emphasizing their total control over the situation but also forming a beautiful and striking outline against the blue sky. Appearing from nowhere, it is as if the Mexicans spring forth from the architecture or the landscape itself. These shots seem to echo scenes in *Viva Zapata!* that see peasant revolutionaries in the same dress, appearing from hiding places in the mountains. Despite the striking similarities in visual representation, the films' very different political positions on revolution demonstrate the malleability of this image of the Mexican revolutionary in cinema.

Figure 4.1 Juaristas are closely connected with the traditional architecture and Mexican landscape in *Vera Cruz*'s stylized vision of the peasant revolutionaries.

Concurrent with *Vera Cruz*'s celebration of Mexico through its mythic landscapes and representation of the Juaristas as a noble people, the film also has an obvious concern with preserving an authentic, ancient Mexico. As Edward Said argues of Orientalism, *Vera Cruz* makes Mexico speak, describes it and "renders its mysteries plain" for US audiences.[29] The film inherently participates in "dominating, restructuring and having authority" over Mexico and it cannot escape these discourses, as demonstrated through its focus on the plight of the American characters.[30] Although the Juaristas are presented as moral, stoic soldiers, they are unindividualized and treated as a uniform collective unlike the American stars who are distinct individuals. Because they are always shown as a collective, the Juaristas are on the very periphery of the narrative and even the shot composition. They line the edges of the screen, literally serving as a background for the American hero and antagonist. While they appear stoic and noble rather than menacing or threatening through these stylized representations, they do not ultimately challenge the positions of Cooper and Lancaster as the stars of the movie. Although it clearly endorses the Juaristas' collective socialist ethos, *Vera Cruz* also celebrates its individualized American star characters, both the good and the bad.

Left-Wing Politics and Revolutionary Mexico

Vera Cruz was produced by Lancaster and Harold Hecht's company Hecht-Lancaster and released through the independent studio United Artists. It was the second Western in a row for the studio which brought Lancaster and Aldrich together, following *Apache*, which was made the same year.[31] The movie had a budget of $3 million and was "filmed at the relatively leisurely pace of two and a half months."[32] It was Aldrich's first major film as director and by dint of his growing power and status in the industry it was a relatively grand affair. Aldrich took one hundred cast and crew members with him to Mexico, and according to the fairly extensive press coverage the production received, he hired a further two hundred locals on arrival.[33] Filmed at considerable expense in both Technicolor and SuperScope, *Vera Cruz* was under pressure to perform at the box office; the company pulled out all the stops in the press pack by advising exhibitors to hire actors to dress as characters from the film and parade through the streets near their cinemas. The movie went on to be Hecht-Lancaster's biggest film thus far, with initial release earnings of more than $9 million.[34] The film's commercial success was therefore very important for its producers. However, the involvement of several key left-wing Hollywood personnel also seems significant and suggestive of a connection between *Vera Cruz*'s vision of revolutionary Mexico and left-wing politics.

Vera Cruz's director, Aldrich, is famed for the left-wing political nature of his films, which have been described as "iconoclastic, anti-authoritarian, even revolutionary in message."[35] As the first major film he directed with a substantial budget, coupled with the fact that United Artists was founded upon the premise of granting of autonomy and creative freedom to filmmakers, it is likely that *Vera Cruz* offered Aldrich the opportunity to explore his personal and political interests.[36] Aldrich came from a powerful wealthy family who were politically conservative, but he struck out against this background through his outspoken socialist ideology. For example, as national vice president and subsequently president of the Directors Guild, Aldrich made the position an explicitly political one—in his own words, he "thought of the guild as a political instrument for the betterment of its members" in contrast to many of his predecessors in the role.[37] Aldrich spent the formative years of his career at the left-wing independent Enterprise Studios, working alongside figures such as Abraham Polonsky, Robert Rossen, John Berry, and John Garfield, forming a close-knit community of liberal and leftist filmmakers. These four were among those blacklisted for suspected links to communism by HUAC at the time of *Vera Cruz*'s production.[38] In addition, both the film's presenter, Hecht, and one of the scriptwriters, Roland Kibbee, were summoned by the committee in 1953 under suspicion of links to left-wing and communist factions.

Lancaster too was a prominent left-wing figure in Hollywood at the time of the film's production. Gary Fishgall argues that Lancaster's "long public commitment to liberal causes" began in the early 1950s with his involvement with the Committee for the First Amendment, Hollywood's movement against the HUAC investigations.[39] Although not called before HUAC, Lancaster was considered a potential subversive and had his passport confiscated. He later attested that as a result of his political stance, "in a very small way, certainly not comparable to what others had suffered, I was on blacklists."[40] Lancaster would later return to revolutionary Mexico in *The Professionals* but this time to be won around to the revolutionaries' cause. Cooper also had direct contact with the HUAC proceedings when in 1947 he voluntarily attended a hearing to provide information about communists working in Hollywood. According to his biographer Lary Swindell, Cooper "never recanted his testimony, or said he regretted having been a friendly witness."[41] In 1944 Cooper had joined prominent Hollywood conservatives such as Cecil B. DeMille, Walt Disney, Ronald Reagan, Ginger Rogers, Hedda Hopper, and John Wayne to form the Motion Picture Alliance for the Preservation of American Ideals (MPA). The MPA was formed specifically in order to combat communism in the film industry with a mind to providing willing witnesses for the HUAC investigations.[42] Cooper's famous conservativism thus adds interesting complexity to the politics of *Vera Cruz*.

Because of the left-wing politics of key members of the cast and crew, the production of *Vera Cruz* was directly affected by HUAC investigations into communism in Hollywood. Tony Williams argued, "Although far removed from the 1950s by its historical setting, *Vera Cruz* foreshadows that later blacklisting era, which saw many examples of personal and political betrayals."[43] Indeed, *Vera Cruz* can be read as an indictment of the HUAC blacklisting through its political figuring of Mexico and Mexicans. The team working at the heart of the production included prominent Left and liberal figures who were concerned about HUAC's intervention in Hollywood. Their colleagues were blacklisted and the film's writer and presenter were called before the committee itself. As an independent and personal project for Hecht, Lancaster, and Aldrich, the film can be seen to reflect the filmmakers' experiences with the oppressive presence of HUAC in Hollywood at the time. However, *Vera Cruz*'s leftist vision of revolutionary Mexico is ambivalent and conflicted. Although the American character Trane denounces individualistic wealth and colonial rule in order to join the revolutionaries, the actor Cooper cooperated with HUAC investigations in order to help oust communist ideals from Hollywood entirely. Rather than simply reflecting HUAC oppression, the film also evokes a sense of the unstable and heterogeneous status of politics in the Cold War. Although the terms of cold war debate may have been the same across the political spectrum, seen here through the image of the Mexican revolutionary, *Vera Cruz*'s conflicted vision nevertheless indicates the way in which cinematic border crossing enabled a variety of different ideological positions to flourish.

Conclusion

This chapter has argued that although it is often classified as a Western, *Vera Cruz* does not exhibit the frontier mythology that Slotkin argues pervades cultural representations of the American west but rather establishes a specifically Mexican mythology. Through its celebration of Mexican landscape and heritage, the film questions French and American colonial claims on the continent. Further, *Vera Cruz* interrogates ideas of individualism and collectivism in relation to Mexican revolutionary movements and the overthrow of colonial leaders. Individualist capitalism is set against the Juaristas' moral communitarian cause and the film presents a debate around individualism, which is articulated through the complexities of revolution rather than a simple expansive frontier mythology. Revolution is a central theme of many American films that cross the border into Mexico in the Cold War and *Vera Cruz*'s production crew includes key left-wing Hollywood figures. Perhaps echoing the flood of left-wing writers, artists, and intellectuals to Mexico City to escape persecution by anticommunist factions at this time, *Vera Cruz*'s Mexican landscapes create a "space of critique" where debates around revolution and radicalism can take place.[44] This cinematic Mexican space is taken up in a wide range of films that look to revolution as a way to work through the political complexities of this period and that present a wide range of different and conflicting positions. It is through Mexican revolution and the overthrow of the French empire that films such as *Vera Cruz*, *The Treasure of Pancho Villa*, and *Viva Zapata!* foreground debates about colonialism, which were central to the cold war political climate.

Chapter 5

Territory, Colonialism, and Gender at the American Frontier

Westerns have long been associated with a very specific spatial terrain of vast, open landscapes, and these expansive spaces have been the subject of much critical attention. André Bazin has argued of Westerns, "Transformation into an epic is evident in the set-up of the shots, with their predilection for vast horizons."[1] For Bazin, it is precisely the images of open landscape that create the mythic properties of Westerns. Scott Simmon claims that it was through the genre's shift from its early origins in the east to films made in the west that the "wide, bright, harsh, 'empty' landscape of the west was constructed."[2] Similarly, in his analysis of masculinity and the genre, Lee Clark Mitchell asserts that the Western hero is "ineluctably a part" of the wide-open spaces and landscape that characterize the films.[3]

The landscapes of the Western were also a key concern for critics who were writing in the 1950s. Henry Nash Smith argued that "the notion that our society has been shaped by the pull of a vacant continent drawing population westward" had a central influence on American literature and society.[4] Clearly drawing on Frederick Jackson Turner's frontier thesis, Smith's analysis of the West and Westerns is developed through space and specifically through the expansion of US national territory at the frontier. However, through close analysis of the film *Border River* (Sherman, 1954), this chapter will argue that this film's terrain is not wide or open, and it does not express any "inevitability" of American expansion. Further, *Border River* does not easily fit within the mythology of the frontier that scholars from Smith to Bazin, Simmon, and Corkin find at the heart of the Western genre.

The cold war period saw a significant renegotiation of the United States' place in the world as it sought to establish itself as global leader. Historian Thomas J. McCormick has argued that during the 1950s, US leaders believed that "the rest of the world would win more than it would lose by acquiescing in American hegemony."[5] This unquestioning assumption of the United States' position as leader of the Western world promoted an exceptionalist and expansionist view of the nation among its leaders, which assumed that the United States was the exception to the rule; it led the world and expected it to follow. The country underwent massive economic expansion during the Cold War and this was naturalized by economists like John Galbraith as the continuation of a distinctly and intrinsically American expansive impulse. Holding clear echoes of Smith's work, the "expansive mood" of the economy that Galbraith described was linked directly to the frontier.[6]

American economic expansion during the early Cold War was felt particularly keenly in Mexico, in large part through the recruitment of temporary Mexican workers to the south of the country to support the farming industry. The American press responded with alarmist reports of invading migrants that drew on the threatening language of tides and floods. However, this commercial connection with Mexico was nothing new; the United States had been economically expanding into the country ever since the two nations were established, and with increased intensity following the closure of the Western frontier in 1890. One of the reasons that the 1910–20 Mexican Revolution was followed so closely in the United States was the high level of economic and territorial interest in the country. Linda Hall and Don Coerver have argued, "By 1910, foreigners—mostly Americans—owned about one-seventh of the land surface in Mexico."[7] Beginning soon after the official closure of the Western frontier, the Mexican Revolution posed a threat to this American-owned land; one of the key aims of the revolutionary movements was to reclaim land sold to foreigners by President Díaz for the Mexican people.[8] Thus American economic interests beyond the border became colonial issues, questions of land ownership, imperialism, and revolution.

Directed by veteran B-Western director George Sherman in 1954 for Universal-International, *Border River* is set in a rogue free zone along the Mexican side of the border known as Zona Libre. Although ideas of land and territory are important in the film, it is not centered on or contingent upon expansive vistas and open landscapes but is rather concentrated in closed spaces. The way in which *Border River*'s landscape is enclosed is related to the way in which the central female character is represented in the movie. Attempts to map and bind her into place fail, and through her Mexican heritage and the Mexican landscape, she becomes a politically active driver of the film's narrative.

Closed Landscapes and Revolutionary Territory

Border River tells the story of General Mattson (Joel McCrea), a Confederate soldier who crosses the border into Zona Libre to purchase supplies for the war with stolen Union gold.[9] He makes a deal with General Calleja (Pedro Armendáriz), the corrupt dictator of the separatist state, who soon learns of the gold and wants it for himself. Meanwhile, Mattson grows closer to Carmelita Carias (Yvonne De Carlo), Calleja's girl. When Calleja realizes he is in danger of losing her, he attacks Mattson, attempting to take his gold and withhold supplies. Overpowering him in treacherous quicksand on the banks of the eponymous border river, Mattson leaves Calleja to sink into oblivion as he rides off with Carias through the free zone, which has been liberated by Juarista revolutionaries.

Critics have identified an expansive mood within cold war Westerns, particularly those set in Mexico; this has often been understood as a simple transference from the westward expansion of the frontier days to ambitions for southward extension. The French intervention in Mexico (1862–7), which is dramatized in *Border River*, *Vera Cruz* (Aldrich, 1954), and later pictures such as *Major Dundee* (Peckinpah, 1965), took place during the final phases of frontier settlement, and beginning in 1910, the Mexican Revolution followed soon after the closing of the frontier. Camilla Fojas has argued that after closure, "the southern line replaced the western frontier as a major organizing symbol of popular culture because it defined the nation on different, more modern terms: the United States was now bounded, limited, and exclusive."[10] However, at the time of the 1910–20 revolution, US attitudes toward the southern border were not defined in terms of territorial expansion or frontier spirit but rather by economic interests. The revolution specifically targeted American land holdings and businesses in Mexico. President Díaz, who would be overthrown in the upheaval, had sold off land and resources to foreign businesses, and revolutionaries sought redress through the redistribution of this wealth to the Mexican people. John Britton has argued that the issue of most concern to the US government during the revolution was preventing damage to its "economic connections" in Mexico.[11]

Much like the opening of *Vera Cruz* and many other Westerns of the period, *Border River* begins with long shots of vast, open landscape. A series of explanatory titles clearly situate the action in the period of the French intervention in Mexico and the American Civil War, on the banks of the Rio Grande. The opening titles play over a long shot of a river, presumably the border river, flowing past monumental rock formations. As the titles fade, the shot continues and the camera remains fixed on this landscape. Then, from behind where the text was located comes a lone rider, scrambling down the rocky cliff toward the river. His entry into the scene having been thus obscured, this character appears to spring straight from the text, situating him directly in the realm of epic narratives and lending a mythic feel to the opening. The rocky cliffs give way to an expanse of scrubland that recedes from the river all the way back into the open sky behind. These American spaces are only seen from across the river, as the camera remains situated on the Mexican bank. As the rider moves more clearly into view from beneath the titles on the screen, he heads toward the river and begins to move across it. The long shot persists and the camera does not move as the rider and horse slowly make their way through the water. Even as gunshots are heard and pursuers appear on the northern bank, the camera does not shift, allowing only a very limited view of events. Because of the long focal length of the shot, the rider's progress across the river is flattened and stunted; the closer he gets to the Mexican side of the water the slower his progress becomes; it is as if he is thus immediately entering a more enclosed, restrictive space. As the action finally cuts away from the American rider, it is revealed that this space is controlled by the characters watching on the Mexican bank. General Calleja and his entourage view the events on the river with great interest to see if the rider makes it across the central point, bringing him into Zona Libre.

This close watching of the border river recalls the fact that people gathered on the American side of the Rio Grande during the Mexican Revolution to watch the fighting.[12] Spectators were sometimes injured as stray bullets flew across the river. Claire Fox argues that this was because people were "behaving as though they were watching a play or a movie rather than a war."[13] Upending this historical observation, *Border River* sees Mexicans looking north and gleefully watching on as the American Civil War plays out. With the action now on the Mexican side of the border and in Zona Libre, the dialogue and filmic space focus on questions of land, soil, and territory through the film's continually closed and enclosing spaces.

Following this opening sequence, much of the film's action takes place in Zona Libre; in contrast with the broad vistas of the opening shots, Zona Libre is largely comprised of a series of interior sets including the bar room, General Calleja's office, and characters' apartments. All of these sets are overcrowded with people and objects and give a sense of constraint and oppression. Calleja's office is filled with opulent patterned rugs and ornaments, which stand in the way of the camera as he is framed between pairs of brass candlesticks and gilt mirrors. The bar too is crowded, as the frames of the building, furniture, and people all close in on the screen. At one point the camera looks through the spinning wheel of a casino game at characters beyond, the wooden spokes framing the action in the room and enclosing the characters. Within Zona Libre, the camera is always trapped inside a network of rooms and partitions, moving from one establishment to another through the tight streets of the township but never into an open, expansive landscape. In these interior spaces, rooms and objects press in on the edges of the screen claustrophobically. In this way, the film recalls the oppressive spaces of *Rio Bravo* (Hawks, 1959), another film that is concerned with the history of the US-Mexico border. For this movie too, the action takes place within the tight confines of a small border town, with many scenes set inside the small Sherriff's office and jailhouse and the Alamo Hotel. Trapped within the town by the brother of jailed criminal Joe Burdette (Claude Akins) and a gang of hired guns, the plight of Sheriff John Chance (John Wayne) and his motley crew of deputies is played out spatially through the claustrophobic interiors and tightly enclosed streets.

Similarly, even when *Border River* ventures outside the Zona Libre township, the land is not open or conquerable but rather is already and naturally closed. The banks of the river are laced with pools of quicksand, which nearly engulf Mattson's unsuspecting horse at one point. In the final standoff between Mattson and Calleja, they fall fighting into quicksand, which claims the life of the land-grabbing Calleja while his former girlfriend helps pull Mattson out from the churning earth. Swallowing the leader who pursued Mexican terrain for individualist ends, it is the landscape that sees Calleja overthrown. Closing in on itself, the pit of quicksand is enclosing and entrapping. The terrain rids itself of those who would seek to control it, presenting a landscape quite unlike the expansive and conquerable vistas of much Western genre criticism.

American cold war culture has previously been described by critics using a similar concept to that of the closedness described above, but one that I wish to differentiate the territorial concerns of *Border River* from. Alan Nadel has argued that a culture of "containment" pervaded the United States in the cold war period.[14] This idea is derived from US foreign policies during the Cold War, which sought literally to contain communism and prevent it from spreading further across the globe. These strategies of containment were implemented by the Truman administration; historian John Lewis Gaddis explains that in practice they included employing policies of limiting the external influence of communist countries.[15] Nadel and other critics such as Elaine Tyler May see the effects of these strategies of containment played out on both foreign territory and home turf. For these scholars, narratives of containment also sought to contain and control cultural institutions and identities such as the family, sexuality, race, and gender.

For example, May argues that the American government saw secure families and homes as a key element in the fight against subversion within the country. Simultaneously, she claims, gender issues played a defining role in cold war rhetoric and became a vital element of the discourse separating the United States from Russia and elevating it above its rival:

> American women, unlike their "purposeful" and unfeminine Russian counterparts, did not have to be "hard working," thanks to the wonders of American household appliances. Nor did they busy themselves with the affairs of men, such as politics. Rather, they cultivated their looks and their physical charms, to become sexually attractive housewives and consumers under the American capitalist system.[16]

For May, American women and their bodies thus became a battleground in the ideological war against communism. The 1950s did indeed see surprising levels of marriages and births; 96.4 percent of women and 94.1 percent of men were married—the highest levels ever recorded—and in addition, "most couples had two to four children, born soon after marriage and spaced closer together than in previous years."[17] Following this argument, we might expect to see such narratives of containment reformulated, replayed, or contested in popular culture from this period, and indeed, Nadel and May cite convincing examples of films and literature that support their assertions. However, for *Border River*, a movie borne out of this very same environment, the themes of space and control are rather bound up with colonialism and revolution. The film is concerned with rightful land ownership and explores what happens when territory is colonized, taken over, and controlled. Further, for its lead female character the story is more complex than simply one of containment and control. Carias has an active moral sensibility and her political awakening is central to the film's plot, enabling her to take an active role in the narrative.

The United States had always stood against old world empires, and during the 1950s it criticized the efforts of the Soviet Union to expand its power across Eastern Europe in colonial terms.[18] However, at the same time, its intense political involvement with other countries, particularly those in Latin America, was becoming more and more akin to a colonial presence. Britton has described this approach as "informal imperialism, using military intervention, threats of military intervention, diplomatic pressure, and economic clout to influence and at times to manipulate events."[19] Mexico, in particular, was the target of these US attentions, not least because of fears that the long, porous border between the countries could grant "easy access to subversives."[20] Challenging containment accounts of US foreign policy during this period, Greg Grandin argues that US intervention in Latin America was actually more concerned with eliminating concepts of social democracy than containing communism, in order to protect American investments and future oil and labor supply.[21] It is this concern with the United States' intervention in other countries that is far more relevant to *Border River*'s narrative as it explores the consequences of imperial occupation and subsequent revolutionary uprising.

Cartographic Colonization, Gender, and Ethnicity

In prerevolutionary Mexico, American appropriation of Mexican land and resources formed a process of colonizing through mapping, where property was established through cartography and the overwriting of the land. However, landscapes are always changing and resisting cartographic fixing, as illustrated by the impossibility of definitively mapping the borderline. In time, the revolution saw much of this American-owned land returned to Mexico. *Border River* is similarly concerned with the failure to map, order, and control land. In the film, Calleja's attempts to control the spaces of Zona Libre are visualized explicitly through the character of Carias. As Calleja's love interest, she is constantly subject to gridding and mapping, while the tight spaces of the town literally close in on her as Calleja attempts to tighten his control.

Cartography was a key tool for the colonizers of the Americas, enabling them to map uncivilized territory, pushing back the frontier and incorporating land into the nation. Drawing on cartography's colonial history, many critics such as J. Brian Harley, Tom Conley, and Karen Piper have argued persuasively of the ideological power of maps and the ways in which they are transformative rather than reflective.[22] Harley contends,

> Far from holding up a simple mirror of nature that is true or false, maps redescribe the world—like any other document—in terms of relations of power and of cultural practices, preferences, and priorities.[23]

In the case of colonization, mapping was put to a particular end: the acquisition of land and territory. In his study of colonization in the Americas, Cole Harris finds that "maps were tools in the process of land allocation. Property required a location, and maps were the means of establishing it."[24] This overwriting of the landscape in perspectival cartography "conceptualized unfamiliar space in Eurocentric terms, situating it within a culture of vision, measurement, and management."[25] It removed indigenous knowledge, replacing it with an ordered, measured European vision.

Piper argues of the process of colonial mapping that "'territory,' . . . was something haunted from within by the 'primitive,' which had to be perpetually overcome by the sovereign subject."[26] This always masculine sovereign subject, signifying order, rationality, and civilization, was set in opposition to an explicitly feminized primitive landscape, "viewed by the colonizers as infected with fear, superstition, enchantment or fancy."[27] Many early maps were accompanied with allegorical pictures that personified the continents as women. For example, the frontispiece from Joan Blaeu's *Le Grand Atlas* boasts a striking depiction of geography and the four continents as women.[28] Assessing the prolific personification of continents as virgin women, Caterina Albano concludes that "cartography selects an image of femininity which can be conquered, subdued and handed over."[29] In the United States, the notion of the land beyond the frontier as unruly, disordered, and irrationally feminine constructed the vision of a land ready to be taken and conquered. For *Border River*, through the closed, interior, and overwhelmingly domestic spaces of Zona Libre, Mexico too seems to be figured as a feminine site. But in the character of Carias the conquering of this landscape is contested and challenged, and although Calleja attempts to seize and control the territory and women of Zona Libre, he is not successful in either pursuit.

Despite playing a central role in the narrative, Carias is nevertheless subject to the same effects of Calleja's colonization as the land with which she is identified. For almost the entire film she is only shown inside Zona Libre and within the domestic spaces of her apartment and Calleja's rooms. She owns a 50 percent stake in the town's saloon, revealed when characters discuss her portrait that hangs behind the bar. As though being enclosed within the filmic frame is not enough, Carias is pressed into the picture's frame too, a double-binding that maps her in place as an object to be looked at and controlled, set within the ordered gridlines of the colony. Images of gridding are repeated throughout the film through the presence of divisions and partitions in the spaces of Zona Libre. For instance, within Calleja's apartment and the barroom there are areas separated off by vertical bars. In the same way in which she is contained by the painting, Carias is often shown behind these bars. The gridding of the image divides her figure, mapping her body and attempting to put her under Calleja's control. However, despite these efforts to contain her in the filmic space and narrative, Carias plays a key role in the movie. Toward the end of the film, she leaves both Zona Libre and Calleja, undergoing a political awakening through a rediscovery of her Mexican heritage. With distinct echoes of the representation of Nina (Sara Montiel) in *Vera Cruz*, it is through her Mexicanness and ostensibly innate sense of political justice and socialism that the film constructs an active and participatory role for Carias.

Laura Mulvey has written about the complexity of female roles in Westerns, arguing of the film *Duel in the Sun* (Vidor, 1946) that the character Pearl demonstrates the way in which many female characters engage with archetypal Western gender roles. Rather than a flat, one-dimensional character, Pearl embodies both the passive virtuousness and active sexuality identified as opposite character types in earlier criticism.[30] Through this dual role, Pearl experiences both "passive sexuality, learning to be 'a lady,' above all sublimation into a concept of the feminine that is socially viable," and "sexual passion...a boy/girl mixture of rivalry and play."[31] Mulvey's model identifies a Western woman in-between, one with active choice and self-determination within the narrative, albeit through her relationships with male characters.

Likewise, Carias's involvement with the two male leads in *Border River* highlights her multiple and complex femininities. With General Calleja she is passive and restricted. The scene in which he presents her with a necklace provides a telling example. A side-on shot shows Calleja ordering Carias to turn around. He reaches for the necklace behind her and as he places it around her neck, the action cuts to a medium close-up of the two characters shown in a mirror. Now seen front-on, Calleja's presence behind her is oppressive and an aggressive hand on her shoulder pins her in place (see figure 5.1). Carias's entrapment is again emphasized through the framing device of the mirror. The shot appears flattened and cramped as the mirror's frame expands to the edge of the screen. The presence of the vertical bars of the gated section of the room seen within the mirror also serves to emphasize her incarceration.

In contrast, when Carias learns of the plot to ambush Mattson at the river and take the gold, she fools Calleja's henchman Captain Vargas (Alfonso Bedoya) and escapes through the backdoor of the bar to warn Mattson. She is shown galloping on a horse along a narrow ravine and rather than sporting her usual luxurious gowns for this sequence, she dons trousers and a buttoned shirt. Carias's active role in the plot is also explicit in her physical rescues of Mattson. In addition to running to his aid in the river at the film's opening, toward the end of the picture she saves his life again by pulling him out of quicksand. It is through Carias's Mexicanness that she is politicized and given this morally and physically active role in the story. The decor of her apartment is centered on portraits of her father and brother who died fighting to free Mexico's terrain from imperialist French occupiers. Carias's Mexicanness is equated with a romanticized political radicalism; forming the turning point in her narrative, when she is reminded of the sacrifices her family

Figure 5.1   Attempts to control and contain Carmelita Carias are figured through repeated frames and divisions in the filmic space in *Border River*.

made for their country, she recovers her political ideology. Moved to action as she recalls the pain of losing Mexican territory to the United States in the Treaty of Guadalupe Hidalgo, Carias's political awakening is thus situated in a specifically Mexican experience of land and space, seeking to reclaim what rightly belongs to the people, not expanding or expansive.

The character of Carias has striking parallels with the lead female role in *Vera Cruz*. Nina, the surname-less Mexican love interest for Ben Trane, plays a vital part in *Vera Cruz*'s narrative. She works undercover as a Juarista agent, gathering information and funds for the rebellion and plays an instrumental role in the revolutionaries' victory over the French. Nina infiltrates the American party en route to Veracruz, passing information about the gold to the revolutionaries, while pretending to be only interested in stealing the French countess's dresses. When Trane confronts her, declaring he realizes she is "not only a thief...a Juarista," Nina boldly counters that she knows Trane is not like the other Americans as he understands the gold belongs to Mexico. Leaving Trane to ponder this, Nina joins the revolutionary leaders in the thick of the action in the film's final fight. In the movie's closing scenes it is revealed that Trane chooses Nina and her revolutionary cause over taking the gold for himself. As the film ends on an image of Trane joining Nina on the bloodied battlefield, her vital role in politicizing the American soldier is revealed.

Nina is played by the Spanish actor and singer Montiel, again demonstrating Hollywood's easily flexible approach to ethnicity at this time. Montiel had already gained considerable fame for her films in Spain and Mexico before making her Hollywood debut with *Vera Cruz*. Similarly, *Border River*'s lead Mexican female Carias is played by De Carlo, a Canadian-born actor.[32] Carias neither speaks Spanish nor does she dress in traditional Mexican clothing, instead mostly wearing dresses befitting a royal courtesan that are very European in flavor. She speaks a well-pronounced English and her skin is markedly lighter than that of the other Mexican characters in the film. Neither Carias nor Nina resemble any of the most common types of Mexicans seen in American film as identified by Charles Ramirez Berg; they are not easily classifiable as either "harlot," "clown," or "dark lady."[33] That these characters are played by Canadian and Spanish actors seems to mark them as in-between and ethnically ambiguous, complicating the characters' positions as Mexican.

Clara Rodriguez has argued that the 1950s saw a decline in the number of depictions of Mexicans on-screen in leading "Latin lover" and "bombshell" roles because of the changing "public values" of cold war culture.[34] The 1930s had seen greater numbers of Mexican and other Latin Americans on Hollywood screens and Peter Stanfield has argued that the perceived threat from the sexual potency of Latin lovers and bombshells in this earlier period was tempered through comedy. Conversely, by the mid-1950s and the release of *Border River* and *Vera Cruz*, the lead Mexican females are made acceptable precisely because they are not played by Mexicans.[35] American enough to unite with Mattson, Carias retains enough Mexicanness to discover her political self-determination and act on it. Negotiating the borders of nationality, Carias enjoys a powerful and active role in this Western that complicates traditional archetypal female roles of the genre. Similarly, drawing on Montiel's powerful European stardom, Nina breaks out of typical Mexican female roles. Although she is casually sexualized at points in the narrative (for instance, the nickname "papayas" is cheerfully bandied about at the film's outset), Nina also plays a powerful political role in the narrative. Seen outside of the frontier myth, both of these characters respond to the Mexican Revolution and are concerned with the return of money and land taken by colonial oppressors. Although the spaces of *Border River* initially seek to control and enclose her, in becoming politicized and literally breaking free from Calleja, Carias takes control of the spaces of the film, determining the narrative through her actions. The complex and politically active nature of these characters points to their "centrality" in the films, which, as Stanfield has argued of Westerns of the late 1940s, is often overlooked in accounts of the genre.[36]

Mexican Revolution and Political Contexts

Border River appeared to its contemporary audience to be a conventional civil war Western, that is, all except for its Mexican location. *Today's Cinema* highlighted the film's "novel setting," writing that the "narrative effectively breaks away from [the] more familiar Western pattern by placing its action in [the] colourful setting of [a] corrupt Mexican township." *Variety* too declared it was the fact that "[Universal's] cameras move south of the border" that distinguished the picture. Likewise, for *The Hollywood Reporter*, *Border River* was "a standard western given extra value by its setting."[37] The Mexican backdrop was the single most important characteristic of the film for its contemporary critics, and it is through Mexican landscapes and characters that the film negotiates issues of colonialism and revolution. *Border River*'s Mexican setting also appears to have been significant for director Sherman. A prolific and prominent B-movie director, Sherman repeatedly returned to Mexican locales and themes throughout his career. His Mexican titles include *South of the Border* (1939), *Mexicali Rose* (1939), *The Treasure of Pancho Villa*, and *Last of the Fast Guns* (1958). Later in his career he would also direct pictures for Mexican and Spanish production companies.

Criticized by Richard as simply a "let's generate sympathy for the south in the Civil War film," on closer reading, *Border River* is considerably more ambiguous in its political position.[38] Its alignment with the US south is called into question through comparisons drawn between the Confederacy and Zona Libre's status as a separatist zone at war with the Mexican government. Bedoya's Captain Vargas sneers that just as the Americans have two governments in Lincoln and Davies, so too can Mexico. The separatist state of Zona Libre thus becomes equated with the Confederates' wishes for secession from the United States. The final taking of the town by the Juaristas also mirrors the impending Confederate defeat, which is alluded to throughout the film. The hero Mattson is placed in a questionable position; on the losing side of the war, his imperial desire for independent territory is aligned with that of the film's villain.

Mattson is thus a conflicted hero in the movie. The star persona of actor McCrea only adds to this ambiguity through his carefully crafted image as a classic Western hero. McCrea made Westerns a specific career choice and only acted in one non-Western film after 1945. He explained this choice in a 1978 interview saying,

> I always felt so much more comfortable in the Western. The minute I got a horse and a hat and a pair of boots on, I felt easier. I didn't feel like I was an actor anymore. I felt like I was the guy out there doing it.[39]

His appearances prior to *Border River*'s release included *Saddle Tramp* (Fregonese, 1950), *Cattle Drive* (Neumann, 1951), and *The Lone Hand* (Sherman, 1953). In all of these films, McCrea plays moral and heroic individualist characters at the center of the narratives. Jimmie Hicks describes how McCrea deliberately shaped this image throughout his career as he rejected various offers of parts that did not fit. This included turning down the lead in *The Postman Always Rings Twice* (Garnett, 1946) on account of the poor "moral standards" of the character, to which McCrea's response was that "this isn't the image that I want."[40] McCrea's self-fashioning as a moral and upstanding Western hero sits at odds with the ambiguous position of Mattson in this film.

Biographers of McCrea emphasize his conscious decisions only to play moralistic characters and also how he modeled himself on an older generation of upstanding Western heroes.[41] Robert Nott writes that McCrea particularly admired veteran Western star and Hollywood liberal Will Rogers and the two worked together on a number of films.[42] In an interview McCrea testified, "We stood in awe of [Rogers] and knew what he stood for... he had an influence on every thing he touched. He brought glory to it. The behavior on the set was improved, the attitude towards America, the attitude towards Jews, the attitude towards colored people, he could do all that by his example."[43] McCrea's support for Rogers and the "humorous critique of individualism and capitalism" that Lary May argues pervades his work, suggests that McCrea's love of Westerns and cowboy heroes may be squared against a politically liberal attitude.[44] The conflicted and ambiguous politics of *Border River*, perhaps influenced by McCrea's commitments to both the individualist Western hero and liberal politics, can thus be seen to echo the complex political discourses of the cold war period.

Conclusion

Despite its political ambiguities, the overarching colonial narratives through which *Border River* tells its story and negotiates the political tensions of empire and revolution are clearly identifiable. Rather than exhibiting the wide-open vistas and vast plains we might expect of the Western genre, *Border River* presents a closed set, full of tightly framed shots that control and pin down the spaces of the film. Territory was personified as female in early cartography and art, and so too in *Border River*, Calleja's attempts to control territory are depicted through his power over the female lead, Carias. Her body is mapped, bound by the closed spaces of the film, and yet, just as the territory is returned to the Juaristas, through her Mexican heritage Carias becomes politically active and self-determining within the narrative. Her centrality to the film challenges many prevailing accounts of female characters in Westerns in the cold war period. With two differing takes on the politics of revolution and the US Civil War, *Border River* and *Vera Cruz* are nevertheless both framed by questions of land, territory, and empire. The myth of the frontier is an inadequate explanation for the way in which the films engage with their contemporary cultural contexts.

Part III

Regulation

Chapter 6

Ethnicity, Imperialism, and the Law: Policing Identities at the Border

As *Border Incident* (Mann, 1949) begins, images show Mexican workers waiting to cross the borderline into the United States. A sea of faces stretch out back from the border, as the boundary's two layers of chain-link fencing almost completely obscures their features. The wires of the fence intertwine, filling the screen and seeming solid and impenetrable. As the camera pulls in closer, the Mexican workers appear more clearly, yet still gridded by the wire. Imprisoned by the border, the faces of these men are mapped into place by the fence, their helplessness in the face of the American labor system underscored (see figure 6.1). As a few members of the crowd are called forward to receive work permits, hundreds of others are left dejected, hungry, homeless, and with nowhere else to go. Their only option is to attempt to cross the border illicitly, and the landscape that they must traverse is fraught with danger. For *Border Incident*, this Mexican topography is dark, rocky, and mountainous. Almost always filmed at night, its jagged irregular skylines and shadowed valleys are nightmarish and sinister, threatening the lives of the Mexicans who attempt to cross it.

With this opening, *Border Incident* clearly attempts to evoke a sense of the dangers and injustices faced by Mexican migrants who enter the United States without proper documentation. However, the prevailing media environment of the early 1950s was often considerably more hostile toward both undocumented and official migrants. A small selection of the many headlines featured at this time includes "Peons in the West Lowering Culture," "Wetbacks Cross at Two a Minute," and "Mexicans Convert Border into Sieve."[1] This period in American history saw huge changes in terms

Figure 6.1   The US-Mexico border fence highlights the entrapment facing Mexican migrant workers in *Border Incident.*

of migration and border policy; the wartime Bracero Program persisted long into the post–Second World War period as farmers in the US south continued to need the cheap and flexible labor provided by the Mexican workers.[2] The continuation of the official program also led to increasing numbers of undocumented workers, and the two types of migrant were often conflated in media representations such as the above headlines. *Border Incident* attempts to delineate between the two types of migrant workers and rather than flatly condemning undocumented migration, it presents, as the opening narration pointedly attests, "a tale of human suffering and injustice about which you should know."

Just as they are imprisoned behind the border fence at the film's opening, the braceros' spatial fixity is a visual motif that runs throughout the film. These initial scenes emphasize the border's physical role as a barrier and highlight its function as a regulator of movement. John Urry has written about the connections between mobility and power, arguing that "multiple mobilities become central to the structuring of inequality."[3] While Urry claims that in the twenty-first century "there are increasingly few restraints upon states and private corporations seeking to, and succeeding in, monitoring, regulating and limiting people's right to movement," regulation of movement was also central to the United States' relationship with Mexico in the cold war period.[4] *Border Incident*'s braceros make the connections between these different levels of mobility and inequality explicit. As Peter Adey has argued, mobility is also inextricably related to participation in politics and political movements.[5]

Border Incident takes place at the Calexico-Mexicali borderline and presents a narrative that repeatedly moves back and forth across the international boundary, both within the town that is divided through the middle and in the nearby rural borderlands. The mobility of those able to cross the boundary freely is starkly contrasted with the entrapment of the braceros. The braceros' forced stasis eventually leads to their disappearance into the borderlands, and to death for many. While the film undoubtedly portrays the United States as technologically advanced in comparison to its southern neighbor, *Border Incident* also works to equate the police and government institutions of the two countries. Made shortly after the Second World War, wartime good neighborly foreign policies therefore form an important backdrop to the film's production. While many of the Mexican workers meet grisly ends in the movie, intriguingly, the clear hero of the film is not an American cop but rather his Mexican counterpart.

Colonial Subjectivity

It is surely an indication of the high levels of public concern around undocumented Mexican workers at this time that a film was made specifically about the issue. Set on the border between the towns of Calexico and Mexicali, *Border Incident* tells the story of two police officers, one American and one Mexican, who join forces to bring down a criminal syndicate smuggling undocumented migrants into the United States. The first major Hollywood film to take Mexican migration directly as its subject matter, it sees Mexican officer Pablo Rodriguez (Ricardo Montalban) go undercover as a bracero who is smuggled across the border with other Mexican workers. In the United States, the Mexicans face exploitation and imprisonment at the hands of a criminal gang headed by an American ranch owner, Owen Parkson (Howard Da Silva). The American agent Jack Bearnes (George Murphy) also goes undercover as a criminal with access to stolen crossing permits, which he attempts to sell to the smugglers. Outed as an officer of the Immigration and Naturalization Service (INS), Bearnes is killed while Rodriguez defeats the criminals in a final showdown in the deadly "canyon de la muerte."

In an important early critical study of the Bracero Program, Ernesto Galarza argued that the system formed "the prototype of the

production man of the future" with the individual bracero representing "an almost perfect model of the economic man, an 'input factor'
stripped of the political and social attributes that liberal democracy
likes to ascribe to all human beings ideally."[6] This machinistic imagining of the Mexican workers foregrounds the paradox of bracero
noncitizenship; their bodies are welcomed into the United States but
are stripped of all human rights and attributes upon arrival. Building
on this idea, in her study of undocumented Latin American migration to the United States, Mae M. Ngai argues that the system of
Mexican labor in the US south during the Cold War functioned as
a "kind of imported colonialism, which constructed Mexicans working in the United States as a foreign race and justified their exclusion from the polity."[7] For Ngai, both the official Bracero Program
and the regular use of undocumented migrants by ranch owners
served to construct Mexicans as colonial subjects and outsiders. She
argues that undocumented migrants constitute "a social reality and a
legal impossibility" as subjects "barred from citizenship and without
rights."[8] *Border Incident* is closely concerned with the paradoxes facing undocumented braceros in the United States, although ultimately
it cannot provide any answers to these questions. The film constructs
its braceros precisely as colonial subjects who are subjected to enslavement and exploitation. The fact that the film's action takes place on
territory that formerly belonged to Mexico adds a further imperial
dimension to the injustices faced by the braceros.[9]

In his analysis of *Border Incident*, Jonathan Auerbach argues that
the undocumented braceros occupy a position of "radical geopolitical
dislocation and estrangement" in the United States, which he terms
a form of "*noir* citizenship."[10] Developing this argument further in
his book *Dark Borders*, Auerbach contends that *Border Incident* "is
especially important for articulating [a] condition of statelessness or
dispossession...dramatizing the anxieties of a nation-state intent
on policing itself against uninvited outsiders at midcentury."[11] For
Auerbach, *Border Incident*'s engagement with questions of national
identity situates it at the heart of debates around Americanness and
the un-American in the cold war climate. His discussion of un-
Americanness is also useful for understanding the role of the border
in the film:

> Rather than classifying ontologically a type of person or trait, *un-
> American* functioned strictly by negation, a canceling out or reversing
> of a more nebulous set of ideals. The prefix *un-* is so strange because it,
> unlike *anti-*, cannot signify any specific grounds for difference: to be

un-American is not simply to be hostile toward or positioned against American values from some identifiable alternative perspective, but rather to somehow embody the very opposite of "America."[12]

According to Auerbach's reading, American cold war concerns about infiltration by enemies are played out precisely through the label "un-American," which situates the divide between friends and foe along national boundaries. Although Auerbach makes a strong case for this interpretation of *Border Incident* in the context of film noir's relationship to American politics, my argument here is slightly different. While *Border Incident* can certainly be read as noir with its dark visual palette, detective narrative, and themes of isolation, in this chapter I argue that it is most usefully understood as a border film. Starting from the border, this spatially focused analysis of *Border Incident* will enable an exploration of the political climate of the Cold War through the film's representation of the regulation of the border and its comparison of American and Mexican terrain.

The opening of the film presents a sequence of documentary footage of the border, which presages the main action of the narrative. These initial shots show dark mountains, rocky crevasses, and the ominous barbed-wire fence of the border in silhouette. Next, as the narrative action begins, two men are shown escaping across the border from the United States back into Mexico, only to be accosted by a band of menacing riders, their horses steaming and rearing in the night. The fleeing men are murdered, stripped of their money and possessions, and thrown into a quagmire of quicksand where they are ingested by the churning earth. Auerbach has described this quicksand incident as "a kind of birth in reverse, as the sinking, bloodied Mexicans quite literally return to the motherland from whence they came."[13] But this return to the dangerous Mexican terrain at the behest of villainous Americans also establishes a metaphorical comment on the invisibility of the plight of Mexican workers. Literally disappearing in the borderlands, the film highlights the fate faced by many Mexicans as they attempt to cross into the United States as well as the invisibility of their place in American society.

The journey across the border undertaken by Rodriguez is equally perilous. While posing as a bracero awaiting a crossing permit, Rodriguez befriends a young Mexican worker, Juan Garcia (James Mitchell). After deciding to attempt to enter the United States illicitly, the two are bundled into the back of a truck with other braceros. During their treacherous nighttime journey, one of the men dies, only to be dumped out onto the ground by a criminal henchman and left behind. Upon their arrival in the United States, the men are set to work at Parkson's ranch while they await forged documents and onward shipping. The power and reach of Parkson's empire is significant. With agents on both sides of the border, he not only appears to dominate the provision of braceros to the entire farming industry in the region but also controls bars and shops in both Mexicali and Calexico and a network of smugglers and informants across the whole area.

Parkson is vicious and violent in his pursuit of capitalist gains, manipulating the conditions of the border and Mexicans in order to further his business. Upon arrival at his ranch, the braceros are informed they will only be paid 25¢ an hour—just a third of the 75¢ promised to them before the journey across the border. As Garcia protests about the wages, Parkson's chief stooge Jeff Amboy (Charles McGraw) illustrates the level of estrangement the Mexicans face, shouting, "You come in here like a crook, break our laws and expect to be treated like one of us?" This colonial construction is the perfect arrangement for Parkson and his business; Mexicans desperate for work are tempted with tales of good pay and remuneration to cross into the United States without documents. Even though Parkson facilitates the workers' illicit crossing of the border in the first place, upon arrival, he has only to remind the braceros that they entered the country unofficially in order to reassert total control over them.

Just as the braceros were shown imprisoned by the border fence at the film's opening, there is an emphasis on borders and dividing lines throughout the movie. The filmic space is rife with fences that march across the screen, marking the limits of fields and ranches. Signs are another frequent feature, including notices along the borderline that demarcate the division between the two countries with lines and arrows. In this way, Tom Conley finds that the film shouts "'stop, look, and listen': be aware of the compositional frame, the multifarious borders in the landscape, and note that the spaces and territories embody limit-situations and experiences."[14] The limiting of the braceros' lives and freedoms is clearly played out in the demarcated landscapes of the film. As they work in huge fields, long aerial tracking shots show workers moving along regimented lines of crops. These images emphasize the angular, gridded nature of the fields and the straight line of the canal that runs alongside them. Clearly contrasted with the dark, undulating landscape of Mexico, the ordered and modern US terrain traps the Mexican workers in a different way, enclosing them within the gridlines of the fields.[15] They are unable to escape their position fixed outside of citizenship within this imperialist labor system.

Featuring a similar stateless entrapment set around the US-Mexico border, the 1957 British movie *Across the Bridge* (Annakin) sees Carl Schaffner (Rod Steiger) trapped in a Mexican border town. Sharing a vision of the border as a space of regulation, the Mexican and American police work together to prevent Schaffner from leaving the town. They eventually shoot him in the middle of the bridge across the Rio Grande, where he slumps down dead next to the border marker, behind the gridded ironwork of the bridge. In *Espaldas Mojadas* [Wetbacks] (Galindo, 1953), one of the first Mexican movies to tackle migration to the United States, undocumented migrants attempting to swim across the border river are shot at by the US border patrol. The river is patrolled by searchlights, which seek out Mexicans from atop high towers on the US bank; constructed of similar crisscrossing metal bars, this image of gridding is repeated throughout border films produced by nations internationally.

"Two Great Republics": Policing the Divide

The divisions in *Border Incident*'s filmic space construct the film's central distinction between official, documented workers and illicit undocumented ones. A fine line separates them and the difference lies only in paper work permits. These crossing cards or work permits play a significant role in the narrative of the film. In order to catch the criminals and trace the whereabouts of the undocumented braceros, the immigration service employs the use of marked work permits, sold to the smugglers by Bearnes. The criminal gang is unable to move the undocumented braceros without obtaining these false permits, so it is through the marked papers that the immigration authorities identify and track down the migrants, as well as the criminals smuggling them across the border. *Border Incident*'s permits are titled "Record of Admission and Registration of Alien Laborer," and have spaces for name, address, place of birth, identifying marks, details of the employer, a photograph, and fingerprint. Christian Parenti has identified the rise of police photography, fingerprinting, and the documentation of other such "distinguishing features" as practices that worked to "construct 'insider' and 'outsider' identities."[16] Parenti argues that the history of identification is intrinsically bound up with differentiation between people and the construction of others. He traces the emergence of identification documents in the United States back to the passes that were issued to newcomers to colonies and on through the advent of slave passes in the mid-seventeenth century.[17]

In *Border Incident*, without the correct papers, the Mexican migrants are left at the mercy of criminals as colonial subjects with no recourse to help. Although they are freed from Parkson's enslavement at the end of the movie, the film has no answer for their plight. Cutting swiftly from the scenes in the canyon where the undocumented braceros help kill the villains and save Rodriguez from quicksand, the action moves on to its final sweeping aerial shots of farmland. Presumably, those braceros discovered without correct documentation were deported back to Mexico, to wait with hundreds of other desperate people for a permit that may never come. *Border Incident's* crossing cards police the braceros' identities and bodies; through this documentation they are identified as outsiders in identificatory practices that link back to colonial enslavement.

The braceros' status as outsiders is also foregrounded through their identification as criminals throughout the film: their presence in the country breaks the law and they are positioned as illicit and outside of the US body politic. Historically, migrants and immigrants have always been closely aligned with criminals through practices such as fingerprinting. As Simon Cole has shown, fingerprinting initially emerged for the dual purpose of identifying both criminals and immigrants.[18] For *Border Incident*, the crossing cards not only police the braceros' national identities but also position them as criminals, defining their presence in the United States as criminal. In a move that solidifies the connection between the braceros and criminals, one of the film's central marketing suggestions for distributors of the feature was to display "effective 'WANTED' posters around your foyer using stills of the four 'crooks' in BORDER INCIDENT."[19] The wanted posters provided for exhibitors feature mug shots not only of Parkson, Cuchillo, and Zopilote from the criminal gang but also that of Juan, the bracero. Attempts to criminalize undocumented Mexican migrants are still alive today, with the US government's unsuccessful "Border Protection, Anti-terrorism and Illegal Immigration Control Act of 2005," which sought to define an estimated 10–12 million migrants in the United States as criminals.[20] President Obama's efforts to extend "temporary relief from deportation" to undocumented parents of US citizens and to focus on removing "felons not families" from the country takes a small step toward addressing this huge issue in the United States today.[21]

For *Border Incident*, differences between Mexicans and Americans and their respective nations are inscribed both in the landscapes of the countries as well as through the presence of technology and objects of modernity. While many critics have since identified it as film noir,

Border Incident is also usefully considered alongside critical work on semidocumentary police procedurals. In addition to the fact that it was classified as "semidocumentary" and "realistic" in its contemporary reception, the film proclaims itself based on true events, adopts a realist filmmaking style, and features an emphasis on technology and institutions.[22] Mann attested that the template for the movie was indeed drawn from his earlier film, *T-Men* (1948), and there are certainly major similarities in the narratives—both feature government officials working to catch criminals and solve crimes.[23] Both movies focus on the technologies of police work and often center visually on radio equipment, monitors, and other machines. This "special emphasis upon technologically advanced surveillance techniques" is a crucial identifier of the police procedural for William Luhr.[24] The procedural and semidocumentary forms were also inexorably linked at this point in time. As Will Straw argues, "Virtually all the semi-documentaries of the postwar period revolved around public institutions."[25]

Martin Rubin has claimed that in this focus on public institutions semidocumentary and procedural films "carr[y] over wartime spirit into postwar life."[26] Comprised of both semidocumentary and procedural elements, *Border Incident* can, like *T-Men*, be seen as part of a wave of post–Second World War movies that continued to foreground the importance of the work and modernity of state institutions such as the police. In his more historically grounded account of the genre, Straw argues that while semidocumentaries lauded the work of such institutions, they also bore out progressive filmmakers' efforts to "produce films that exalted collective over individual action."[27] Although *Border Incident* certainly does emphasize the importance of institutions and collective actions, the film also has a clear individual hero in Montalban/Rodriguez.[28] Through his ethnic and political identities, Montalban/Rodriguez transcends Frank Krutnik's formulation of individuals as simply "necessary but necessarily regulated" parts of the system in semidocumentaries and procedurals.[29] Through Rodriguez, as well as the objects of modern technology used by both government institutions and individual criminals, the film's interaction with ideas of individualism and collectivity is more complex. For *Border Incident* the interrogation of these issues is used to distinguish different filmic spaces and to explore the relationship between the United States and Mexico at the borderline.

It is not just the police who make use of modern technologies in *Border Incident*, as there is also a great emphasis on the objects and machinery used by the criminals. A police control room receives special focus as professional knowledge embodied in shiny metal banks of machines helps officers track the criminals' whereabouts. But Parkson and his stooges also make use of complex technologies collectively to run their operation. In order to get across the border safely, networks of lookout scouts hide up in the mountainous Mexican landscape, signaling with a system of lights and radio handsets to let the driver of the bracero truck know when the coast is clear. Parkson uses a recording machine in his business dealings, which, when discovered by Mexican henchmen Zopilote (Arnold Moss) and Cuchillo (Alfonso Bedoya), replays a message dictated by him concerning the price of braceros. However, further emphasizing the gap between the United States' technological superiority and Mexico's primitiveness, the bandits are mystified by the disembodied voice and unable to operate the machinery properly. Technology and collective actions also bring about Bearnes's demise; it is the spread of Parkson's networks across the country that enables his contact in Kansas to uncover the INS plot. When this contact phones through his information, Parkson orders Bearnes brutally murdered.

In this sequence, Bearnes is marched out into a dark field that is flat and still with regimented furrows of dirt spanning across the screen. Parkson's henchman Amboy shoots Bearnes as he tries to escape and then starts a nearby tractor towing a plough. The tractor lights bear down on Bearnes, disabled by the gunshot, as successive quick camera shots draw the menacing machine ever closer to him. The plough starts and the camera closes in on its sharp shining blades as they churn and slice the earth. After an excruciating wait, the tractor slowly reaches Bearnes and passes over him. With his last terrible expression of tortuous horror, he is ploughed into the earth, the very same fate met by the braceros on the Mexican side of the border as they disappeared into the roiling quicksand. The tractor burns bright with horrific lights and shunting metalwork, revealing objects of modern technology to be dangerous and deadly in the wrong hands. When not policed and used within the law, modern technology proves fatal.

Despite clearly positioning the United States as a more modern and technologically advanced country than Mexico (although such technology is not always put to positive use), *Border Incident* also stresses the similarities between the two nations and the effectiveness of their collective efforts to catch criminals. Just as the semidocumentary and procedural elements of the movie lend a wartime spirit of the celebration of government institutions, wartime efforts by the film industry to appeal to Latin American markets also seem to permeate its narrative. During the Second World War, movies such as Orson Welles's unfinished *It's All True* (1942–3), and Disney's *Saludos Amigos* (Jackson et al., 1942) were specifically commissioned by the US government to build support for the war effort in Latin America.[30] It was critical that Latin America sided with the Allies, so efforts were made to build alliances within the continent by presenting positive cultural images of the United States to Latin America, and, at the same time, showing positive images of Latin Americans within the United States. Thus, Hollywood was engaged in President Roosevelt's Good Neighbor Policy. So much so, that, as Brian O'Neill notes, it "came to be known unofficially as Hollywood's Good Neighbor Policy."[31] In line with this policy, alongside its remit to monitor images of sex, violence, and amorality, Hollywood's self-regulator, the PCA, was engaged with "equal fervor" in improving images of Latin Americans in Hollywood films at this time.[32]

Hollywood also had clear economic motives in ensuring that films would sell in Latin America as it was fast becoming one of the industry's most important foreign markets. In a special feature on Latin American stars, a movie magazine declared that faced with "shrinking markets elsewhere, the courtship between Hollywood and Latin America is on again. Latin American stars are being imported by the boatload."[33] Alfred Richard has argued that the PCA was at its most effective between 1935 and 1955 and that during this time, it "affected every [Latin American image] portrayed."[34] *Border Incident* was, according to Richard, greeted by the PCA as a "sympathetic treatment of the issue" of Mexican migration, which was very much in line with their agenda.[35] He argues that the office sought to promote themes of "the unity and likeness of peoples in both hemispheres," an ambition that perhaps directly influenced *Border Incident*'s narrative.[36]

Although the film does construct differences between the United States and Mexico in landscape and technology, it also displays a striking effort to emphasize the parity between the police and governmental forces of the two countries, possibly as a result of these wartime governmental policies. One of the central ways in which this takes place is through the comparison drawn between the two officers, Rodriguez and Bearnes. At the start of the film, the police officers are both shown traveling to their meeting at the border by airplane, in almost perfectly symmetrical sequences. It is at this point that the narrative makes the cooperation between the two countries most explicit as the officers confer and decide to "work together to enforce the law." The meeting takes place around a glass-topped table and the officers sit facing one another, framed to appear like mirror images, an effect that is further emphasized by their reflections in the table surface. The script in this scene is full of metaphors of circularity that operate to depict the two countries working in a perfect, equal symbiosis. The Mexican Colonel Raphael Alvardo (Martin Garralaga) explains, "Since the criminals work in a circle, we will cover the circle," as a globe in the room looms large in the shot. The collective, global emphasis of the police institutions' efforts is aligned with the image of the continent of America as a whole, diminishing the separation between the United States and Mexico.[37]

Border Incident is bookended by such narratives of equality, with a similar final ceremony showing officers of both police forces congratulating each other as Rodriguez and Bearnes (posthumously) are awarded medals. The crossed flags of the two countries fill the screen as the camera pulls back, celebrating an equal partnership and the collective work of the two states. As the image then fades to reveal aerial tracking shots of braceros working in geometric American fields, the voiceover intones that these Mexicans workers are now "safe and secure living under the protection of two great republics." For *Border Incident*, when the two nations are operating as equal partners, the exploitation of braceros is eradicated and they are treated fairly. However, the movie cannot offer any solution for its undocumented workers who are simply ejected from the United States and apparently forgotten. The film's publicity materials also emphasize the equivalence of the two male police officers; Montalban and Murphy are given equal billing on the posters, which feature their faces framed again as mirror images of each other. But despite their similarity in the promotional materials, it is certainly Montalban's character and performance that steals the show itself. While the film celebrates the effective collaboration of the United States and Mexico and lauds the collective efforts of the police forces, it nevertheless presents a clearly individualized Mexican hero.

Representing Mexicanness: Identity Politics

Modern farm technology may have led to the untimely demise of *Border Incident*'s American agent but his Mexican counterpart lives to see the end of the movie and defeats the bad guys in the process. Bearnes is subject to repeated beatings and torture in the film and remains imprisoned for much of the time at Parkson's ranch. In contrast, Rodriguez is active and mobile throughout, occupying a far more significant role in the film's narrative. Montalban conspicuously outplays his American partner, and it is his name that appears first in the closing credits. Clara Rodriguez has argued that Latin American characters, and lead characters in particular, were becoming far less prevalent in Hollywood films after the Second World War. Moving away from the more "positive" images of Latin Americans, which she contends characterize 1930s and 1940s Hollywood movies, in the 1950s, "many of the films that featured Latino characters...focused on social problems and were steeped in historical myths, machismo, or stereotypes of Latin lovers and Latina bombshells."[38] Not mythic, macho, or a "Latin lover," Montalban's character in *Border Incident* is thus an unusual lead role for this time.

Rodriguez asserts that the Latin American actors working during this period could choose either to "Europeanize their images" or "play up the stereotypes" in order to get work in the industry.[39] She claims that although the Latin lover and bombshell roles "were in many ways desirable," the roles were often "morally inferior and ended up reinforcing the comfortable American status quo that relegated [Latin American actors] to the back seat."[40] Despite this increasingly difficult climate for Latin American actors in Hollywood, Rodriguez contends that Montalban worked to fashion a career and star persona that enabled him to embrace his Mexican heritage, become a respected actor, and pursue political activities.[41] Before he was cast as the lead in *Border Incident*, Montalban's earlier films with MGM, *Fiesta* (Thorpe, 1947), *On an Island with You* (Thorpe, 1948), and *The Kissing Bandit* (Benedek, 1949) saw him singing, dancing, and lovemaking in what Rodriguez has described as "quintessential Latin lover" roles.[42] *Border Incident*'s press strategy focused on the fact that he was now moving away from such roles to become a serious actor. Yet the narratives around Montalban's presence in the film do not make his Mexicanness invisible but articulate it in a new way. Publicity articles published in the film's press kit seek to move Montalban away from his erstwhile Latin lover image, instead, inaugurating his "brand-new Hollywood career as a dramatic actor."[43] Tropes of Mexicanness are drawn upon through the evocation of a fiery Latin spirit and claims that his dramatic talent "blazed" onto the screen. Montalban's Mexicanness is also emphasized through the film's claims to Mexican authenticity. The fact that he was born in Mexico City is highlighted elsewhere in the publicity material while he is also bestowed with the moniker of "Mexico's film idol."[44]

An article in *Picturegoer* magazine published just before *Border Incident*'s release similarly recognizes Montalban as the exemplar of a "new approach to the Latin star."[45] Titled "The End of the Latin Lover?" the article postulates verbosely that

> the proverbial Latin lover of the prewar days...is a thing of the past...The new generation of Latin stars taken to Hollywood are more remarkable for their dramatic ability than for any particular ability to gaze at their leading ladies with the soulful eyes of a love-sick gazelle.[46]

Featuring a photograph of Montalban and his wife Georgina at home with their baby daughter, the article presents an image of him as a serious Mexican actor set to take Hollywood by storm. His Mexicanness is not played up or made invisible and his heritage and acting prowess are emphasized through reference to his successful Mexican productions, notably *Nosotros* [Us] (Rivero, 1945) for which he won a major award. Montalban would later go on to found the political campaign group Nosotros, which pressured the film industry to "change the portrayal of Chicanos on screen."[47] The group campaigned for equality in casting for Mexicans and Chicanos and, in his own words, "simply asked that such people be *considered* for acting opportunities."[48] Victoria Thomas stresses that Montalban's important strides in advancing Chicano rights within the film industry date from his first arrival in Hollywood, throughout his early Latin lover roles and beyond.[49]

Given *Border Incident*'s subject matter we can perhaps assume that Montalban approved, to some extent, of the character of Rodriguez, as well as the narrative highlighting the oppression of undocumented braceros. Indeed, it appears that the script was chosen by its filmmakers specifically because of its social concerns and liberal approach. Produced by veteran social problem filmmaker Dore Schary, Auerbach argues that "*Border Incident* presumably appealed to the liberal Schary less for its police plot...than for its representation of a disadvantaged group's oppression."[50] Mann too was a prominent liberal figure in Hollywood, and part of a group of newly emerging directors in the postwar period who championed "social realism and left-liberalism," according to film historian Thomas Schatz.[51] With a "progressive political agenda and a strong interest in film realism," these filmmakers strove to make movies that dealt with social problems and issues in a realist style.[52] During the HUAC investigations of the early 1950s, both the film's assistant director Howard Koch and actor Howard Da Silva were blacklisted because of their left-wing activities.[53] *Border Incident*'s filmmakers therefore seem to have been drawn to it because of its progressive themes and their left-wing political agenda likely impacted on the focus on oppression and ethnicity as well as the semidocumentary style. Although it was almost certainly influenced by good neighborly and economic imperatives to present images of Latin America that reflected the unity of the continent, *Border Incident* also appears to have been a project of political importance to its filmmakers.

Despite the liberal influences of the PCA alongside input from Montalban, Schary, Mann, and others, *Border Incident* retains several crude Mexican bandit characters. Played by regular character actors Moss, Bedoya, and José Torvay, characters Zopilote, Cuchillo, and Pocoloco embody the typical dirty, sleazy, and dangerous bandidos found in the mountainous regions of Hollywood's Mexico. Although just three women feature in the entire picture—and each only very fleetingly at that—the crooks still find time to slobber at them while keeping up with their day job of cutting the throats of unsuspecting braceros. This trio of actors features regularly in American films set on or south of the border and appear in several other movies analyzed in the book.[54] It is often the character actors who are highlighted in *Border Incident*'s contemporary critical reviews, where they are praised for their efforts in spite of the brutish roles they are ascribed. *Variety* found Moss "firstrate" in *Border Incident* while the *New York Times* highlighted Moss and Bedoya for their "amusing" portrayal of "venal Mexicans."[55] The characters' names too seem so exaggerated as to be caricatures, with Zopilote, Cuchillo, and Pocoloco translating respectively as "vulture," "knife," and "a little mad." Although the characters they play are exaggeratedly vile bandidos, the performances of these character actors were not always taken at face value by either critics or filmmakers; despite the limits and constraints of the roles, the actors' craft and the excessiveness of their caricatured characters seem to have been at least partially appreciated and understood.

Conclusion

Border Incident is a film made by liberal filmmakers that uses the border to question the policing of migration and employment practices relating to Mexican workers in the US south. Condemning the exploitation of braceros who cross into the United States without official documentation, the film portrays these workers as colonial subjects, entrapped by a corrupt American capitalist, and without any chance of escape. The braceros are stuck, fixed in place with no recourse to aid. However, once Parkson and his criminal gang are defeated, the film ends with an endorsement of the use of Mexican labor when it is overseen by Mexico and the United States together. Unable to address the plight of the undocumented braceros, the movie concludes instead with a celebration of the very governmental institutions that eject the Mexicans from the country and fix them outside of citizenship.

Despite emphasizing the United States' superiority in terms of technology and modernity, the film also stresses the parity between the police forces and governmental institutions of the two nations. Not only does a Mexican actor star alongside an American but he also steals the show and takes top billing. Forming a key turning point in Montalban's career, this first foray into Hollywood drama set the tone for a life that would be spent fighting for Chicano rights and opportunities within the film industry. *Border Incident* uses images of the US-Mexico border for political ends, perhaps as a result of its filmmakers' political interests, good neighborly influences, or Hollywood's economic imperative to appeal to Latin American markets. The connections between the United States and Mexico depicted in the film are also indicative of the changing relationship between the two countries in the Cold War. *Border Incident*'s conflicting emphases on the cooperation of the two countries and the differences between them seem to capture some of the complexities of the US-Mexico relationship at the time.

Chapter 7

Border Cities as Contested Space: Postcolonial Resistance in Tijuana

The city of Tijuana has been profoundly affected by the influence of the United States throughout its history, and by the American film industry in particular. In 1915 Tijuana had just 1,000 inhabitants, but by 1960 it had become a bustling border city of over 185,000 people.[1] American tourism to the city boomed initially during the 1920s and 1930s, as prohibition drove thrill seekers south of the border to indulge in drinking and gambling. Large casino and racetrack complexes were built in response to the rapidly increasing numbers of tourists. Visitors often included Hollywood stars, and so the resorts featured regularly in American press. Paul Vanderwood has described the mythic status that Tijuana has acquired in the United States as a form of "persistent lure" for Americans.[2] Vanderwood writes,

> Tijuana seems to nudge, even challenge, something quite profound in the American psyche. Crossing the border evokes a feeling of "freedom," not just raising hell and having a good time, but as *Liberty* put it, a sense of "playing hooky from the world's greatest supervisor of morals—Uncle Sam."[3]

Tijuana's tourist industry prevails to this day and the city remains a popular destination for Americans, despite fluctuations in numbers over time and recent challenges to the industry as a result of narcoviolence.

Tijuana has also been a frequent fixture on American movie screens since the beginning of the twentieth century. Across a variety of genres such as Westerns (*The Border Raiders* [Paton, 1918]), racing stories (*Riders Up* [Cummings, 1924]), and police dramas (*Federal*

Man [Tansey, 1950]), Tijuana has held a lasting appeal for Hollywood filmmakers perhaps because of this sense of amorality. In his study of the relationship between Tijuana and Hollywood, Tim Girven has claimed that cinematic images of Tijuana produced in the 1920s and 1930s set the tone for a representation of the city as dark, seedy, and dangerous that would persist throughout the century.[4]

Tijuana has been the focus of a substantial body of academic work alongside the sustained attention it has received from the American film industry. As Josh Kun and Fiamma Montezemolo have argued, the city has variously been described as "'hybrid,' 'not Mexico,' 'the End of Latin America and the beginning of the American Dream,' 'the happiest place on earth,' 'a laboratory of postmodernity,' 'a third space,' 'a porous border,' 'a Walled City,' a 'drug capital.'"[5] Among the many different writings on and about Tijuana, the inability to define this city through any single lens or mythology is the one consistent theme. For Humberto Félix Berumen, "[Tijuana] is a kind of palimpsest made up of multiple voices that have contributed to diversify its own social physiognomy."[6] Similarly, Santiago Vaquera-Vásquez describes Tijuana as a place of "fragmentation: there is no conception of a total Tijuana. In this sense, Tijuana is known, but only in passing, never as a unit."[7] Drawing on this idea of fragmentation and multiplicity, Tijuana has also been hailed as a quintessentially postmodern city by authors such as Néstor García Canclini, Guillermo Gómez-Peña, Santiago Vaquera-Vásquez, and Lauro Zavala.[8] As a no-place or *ciudad de paso*, Tijuana is figured as a liberatory manifestation of globalization through its cultural mixing and hybridity. However, following Kun and Montezemolo's approach, these romanticized images of the city seem to reduce it to only a border crossing. Understanding the city instead as a real space that is home to its many inhabitants, this chapter aims to engage with and build on critical frameworks developed from within Tijuana.

Despite critics' repeated emphasis on the impossibility of defining Tijuana, many have denounced Hollywood representations of the city as responsible for creating and perpetuating the very singular black legend or *leyenda negra* surrounding Tijuana. Making a similar argument to Girven, Berumen asserts, "The myth of Tijuana as the ultimate city of vice is the result of the articulations and distribution of American cinema in the 1920s and 1930s."[9] Berumen contends that many of the films about Tijuana use the city's name in their titles "as if it were the unquestionable symbol of vice and indulgence."[10]

However, some of Hollywood's cinematic visions of Tijuana are also are concerned with exploring the relationship between the legend and the real experiences of those inhabiting the city, despite being ultimately bound up in this mythmaking. *The Tijuana Story*, a film directed by Leslie Kardos in 1957 is one such movie. The tagline used on the film's promotional material, "the most notorious sucker-trap in the western hemisphere," explicitly evokes the city's seedy reputation. Alongside the title, which seems to use the city's name precisely as an "unquestionable symbol of vice and indulgence," the film's poster shows a woman dressed in red patrolling a street lit by cantinas and bars. Despite these efforts to evoke a sense of infamy and seediness, the promotional material accompanies a story that combines semidocumentary sequences showing the urban spaces and people of Tijuana with a narrative focused on the local community's fight against organized crime.

The Tijuana Story is based on the true story of Manuel Acosta Mesa (played by Rodolfo Acosto), a Tijuanan journalist murdered by a criminal cartel in 1956 as he strove to clean up the city. The cartel terrorizes the town, beating a schoolteacher to death for reporting the selling of drugs to children, and intimidating Acosta Mesa and his family. The violence against Acosta Mesa escalates as he refuses to stop condemning the gangsters in his editorials, eventually leading to his assassination. After his death, Acosta Mesa's son continues his work and rouses the community to pull together to defeat the criminals. At the journalist's funeral, Tijuanans turn out to pay their respects and show their support for his ideals.

The Black Legend of Tijuana

In 1929, a United Artists executive remarked, "There is a difference between using the name Tia Juana [*sic*] and some other name that is not known, because it has certain connotations—it has a meaning to the audiences and brings a reaction in them."[11] Tijuana has appeared in US film footage from at least as early as 1915, when a newsreel filmed the opening of a new racetrack and American filmmakers have persistently returned to the city ever since.[12] Girven argues that Tijuana's image as vice-ridden and corrupt was cultivated during the period between 1924 and 1935, producing the "prototypical" US vision of Tijuana.[13] Girven attests that these films enacted an imperialist gaze that sought to fix Tijuana as other, which has persisted in US cinematic visions of the city ever since.

Alongside cinematic representations of Tijuana, the close connections between the city and Hollywood personnel contributed to the creation of a licentious image of the place at this time. Hollywood stars and the media circulating around them also played an important role. Hollywood luminaries including Charlie Chaplin, Dolores del Rio, and Roscoe "Fatty" Arbuckle frequented early Tijuanan luxury resorts such as Agua Caliente. This famous casino and racetrack complex was also where Marguerita Cansino—later Rita Hayworth—was first discovered as a teenage dancer. Press images of stars cavorting in the grand casinos brought the city national attention in the United States. For Girven, Tijuana thus became "a space in which the personal lives of screen idols [were] publically played out."[14] Newspapers and fan magazines featured shocking stories of stars' behavior as they drank and gambled across the border while these activities were banned at home. In addition, scandalous celebrities such as Olive Thomas, who died of a drug overdose in Paris, and Fatty Arbuckle, tried three times for manslaughter, were such frequent clients of the casinos and racetracks of Tijuana that they became inextricably associated with the place.[15] Celebrity scandals like these became known as Tijuana bibles, the same name given to the pornographic comics that often featured famous actors and also emerged around this time.[16] While the press regularly featured coverage of stars holidaying in Tijuana, Hollywood celebrities were also invoked in the marketing of the city's glamorous hospitality and adverts for the resorts featured images of celebrities such as Clark Gable, Bing Crosby, Helen Twelvetrees, and Jean Parker relaxing south of the border.[17] The Tijuanan resorts were therefore intimately linked with Hollywood glamour through these advertisements. Widely displayed through this press coverage, the stars' scandals and the city alike became known across the United States.

It was also no coincidence that the physical growth of the city of Tijuana coincided directly with both the advent of Prohibition in the United States and the rise of Hollywood filmmaking; the city first began to increase rapidly in size in response to US demand for alcohol, gambling, and prostitution. The rising interconnectedness of Tijuana and Hollywood also played a major role in boosting general US tourism to the city. John Price has claimed, "Tijuana was born solely of…trade and tourism. It has no history prior to the creation of the border."[18] In this way, Tijuana can be understood as the dialectical product of interaction with the United States. Because of the significant influence of the Hollywood industry during this period of rapid growth in Tijuana, cinema is also deeply implicated in the construction of the city and its image.

Price suggests that the view of Tijuana that developed in the United States through the 1920s and 1930s was of "a city of vice where prostitution, pornographic movies, live sex demonstrations, and drug traffic were unequalled."[19] Other scholars agree that the city's reputation has played an important role in its history and its relationship with the United States. Jennifer Insley has argued that "according to popular US discourse, the city is the ultimate symbol of Mexican lust, dishonesty, and darkness."[20] Whereas Diana Palaversich finds the "leyenda negra de Tijuana" (black legend of Tijuana) to be the most persistent and pervasive discourse about the city.[21] The phrase "leyenda negra" dates from criticism of Spanish colonization of the Americas, and was first coined by Spanish intellectual Julián Juderías in 1914 in order to protest "the characterization of Spain by other Europeans as a backward country of ignorance, superstition, and religious fanaticism that was unable to become a modern nation."[22] Rafaela Castro argues that the black legend has continued to influence attitudes toward Hispanics and Mexicans since then, finding it responsible for widespread "derogatory stereotyping of Mexicans" and "the uncivil treatment of Mexicans and Califonios" during the war of 1846–8 between the United States and Mexico.[23] Many scholars have argued that Tijuana's leyenda negra was "initially constructed on the celluloid screen," explicitly implicating the American film industry in the creation of this pejorative mythology.[24] Further, Palaversich's argument specifically foregrounds the role of American imperialism in the production of the city and its mythic status. Because it recalls the war between the two countries, which saw the United States take control of a huge proportion of Mexico's territory, the American legend of Tijuana foregrounds its own colonial effects, positioning the United States' imperial actions in a continuum with those of colonial Spain. Colonialism and the critical work of postcolonialism are therefore invoked in Palaversich's emphasis on the historical roots of this American vision of Tijuana.[25]

Jane Jacobs has emphasized the important role that the city often played in the regulation of colonies, attesting that "it was in outpost cities that the spatial order of imperial imaginings was rapidly and deftly realised."[26] But despite the city's role in establishing imperial power and order, the very nature of these complex, multifarious places means that they are also spaces of contestation. Jacobs continues,

> Imperialist manipulations of space never had an unchallenged surety, either in the past or the present. Precisely because cities are sites of "meetings," they are also places which are saturated with possibilities for the destabilisation of imperial arrangements.[27]

Just as Tijuana was not simply constructed by Hollywood but in dialogue with it, there also exist spaces of challenge and "destabilisation" both within the city and in representations of its legend. *The Tijuana Story* is one such space of resistance that challenges prevailing American visions of the city through its content and form.

The Cinematic City: Destabilizing Spaces

The Tijuana Story explores different stories and experiences of the city and the film highlights a wide range of different viewpoints and perspectives within its cinematic space. The word perspective invokes ideas of personal opinion and physical position: both the ideological and the geographic. Giuliana Bruno argues that the development of perspective in art in the fifteenth century enabled new, shifting visions that broke away from the linearity that had previously pervaded visual culture. This enabled the later development of perspectival cartographic practices such as bird's eye view and a mobile visual culture replete with multiple, moving viewpoints, which in turn led to the emergence of cinematic vision. Bruno claims,

> Cinematic vision bears the destabilizing effect of a shifting, mobilized field. The product of the history of space, filmic space is a terrain of shifting positions—the product of multiple, incorporated, and mobile viewpoints.[28]

For Bruno, cinematic images always incorporate multiple, flexible, and shifting perspectives that do not present a totalizing vision but rather a destabilizing one. Despite its thematic focus on corruption and criminality, *The Tijuana Story* breaks down a hegemonic imperial account of the city and instead presents a multitude of mobile, shifting perspectives that are unfixed and detotalizing, offering a multiperspectival experience for audiences.

A documentary sequence narrated by Los Angeles newspaper reporter and television personality Paul Coates opens the film and the first image is a long shot of Tijuana's main strip, Avenida de Revolución. The view shifts to a high-angle long shot of the border crossing shown from the American side as cars stream under arches into and out of Mexico, while Coates tells of the 12 million American visitors to the city in 1956 (see figure 7.1). In an unusually dislocating cut, the camera is then suddenly positioned under one of these arches in the dark, as the cars drive through from the United States toward the screen. This edit almost violates the traditional 180-degree axis

Figure 7.1   Cars stream across the border into Mexico in *The Tijuana Story.*

of action of classic Hollywood cinema, which the rest of the movie adheres to. This shift in position physically transports viewers through the border, and with its dislocating jolt of unconventional editing, the audience is thrown off-balance in a liminal borderline space.

The Tijuana of *The Tijuana Story* is marked by constant movement within the cinematic frame. Cars are always shown in motion, moving up and down the streets as tourists walk along pavements filling the frame with movement in multiple directions. The film shifts its national territory too, switching between the US and Mexico in the space of a cinematic cut, recalling the dislocating border crossings of *Borderline* (Seiter, 1950). Multiple perspectives are also presented through the cinematic architecture. This opening sequence contrasts different viewpoints and angles on the city's streets and buildings, presenting a constantly moving and dislocating effect. Exterior shots of Tijuana repeat throughout the film and construct a border city architecture that is ephemeral as each shot fades into the next. This cinematic city is always in motion as the camera moves through streets and switches from one angle to another, from long shot to close-up of the city.

The concept of border architecture developed by Eloy Méndez Sáinz and Jeff Banister is useful in understanding how these spaces of Tijuana operate. They argue,

"Transitional architecture" is a contradiction in terms in which the natural inclination toward permanence sinks into the waters of the

> ephemeral...Transitions favor the meaningless, the non-place. And
> border cities are international ports destined to combine the various
> conditions of passageways, or areas of transition.[29]

The idea that border cities are comprised of transitional architecture
and spaces that are always changing and in motion, is articulated in
a filmic language. Likewise, *The Tijuana Story*'s city is seen from
a multiplicity of moving perspectives. This cinematic city is also
marked as a non-place through the camera's focus on neon signs.
The clubs and bars that these signs belong to do not appear at all
in the background of the shots, and neon lights alone are shown
in extended montages one after the other, surrounded by an empty
black screen. The camera angles change with each new neon sign in
a sequence of extremely canted shots, producing a jarring discon-
nect in the filmic space. Through this ever-moving and changing
transitional space, the filmic border city becomes unstable with its
diverse, conflicting, and shifting perspectives. Thus, the film seems
to support Michael Dear and Gustavo Leclerc's assertion that "the
principal trope in artistic, cultural, and intellectual representations
of Tijuana is space."[30] However, in this cinematic representation of
the city, space is rendered paradoxical and transitional. The different
geographic perspectives offered on the city seem to echo the contradiction between the film's mythologizing marketing and its central narrative, which attempts to present filmgoers with Tijuanenses's
own views of their home.

The view of the city offered by *The Tijuana Story* is further destabilized through the constant shifting of its framing narratives. The
film opens with an American telling of events provided by the Los
Angeles reporter. After the first sequence of documentary images
of Tijuana and the border crossing, a new scene shows newspapers
being printed. The voiceover describing the courageous journalism of Mexican hero Acosta Mesa clearly suggests that these are his
papers going to print. Yet as the camera pauses for a close-up on
one of the printed newspapers, it is revealed that it is in fact Coates's
paper, the *Los Angeles Mirror*. As the film's credits and title are
superimposed atop the printing machines rattling off copies of the
US paper, it suggests that the Tijuana story is the story of Coates's
own journalism. Coates is then shown at his desk, apparently in the
middle of his work, reading out headlines from *El Imparcial*, the
Mexican newspaper. Presented through the prism of the US journalist's reports, this initial framing device appears to offer audiences a
highly mediated view of Tijuana.

Following these introductory sequences, Coates reappears in the middle of the film, enacting a similar dislocating shift as it moves the action from the Mexican center of the story in Tijuana back to his newspaper offices in Los Angeles. His voiceover also bursts back into the movie to provide narration for a scene that shows Acosta Mesa deciding to reinstate his newspaper in the face of intimidation from the gangsters. Coates speaks for Acosta Mesa here, his voiceover providing the words as the Mexican journalist's soundless mouth moves on the screen. Having been immersed in the Mexican tale, audiences are suddenly pulled back to Coates's story in the United States. The film's repeated and abrupt switching back and forth between the two countries draws attention to this framing device and thus begins to question Coates's perspective and position as the narrator. The story resists framing by the US journalist as it highlights the artificiality of his narration and the film refuses to offer a unified perspective on the city.

The performance of Acosto in the title role further challenges American perspectives of Tijuana in the movie. Acosto was known for playing bad guys and bandits as a character actor in movies such as *The Fugitive* (Ford, 1947), *City of Bad Men* (Jones, 1953), and *Bandido* (Fleischer, 1956). *The Tijuana Story* marked his first and only lead role in American cinema and the strength of his performance was certainly not lost on the film's contemporary critics. Acosto was almost unanimously regarded as the highlight of the film, and the fact that he presented an authentic "native Mexican" voice telling a Mexican story was far more significant for commentators than Coates's appearance.[31] *Kinematograph Weekly* found Acosto's portrayal "powerful and sensitive" and that the film "frequently touches the heart."[32] For *The Hollywood Reporter*, Acosto was "particularly impressive," and *Variety* found his performance "outstanding" in its "dignity and force."[33] Acosto offered audiences an important and believable Mexican voice in the film, which challenged the narration and perspective on events offered by Coates.

As J. Brian Harley has argued, the act of mapping is never deployed without some form of political power.[34] Similarly, cinematic representations of places are never devoid of political impact. Alongside its formal challenge to imperial accounts of the city, the thematic content and visual style of *The Tijuana Story* also conveys political contestations. At moments, the film bears a resemblance to *The Grapes of Wrath* (Steinbeck, 1939) and *Salt of the Earth* (Biberman, 1954), two cultural texts that are renowned for their revolutionary sentiments. During one of his rousing speeches in the movie Acosta Mesa declares that "when a decent man is hurt, I feel it." The line cannot help but recall Tom Joad's final speech in *The Grapes of Wrath* in content, tone, and rhythm: "Wherever there's a fight so hungry people can eat, I'll be there. Wherever there's a cop beating up a guy, I'll be there."[35] The lines given to Acosta Mesa's publisher (Michael Fox) also echo this revolutionary and communitarian sentiment. His final speech in the film makes explicit the film's collective, socialist ethos: "Manuel was right, there is no power in the world stronger than us. Together we can clean up Tijuana, all it takes is the will."

During the film's closing funeral sequence, the stylistic influence of *Salt of the Earth* can also be felt. Given the similar focus on the plight of oppressed Mexican communities, this further visual similarity seems to draw a clear comparison between the two films. *The Tijuana Story*'s funeral procession shows Acosta Mesa's family, friends, and members of the community passing through the streets of Tijuana. Intercut with long shots of the slow-moving procession are distinctive close-ups of townsfolk, showing their faces and expressions to demonstrate their empathy with Acosta Mesa's cause. Recalling the slow, documentary-style close-ups used to show the determination and nobility of the strikers in *Salt of the Earth*, these images lend *The Tijuana Story* a further socialist and revolutionary ethos, presenting Tijuana as a moral and politicized community.

Series Exposés, Populism, and Politics: Production Contexts

The Tijuana Story was directed by Kardos and produced by Sam Katzman in 1957. During the 1950s, producer Katzman was best known for the *Jungle* series of movies (earning him the nickname "Jungle Sam") and for making breakthroughs into teen audiences with controversial youth rebellion features *Rock around the Clock* (Sears, 1956) and *Don't Knock the Rock* (Sears, 1956). Katzman is widely credited with a talent for spotting contemporary issues with potential for exploitation at the cinema, such as the rise of rock and roll.[36] As Wheeler Winston Dixon argues, during the 1950s, "with the exception of one or two ill-conceived projects [Katzman's films] attracted the public's attention and reaped substantial returns at the box office."[37] Katzman was known as one of "the most cost-conscious—and because of this, one of the most controversial—producers working in Hollywood in the 1950s."[38] Throughout the decade he produced an average of 3 serials and 17 features a year. Films were often made in just 6 days and for budgets of less than $100,000.[39]

The producer publicly professed his lack of interest in the artistic merit of his pictures, declaring his own "moviemaking philosophy" in the *Life* magazine feature "Meet Jungle Sam": "I'll never make an Academy Award movie but I am just happy to get my achievement plaques from the bank."[40] Despite the cultivation of this philistinic moneymaking image, Katzman has been lauded as one of the very first independent filmmakers in the United States who granted considerable artistic freedom to directors and writers.[41] More so than any other producer of the time, he also made regular use of crewmembers blacklisted by HUAC.[42]

The Tijuana Story was made by Katzman's company Clover Productions for Colombia Pictures and formed one in a series of crime exposés set in different cities. Previous Clover Productions flicks *The Houston Story* (Castle, 1955) and *Miami Exposé* (Sears, 1956) were also centered on social problems in the cities but had a very different tone. Being dramatic stories of corruption, murder, and betrayal, these films threw a sensational light on violent scenarios, forming part of what Will Straw has identified as a cycle of lurid "city confidential" films. Drawing upon "the traditions of the semi-illicit stag film, the police procedural, the semi-documentary instruction film, the vice exposé movie and the low-budget mystery," the city confidential cycle is comprised of exposés set in various American cities.[43] Straw argues that the films' "narratives... are secondary to their cataloguing of vice, and to the formal organization of these films as sequences of scenes in night-clubs, gambling dens and along neon-lit streets."[44] Perhaps unsurprisingly, *The Houston Story* was slammed by contemporary reviewers as a "machine-made racketeer picture which lacks distinction in all departments."[45] *The Tijuana Story*, however, stands apart from Clover Productions' other exposé flicks as well as the wider cycle of city confidential films. Described by Kun as "a rare case of responsible Hollywood filmmaking about border life," the film's social realist style, similarities to explicitly left-wing films, and narrative of morality and community positions it as a more complex picture that engages with the tensions between American mythologies of Tijuana and the lived experience of the city's inhabitants.[46]

Although *The Tijuana Story* shifted the exposé series outside of the United States into a Mexican city for the first time, the interdependence of the two countries in the border region is emphasized through the fact that Coates provides the film's narration. Coates regularly wrote about Tijuana in his "Confidential File" column in the *Los Angeles Mirror* and helped bring national coverage to the events surrounding Acosta Mesa's death, stories that perhaps caught Katzman's eye and led to the production of the film. Indeed, in his columns Coates depicts the situation in Tijuana in cinematic terms, drawing on classic iconography of Westerns and Mexican bandidos. He writes that the community of vigilantes in the city "wear no broad sombreros, no special uniforms, no shiny badges. They pack no pistols."[47]

The Tijuana Story was received as a film with clear political aims, unlike the other movies in the exposé series, despite its own rather lurid marketing strategy. The *Monthly Film Bulletin* found that "the film is at pains to ask Americans not to judge Mexico by its border towns."[48] Its semidocumentary style and authentic setting was also highlighted as a key part of the film's appeal by reviewers.[49] In addition, the actors' Mexicanness was important, and *The Hollywood Reporter* found "added interest" in the fact that "Mexican players look and act like Mexicans even when portrayed by Americans."[50] The fact that *The Tijuana Story* presented a "true story" ostensibly guaranteed by the documentary style and the authentic Mexican voices was important for the film's contemporary reviewers and connected to their understandings of it as a film with a specific political project. Further heightening the sense that the film was a kind of personal crusade, *Variety* reported that "producer Sam Katzman kept this project on the shelf a couple of years because of threats from certain sinister underworld figures."[51] Notwithstanding the fact that the events in Tijuana took place only a year before he made the film, the image of Katzman braving underworld threats to bring the truth to light on behalf of the Mexican townsfolk is a compelling one.

It seems that the plight of the community struggling to overthrow a criminal cartel caught the American public imagination at the time, given that Katzman chose this particular story for the movie. Additionally, as Coates's *LA Mirror* reports, national press such as the *New York Times* covered the shooting of Acosta Mesa and the story of his newspaper, *El Imparcial*.[52] While it may be the case that *The Tijuana Story* was made in response to public interest in the story, aspects of the film that evoke specifically left-wing themes and stylings perhaps suggest that Katzman and the filmmakers also had personal and political motivations in making the film. Granted freedoms unavailable elsewhere in the Hollywood system, the production crew were able to pursue this unusually themed film, which seems awkwardly positioned within the sensational exposé series.

Straw has argued that during the post–Second World War period, semidocumentary filmmaking style such as that featured in *The*

Tijuana Story emerged from a grouping of filmmakers whose political position lay somewhere between a "progressive coalition" and "left-wing activism."[53] Such documentary film style has its origins in early travel films or travelogues, which Jeffrey Ruoff has described as "an open form" that "offers an alternative to both the linear cause-and-effect structure of classical Hollywood cinema and the problem-solution approach of Griersonian documentary."[54] Drawing on the early form of the travelogue, documentary and semidocumentary traveling films would become a way for filmmakers to move outside of dominant Hollywood narrative frames and structures. Seen as part of this move, *The Tijuana Story* can be understood as a descendent of the travelogue movie. Although it participates in the appropriation of Tijuana for American audiences in the manner of a travelogue, through its semidocumentary style and, its constant shifting of perspectives and frames, it also resists dominant Hollywood visions of Tijuana.

Alfred Bendixen and Judith Hamera have written of American travel writing that it is, "like travel itself,...constitutive, a tool of self- and national fashioning that constructs its object even as it describes it."[55] As a travel narrative, *The Tijuana Story* can indeed be understood as constituting the American nation while it tours the streets of Tijuana. Despite its Mexican setting, the film is preoccupied with and framed by the impact of the events on the United States. Although the narrative takes care to emphasize the connections between the two countries and between Coates and Acosta Mesa as newsmen, differences are also plain. US technological superiority is highlighted through the contrasting newsrooms. Acosta Mesa works at a desk with pen and paper, whereas newspapers are mechanically produced on a massive scale at the *Los Angeles Mirror*. In this sense, *The Tijuana Story* reinforces aspects of American national identity including technological superiority and mass media production, as also seen in movies such as *Borderline* and *Border Incident* (Mann, 1949).

But rather than primarily working to constitute the American nation, *The Tijuana Story* instead interrogates the United States' contradictory war on imperialism through its examination of the border town and the relationship between the United States and Mexico. According to John Fousek, nationalism was vitally important to the United States during the Cold War. He argues that "American nationalist ideology provided the principal underpinning for the broad public consensus that supported Cold War foreign policy."[56] Fousek contends that the Cold War was fought specifically in the name of the nation, rather than capitalism or the West, in order to win over public opinion. He continues to claim that political discourses "linked U.S. global responsibility to anticommunism and enveloped both within a framework of American national greatness."[57] Although nationalism was certainly a key theme at work in US governmental rhetoric, the war was also widely understood in terms of imperialism and colonialism. Christian Appy contends that one of the key tenets of US political discourse at this time was the idea that "freedom was everywhere endangered by a red imperialism of unprecedented power and ambition."[58] For Appy, the threat of Soviet colonialism meant that the United States needed to assume "world leadership and global responsibility—the key phrases by which American policymakers at once denied imperialism and enacted it."[59]

In *The Tijuana Story*, the United States' imperial influence in Tijuana forms a regulatory practice, shaping and controlling the city. However, American legends are challenged and subverted through the film's semidocumentary and travelogue style. The regulation of mobility at the border lies at the heart of *The Tijuana Story*'s narrative, and it is precisely through movement that the film's vision of the city resists dominant American narratives of this space. The film's more open form that operates in the style of a travelogue frees it from standard narrative storylines, and the left-wing lineage of semidocumentary filmmaking also hints at the subversive nature of the picture.

Conclusion

Tijuana has a long history as a cinematic space and the Hollywood film industry played a significant role in both the growth of the city and the production of its mythic status. *The Tijuana Story* is an American-made film that does not simply perpetuate the black legend of the city constructed in American cinema but through its contradictory embracing of both the city's seedy mythology and the perspective of Tijuanan citizens it can perhaps offer new understandings of the city's history. Although the film maps out the city for its voyaging American viewers, it is not with a totalizing imperialist gaze but with a more itinerant and transitional one. We are sure of neither which side of the border we may be at any one time nor which perspective of events we are being presented by the film's ever-shifting narrative viewpoints. As it derails such imperial visions of the city, *The Tijuana Story* opens up a multitude of other possible alternatives, suggesting that there can be no single story of Tijuana but rather manifold shifting and competing narratives. The transitional spaces of this cinematic city, coupled with Hollywood's complex historical connections with Tijuana raise important questions about the extent of cinema's visible, physical effects on the border.

In analyzing the history of American mythologies of Tijuana, I have suggested that these legends foreground their own colonial effects. In examining the production contexts of the film it is also clear that there can be no definitive account of its influences or political persuasions. However, its striking appeal to the style and imagery of explicitly left-wing cultural texts coupled with its difference from the other films of the city confidential cycle suggest that there may have been specific political motivations behind the production. Alongside the other border films examined in this book, *The Tijuana Story* demonstrates that contrary to the "end of ideology" identified by critics in the 1950s, the cold war period bore witness to diverse and politically multifarious cultural texts that looked outside of the United States and beyond questions of nationalism to articulate their positions.[60]

Chapter 8

Imperial Journeys and Traveling Shots: Regulation, Power, and Mobility

In a memo to Universal-International written following a screening of the studio's provisional cut of *Touch of Evil* (1958), Orson Welles argues against the inclusion of a scene that "sweetens" the relationship between newlyweds Susan and Mike Vargas. In the memo, Welles links the growing personal distance between the characters in the middle of the film to the international border, which serves as a backdrop to the movie's action, arguing that "their separation, too, is directly the result of a sort of 'border incident' in which the interests of their two native countries are in some conflict."[1] The relationship between the protagonists here is figured spatially and the border is positioned as a metaphoric divide or collision between them. The choice of language is curious, and the explicit reference to a "border incident" cannot be ignored. It spells out a clear lineage for *Touch of Evil* that connects directly to Anthony Mann's earlier movie *Border Incident* (1949) with its similar narrative and thematic structures, as well as the wider cycle of border films examined in this book.

As in *Border Incident*, *Touch of Evil*'s protagonist is a male Mexican government agent whose heroic actions solve crimes and capture criminals. In both films, the Mexican officers leave their American colleagues by the wayside as they reveal them to be ineffective or corrupt. Likewise, both plots feature police forces working to bring down cross-border smuggling rackets and gangsters who are not afraid to use violence to get their way. The films also look similar, both being shot in black and white with lots of nighttime scenes, combining fast pace and extreme violence. *Touch of Evil* has further similarities with *Borderline* (Seiter, 1950) and *Wetbacks* (McCune, 1956) where traveling across the border to Mexico also brings an escape from the strictures of American law, allowing US police officers to bend and play outside the rules normally governing them. Inexorably linked to Hollywood's earlier border crossings, this chapter argues that *Touch of Evil* must be seen in the context of the whole series of cold war border films.

Set in the fictional border town of Los Robles, *Touch of Evil* tells the story of an investigation into a bomb that kills a prominent American construction tycoon and his girlfriend. The film opens as the bomb explodes and the investigation begins, headed by US detective Hank Quinlan (Welles) and his partner Pete Menzies (Joseph Calleia). The explosion takes place just across the American side of the international border with Mexico, and so Mexican narcotics officer Miguel/Mike Vargas (Charlton Heston) is enlisted in the investigation.[2] However, as the narrative progresses, a second investigation grows out of the first as Vargas becomes suspicious about the integrity of Quinlan's procedures. Caught between these investigations, Vargas's new wife Susan (Janet Leigh) is drawn into events by local narcotics smugglers, the Grandi family, who align themselves with Quinlan in his attempts to use Susan to get to Vargas. In the end, Vargas's detective work reveals Quinlan's corruption, and the US district attorney (Ray Collins) and Menzies assist him in capturing Quinlan's confession on tape.

Touch of Evil has received a phenomenal volume of critical attention; one of the key frameworks this scholarship uses is an auteurist approach that considers the film in the context of Welles's personal talents.[3] For example, writing in *Arts* magazine in 1958, François Truffaut exalts, "You could remove Orson Welles's name from the credits and it wouldn't make any difference, because from the first shot...it's obvious that Citizen Kane is behind the camera."[4] Similarly, André Bazin argues that *Touch of Evil* forms part of Welles's continual artistic development, claiming that "in its underlying thematic pattern, *Touch of Evil* can thus be seen as a masterwork of Welles despite its detective-story pretext."[5] James Naremore's analysis of the film similarly positions it in a narrative about Welles's unique talents, although he also pays some attention to the film's Mexican setting. Naremore argues, "Welles may be the only German Expressionist who is also authentically attracted to Latin cultures, and who is able to appropriate their 'feel' to his style."[6] Again, attention is directed to Welles's individual attributes and his personal "feel" for the topics his movies address.

However, the version of *Touch of Evil* that was released in 1958 was far from a singular Welles vision. Aside from the fact that there were hundreds of personnel involved in the production of the film and contributing to its creation, Welles was pulled from the project in its final stages and new scenes were added, which were filmed under the direction of Harry Keller. Welles's subsequent intervention, in the form of the memo requesting changes to this cut was largely ignored by the studio. In her investigation into the continued desire among critics to attribute authorship of *Touch of Evil* solely to Welles, Brooke Rollins provocatively suggests that "in the case of Orson Welles, our investment in authorial wholeness is inextricably linked to an investment in idealized masculine potency."[7] This chapter seeks not to repeat the mistake of searching for authorship but rather considers the film, in its 1958 theatrical version, as a collaborative product that is constructed both by the personnel and institutions involved and by the cultural, social, and political contexts of its time. Welles's professional and political career is considered as a part of the film's broader cultural contexts, not as a means for asserting authorial authority.

Although it was celebrated upon its release by French critics such as Truffaut and Bazin, *Touch of Evil* did not immediately receive positive reviews in the United States. Howard Thompson at the *New York Times* ended his review not with plaudits but with questions he found unanswered by the movie, finding that "the lasting impression of this film is effect rather than substance." *The Hollywood Reporter*'s Jack Moffitt was most explicitly critical of the film and wrote damningly, "Scripted, directed and acted in by Orson Welles and played by a distinguished cast, this should have been a fine picture. But it isn't."[8] In the years since its release and following the subsequent issuing of two different versions of the film,[9] criticism has generally sought to recuperate and recognize the film as an important piece of work and has covered a wide range of approaches, including psychoanalytic and feminist readings, political analyses, Chicana/o studies, and investigations into the film's soundscapes.[10] Of most import for this chapter are the areas of scholarship that are concerned with postcolonialism, national identity, and cinematic space. Used in part to outline a methodology for the study of the medium of film, Stephen Heath's influential 1975 analysis is interesting because of its particularly spatial focus. Attempting to understand the way film operates as a medium, Heath finds a "shifting regulation," a pattern of "movement held and checked in the diegetic space."[11] He proceeds to literally map out *Touch of Evil*, producing cartographic analyses of the filmic space around and across the US-Mexico border accompanied by maps illustrating the film's movements pictorially. In his 1985 essay, Terry Comito too draws spatial conclusions from the film, understanding it to function as "a network of incommensurable movements—whirling, without stable center."[12] Comito is also prompted to literally map out the film, and includes his own diagram that traces the movements of the movie through space.

The spaces of *Touch of Evil*'s border town have also come under close scrutiny from scholars. Naremore finds the film's location "quite true to the essence of bordertowns."[13] Whereas Comito argues that "Los Robles is the sinister foreign place we discover on the margins of our own world."[14] These critics' views make assumptions that border towns are dark, foreboding places and that the film is an accurate representation of them. William Nericcio takes issue with this position, arguing that it is in fact only a cinematic border town that is evoked by *Touch of Evil*'s location. Accusing other scholars of having "internalized" Quinlan's views of the border and Mexico, Nericcio calls attention to the legacy of visual images of Mexico from which the film and its critics are unable to escape.[15] This is an important point, and one that this chapter seeks to stress: *Touch of Evil* must be understood within the context of other cinematic border crossings occurring at this time. Indeed, what its cinematic border evokes is precisely other such cinematic border crossings.

Homi Bhabha's analysis of the film and interrogation of Heath's work on it is particularly significant for this study because of its postcolonial focus. For Bhabha, *Touch of Evil* maps out "discourses of American cultural colonialism and Mexican dependency," and this understanding of its cinematic terrain informs this chapter.[16] Bhabha argues that colonial discourse "produces the colonized as a social reality which is at once an 'other' and yet entirely knowable and visible. It resembles a form of narrative whereby the productivity and circulation of signs are bound in a reformed and recognizable totality."[17] Knowledge of the colonized thus becomes power over them, and their visibility to the colonizer leaves them powerless. This chapter will draw on Bhabha's formulation of knowledge and colonial power to investigate the connections between colonialism and regulation in *Touch of Evil*. Building on ideas of visibility and fixity, it contends that the film articulates colonialism through the regulation of mobility.

Scholars such as Michael Denning and Donald Pease rightly assert that Chicano politics and Mexican migration to the United States form important cultural contexts for *Touch of Evil*.[18] Indeed, a preoccupation with Latin American locations and themes runs throughout Welles's work, and it is important to understand the relationship between *Touch of Evil* and earlier productions such as *It's All True* (1942–3), the documentary commissioned as part of efforts to unite the Americas in the face of fascism during the Second World War.

As for all of the border films considered in this book, movement and stasis are crucial to *Touch of Evil*'s narrative, where freedom of movement brings knowledge and power whereas constricted mobility leads only to disappearance and decay.

Imperial Journeys: Welles's Latin America

Touch of Evil was by no means Welles's first foray into Latin American themes and locations. His career featured repeated returns to Latin America and these backdrops form a key way in which political concerns are articulated in his work. Upon his initial arrival in Hollywood, Welles wrote a screenplay titled *The Way to Santiago*, which tells the story of an amnesiac stuck in Mexico with Nazi spies and deals explicitly with antifascism.[19] In 1938, he developed screen and radio plays of Joseph Conrad's *Heart of Darkness* (1899), moving the action to Latin America and, as Denning argues, translating the tale into a "parable of fascism" that moved "the imperialist boundary between civilization and the jungle to a boundary between civilization and fascism."[20] Following the release of *Citizen Kane* (1941), Welles worked up an unrealized screenplay called *Santa*, based on a Mexican film of the same name, in which Dolores del Rio was keen to play the lead role. The new version of the script incorporated a clear antifascist slant by including Nazi attempts to overthrow the Mexican government in the plot. Throughout the early 1940s, Welles also presented the *Hello Americans* radio series, which brought political news stories from Latin America to US audiences. Following *The Magnificent Ambersons* (1942), the aborted *It's All True*, and *The Stranger* (1946), his next directorial role in Hollywood was *The Lady from Shanghai* (1947). Just as Welles shifted the action in the novel *Badge of Evil* (Masterson, 1956) to the Mexican border for *Touch of Evil*, *The Lady from Shanghai*'s location was similarly deliberately moved from its New York base in the novel to incorporate Mexico into the film.

In terms of the development of a political connection to Latin American landscapes, the most significant work in Welles's oeuvre is *It's All True*, an unfinished documentary film produced for RKO in 1942–3. Initially conceived as a Mercury Productions picture, the project soon attracted the attention of Nelson Rockefeller, head of the office of the CIAA, who recruited the documentary into efforts to shore up relations between the United States and the rest of the Americas during the Second World War. The CIAA was concerned about Germany's growing influence in countries such as Argentina,

Brazil, El Salvador, and Peru and, as such, its mission was "to provide greater economic cooperation and closer cultural, scientific, and educational ties" within the continent.[21] *It's All True* was to tell a story of pan-Americanism that would unite the hemisphere together in the face of fascism and make allies of the United States' southern neighbors. The version of the film that was agreed upon with Rockefeller comprised three segments: a story called "Bonito" about a bull that is saved from the ring because of his friendship with a young Mexican boy, a section titled "Carnaval," which explores the origins of carnaval and samba in Brazil, and "Jangadeiros," the tale of a group of Brazilian raft fishermen or jangadeiros who successfully campaigned to secure greater rights for workers in their country.

At a governmental level, *It's All True* had obvious imperial ambitions in its aims to influence and bolster relations between the United States and Latin America, something Welles was deeply and personally implicated in through both his close relationship with Rockefeller and his official role as goodwill ambassador to the region.[22] But there is also a focus on social justice and socialism, which runs throughout the segments of the film. Marguerite Rippy has argued that *It's All True* was revolutionary in both political and formal senses. She claims that the "nonlinear narrative ambitiously sought not only to represent but also to create a postcolonial Pan-American identity," contending that the documentary was conceived as a new kind of film format, "rejecting the concept of traditional authorship."[23] As for *The Tijuana Story* (Kardos, 1957), this exploration of a new format that draws on documentary and travelogue practices seems to offer the opportunity to move outside of conventional Hollywood narrative practices. In *It's All True*, the carnaval sequence footage held an unwavering focus on the history and evolution of samba and its relationship with the communities of Rio's favelas. Studio executives and the Brazilian government alike objected to the filming of Brazil's poor, unsightly suburbs, and particularly to the footage of black Brazilians.[24]

The Jangadeiros segment featuring the Brazilian fishermen also has a strong socialist and revolutionary tone. The documentary recreated the true story of four fishermen, who, faced with poverty and hardship, sailed over 1,500 miles around the coast of Brazil on a raft in order to confront the president about their atrocious working conditions. Their epic journey made them famous and upon arrival they negotiated changes to social legislation with the president, improving working conditions and extending medical and death benefits to jangadeiros throughout the country.[25] Denning suggests that "the story of the fishermen from Fortaleza, reenacted by non-actors, is close in narrative and style to Paul Strand's left-wing documentary about Mexican fishermen, *The Wave (Redes)* (1937), and to Luchino Visconti's neo-realist tale of Sicilian fishermen, *La Terra Trema* (1948)."[26] This use of Latin American spaces to tell politically charged stories is evident throughout the wider cycle of border films that this book examines.

While there certainly appear to be left-wing motives at work behind the documentary in the choice of subject matter and its formal experimentation, its government-ordered imperial ambitions complicate the "postcolonial Pan-American identity" that Rippy claims characterizes its representation of the Americas.[27] Although the lack of a single totalizing narrative structure suggests a breakdown of traditional authorship as Rippy contends, the fact remains that the film was produced by Americans for US imperial interests. The documentary's episodic form exactly resembles that of travelogue films, which Jeffrey Ruoff claims bring "together scenes without regard for plot or narrative progression."[28] Like the travelogue, *It's All True* bears an educational impulse, aiming to inform, educate, and influence communities across the continent, bringing distant lands and people home for the American public to see.[29]

Tom Gunning has argued that through such travelogues and travel photography, "travel becomes a means of appropriating the world through images."[30] In its explicit appropriation of Latin American communities intended to inform and educate US audiences, *It's All True* exhibits clear imperial practices alongside its left-wing political themes. As Gunning attests, "the link between foreign views and colonialism needs no deconstructive analysis to be demonstrated."[31] Although it attempts to resist traditional narratives and authorship, *It's All True*'s story of the continent cannot be told outside of the colonial form of the travel picture. The fact that the film takes the form of a travel narrative is crucial, as the United States' imperial influence in the continent is mobilized through Welles's journey around Latin America and through his camera's itinerant motion. In the carnaval scenes, slow-moving panoramas map the bodies of dancers in images that seem unlimited and without borders. Gunning uses the phrase "images without borders" to describe the panoramic and roving views offered by travelogues and their ancestral forms such as panoramas and daguerreotypes.[32] In traveling films, he argues, "the moving camera's ability to seem to surpass its own frame creates another image, which seems to pass beyond its borders."[33] Throughout *It's All True*, the roving camera rolls out such a panorama, always extending beyond the borders of the image, appropriating, controlling, and consuming Latin American landscapes.

As a central and outspoken member of the political Left, Welles's professional work was regularly deeply entwined with politics and his political activities. He was known to the Federal Bureau of Investigation (FBI), who were unable to charge him with membership of the Communist Party but closely monitored his activities and those of his associates, many of whom were card-carrying members.[34] Welles's initial forays into the entertainment world were with the Mercury Players, a socially conscious theater group, which subsequently morphed into the production company Mercury Productions. The Mercury Players sought to bring classical theater to the people and were also closely involved with the Negro Theatre, striving to abolish racism from the stage with productions including a hugely successful Haitian *Macbeth* with an all-black cast.[35] In *The Cultural Front*, Denning positions the Mercury group at the heart of the popular front, a "social movement" born out of the 1930s Depression, which he argues was formed of "a broad and tenuous left-wing alliance of fractions of the subaltern classes."[36] Denning hails Welles as "the single most important Popular Front artist in theater, radio, and film, both politically and aesthetically."[37] Alongside his Mercury work, Welles was active in a large range of political organizations including the Free World Congress, the New Theatre League, the League of American Writers, the California Labor School, and the Progressive Citizens of America.[38]

Latin American political issues were of particular concern for Welles. He was deeply committed to Latin American civil rights movements, and in 1942 served alongside other Mercury members Joseph Cotton, Dorothy Comingore, Canada Lee, and his then wife Rita Hayworth on the Sleepy Lagoon Defense Committee. This committee was formed in response to the trial of 17 Chicano youths charged with the murder of José Díaz at Sleepy Lagoon, a popular swimming location near Los Angeles. As Peter Wollen contends, the Sleepy Lagoon case occurred at a time when Mexican-Americans were already being criminalized in the press, the Hearst press in particular.[39] Wollen attests that "the trial and sentencing led to a new tidal wave of racist propaganda, with statements from the Sheriff's office about the 'biological disposition' of Mexicans to crime."[40] Despite the committee's efforts to raise funds for the defense and to stem growing public antipathy toward Chicanos, the 17 youths were found guilty. They were later acquitted in a court of appeal in 1944. Welles was closely involved in the campaign to defend and release the young men, writing the foreword to a pamphlet increasing awareness about the case, raising money, and serving as spokesperson for the committee.[41]

Both Denning and Wollen argue that the Sleepy Lagoon case forms the most important political context for *Touch of Evil*, claiming the film's central conceit, "the story of the attempt to frame a young Chicano," as Denning describes it, comes directly from Welles's close involvement with the case.[42] At the time of its release, *Touch of Evil* was indeed understood by critics as a political project. Reviewers positioned the film within the Mercury Theatre tradition, linking it to the distinctive style and political agenda the group had forged. The *New York Times* found the "stylized trade-marks of the director's Mercury Players unit" lay at the heart of the movie.[43] Other reviewers criticized it as a "'Big M' of Mercury Theatre monstrosity."[44] Because of the inextricable links between the Mercury group's style and their active political agenda, implicit in the reviews' focus on the Mercury Theatre is also recognition that the movie also had a political agenda.

Although *Touch of Evil*'s reception shows that Welles's left-wing political position was understood as an influence on the film through the associations with the Mercury group, its cultural and political contexts are broader still. Alongside Welles's personal politics and involvement in the Sleepy Lagoon case, the persistence of Latin American images throughout his career is significant. The quasi-imperialist project *It's All True* demonstrates that the relationship between the United States and Latin America could not be articulated outside of colonial frameworks, despite Welles's left-wing and liberal politics. This tension between liberalism and imperialism becomes further complicated in *Touch of Evil*, which imagines the US-Mexico relationship at a time when the American government vehemently denounced the colonial practices of its cold war adversary the Soviet Union. Further, *Touch of Evil* must also be understood as part of the series of border films examined in this book that also engage with ideas of movement, stasis, and the border town.

Border Town in Motion: Movement and Power

Touch of Evil represented a return to Latin America for Welles and a return to themes and forms that were also present in his earlier works such as *It's All True*. The documentary's traveling vision is echoed and exaggerated in the camera movements of *Touch of Evil*, which traverse the border town fluidly, unhampered by the international borderline.

The film's opening shot, filmed in a single take, moves through the spaces of the border town, following a person placing a bomb in a car boot, tailing the car as it drives off, then trailing Susan and Miguel/ Mike Vargas as they walk through the border checkpoint. Shifting from a simple tracking shot showing the bomber sneaking along a wall, the camera suddenly pulls upward into the sky, over the roofs of buildings, before sinking down again into a traveling shot that moves along streets, threading in and out of the paths of pedestrians and traffic. At times seemingly human in its motion, at others the camera's smooth flight into the air and above life on the ground renders it omniscient, a separate witness in its own right within the narrative.

Touch of Evil's camera maps its route through the border town in a very different way to that of *The Tijuana Story*. Unlike the contrasting angles and perspectives of that film which challenge any singular narrative of Tijuana, for *Touch of Evil*, the camera's motion marks out a clear narrative trajectory in Los Robles. The camera investigates, searching for clues, drawing conclusions, and directing the narrative. In the opening sequence it is constantly on the move, directly recalling Gunning's images without borders and the sense that the cinematic frame seems insignificant in light of an ever-shifting field of vision.[45] Rather than destabilized or fragmented, this imagining of a border town is total and controlling, a mobile and shifting vision that constructs the narrative of the movie through its movement. The camera's independent narration and omniscient knowledge within the film situates the border town as a colonized space—as Bhabha contends, one that is "at once an 'other' and yet entirely knowable and visible."[46]

The totalizing effect of the camera becomes most explicit in a scene in which Quinlan interrogates Manelo Sanchez (Victor Millan) in his apartment. Once again in a single long take, the camera tracks around the apartment, searching for clues, moving independently of the characters, and creating its own narrative. It passes by Miguel/ Mike Vargas in the bathroom as he casually knocks a box off a shelf, before heading back into the living room. Later as the camera pauses to witness Sanchez's protestations, Quinlan looms into the frame, ordering Menzies to search the bedroom and bathroom. As the camera remains focused on the interrogation of Sanchez in the living room, Menzies reappears and explains how he discovered the incriminating dynamite in the very same box that the camera found empty during its independent sweep of the apartment. Through the camera's autonomous movement, the story of Quinlan's corruption is made visible and knowable. The camera's knowledge is most often

aligned with Miguel/Mike Vargas's knowledge but through its constant disembodied movement, which swirls around, over and above
the action of the film, it creates a totalizing narrative that maps out
and fixes the border town in place. As the story of an investigation,
the search for knowledge is what drives the narrative forward; it is the
mobility of the camera that gives it control over the filmic space and
knowledge.

Miguel/Mike Vargas is the most mobile character within the spaces
of the film. Lean and supple, *Touch of Evil* frequently sees Vargas
demonstrate his excessive physical mobility, chasing after Grandi gang
members, running back and forth across the border town to check on
his wife, and sprinting upstairs on foot instead of taking an elevator.
Conversant in both English and Spanish, Vargas traverses the border
with ease and passes from one national territory to another fluidly.
As with the camera, it is through his mobility that Vargas constructs
knowledge within the film. In the movie's final scenes, this becomes
explicit as he navigates awkward spaces and dangerous high structures
with acrobatic ease in order to stay within audible range of Quinlan
with his recording equipment. As he pauses to remove layers of clothing in this process, the bodily extent of Vargas's physical abilities is
emphasized. While the two American cops walk slowly around the
canal, Vargas's gymnastic motion allows him to hear Quinlan's confession and record it on tape.

Vargas is also mobile in other ways. Demonstrating the fluid understandings of ethnicity within Hollywood at this time, Heston is made
up to pass as the Mexican officer through makeup, performance, and
language. Yet his all-American star persona colors the character of
Miguel/Mike Vargas throughout the film. In 1950s Hollywood,
ethnicity remained something that was understood as performable
and unfixed but full flexibility in terms of different ethnic roles was
usually only granted to white actors. Only a closed range of ethnic
roles was open to actors of other backgrounds and they rarely played
white American characters. Therefore the extent of ethnic fluidity and
power within the narrative that Heston enjoys comes from the fact he
is a white American playing a Mexican, while Mexican actors do not
play American characters in the story.[47] Also combining American
and Mexican signifiers in his dual name, Miguel/Mike holds power
through this hybridity and fluidity.

Vargas's fluid ethnic identity is highlighted from the very begin-
ning of the film, when Quinlan refers to him as "some kind of
Mexican." His subsequent accusation, "he doesn't sound like a
Mexican" explicitly highlights Heston's awkward Spanish accent. In

his deconstructive analysis of the film, Nericcio finds its representation of Mexico and Mexicans to be contradictory: "One can find
and document how Welles's *Touch of Evil* reinforces predictable stereotypes of the *mexicano* subjectivity and of the Anglo subjectivity.
Closer scrutiny reveals, however, that these expressionistic archetypes
are mined with nuances of difference, which derail the archetype."[48]
This is also true of Vargas specifically. Although the character is an
active, capable, and professional Mexican and the clear hero of the
story, he remains an American actor performing ethnicity. It is the
power of this position that allows him to solve the crime and save his
wife; Heston takes the starring role, not Vargas. Publicity articles in
the film's press kit emphasize this idea, stating that Heston plays an
"unusual role" and appears as "an unfamiliar Heston with dark hair
and moustache."[49]

The character of Tana (Marlene Dietrich) also enjoys some considerable fluidity and power in *Touch of Evil*'s narrative. Like Vargas,
but to a lesser extent, her ethnicity is mobile, seeing the German
actor play the ethnically ambiguous owner of a pianola bar on the
border town's main strip.[50] As Jill Leeper has noted, Dietrich's performance here is something of a pastiche of her previous Hollywood
roles.[51] Indeed, explicitly so, as according to Frank Brady, Dietrich
put together her costume for *Touch of Evil* from clothes and acces-
sories worn throughout her Hollywood career. Brady reports,
"Her black wig came from Paramount, where she had done *Golden
Earrings*, her spangled shoes came from her role in *Rancho Notorious*
[another border film] at RKO, and from Warner Brothers she took
a blouse that she had worn in *Stage Fright*."[52] Dietrich's costume
becomes a cinematic palimpsest within *Touch of Evil*, presenting a
shifting multitude of different characters, which cannot be pinned
down. Through Tana's fluidity, she also holds knowledge of events in
the town; she is a fortune-teller and correctly predicts that Quinlan's
future is "all used up."

The characters that possess power and knowledge in *Touch of Evil*
are those that have the most movement and motion. Vargas is the
most physically and ethnically mobile character, traveling furthest
and undertaking athletic feats of mobility while fluidly able to traverse both sides of the border. Through its free movement the camera
too is able to map out the film's narrative, investigating and uncovering clues and plotting the course of the story as it travels. This
conflation of knowledge, power, and mobility connects *Touch of
Evil* back to *It's All True* and travelogue filmmaking. The characters
exercising the most power within this border town are American not

Mexican; as the camera maps out a narrative through its movements, the town and its other inhabitants are revealed, fixed, and possessed for American audiences.

Static Subjects: Regulation and Mobility

In contrast to the powerful actors within the film who possess movement and fluidity, those rendered powerless are static and trapped within the cinematic space. Disappearance and entrapment narratives are repeated time and again in border films, as seen in *Wetbacks*, *Border River* (Sherman, 1954), and *Border Incident*. This stasis becomes the articulation of difference at the border, as Bhabha argues, "Fixity, as the sign of cultural/historical/racial difference in the discourse of colonialism is a paradoxical mode of representation: it connotes rigidity and an unchanging order as well as disorder, degeneracy and daemonic repetition."[53] Through narratives that regulate movement, colonial dominance is reiterated while the undesirability of the other is rendered visible. This apparatus is clearly seen at work in *Border Incident*, where the undocumented braceros are trapped outside of US society and literally disappear into the borderlands. In *Touch of Evil*, Miguel/Mike Vargas and the roving camera track and fix the border town into place. Outside of clear national territory, Los Robles falls off the map, a place of entrapment that swallows up immobile inhabitants.

The physical spaces of *Touch of Evil* resist any clear national categorization. Originally the film was scheduled to be shot in Tijuana but the Mexican government refused permission because of censorial issues as well as the fact they did not want the film to perpetuate a "scrubby" image of the city.[54] Venice, California, was chosen as a good alternative because of its decaying opulence and grand canal.[55] The border town set closely resembles Tijuana and images from *The Tijuana Story*; arched buildings line the main strip, which is busy and bustling with signs advertising bars, hotels, and clubs filling the screen. The arch is an iconic architectural symbol of Mexicanness and is deployed in most of the films discussed in this book. In *Touch of Evil*, the arches take on a significant role in the filmic space as members of the Grandi gang lurk behind them, preparing to accost Susan Vargas. These covered arched corridors become sinister and dangerous because of their Mexicanness.

Despite all of these signs and symbols identifying the filmic space as a borderline location, the film also flaunts the unmistakably American features of its landscape. Most obviously out of place within a border film are the oil derricks, an iconic feature of the southern

American landscape, which appear throughout the film. As the bomb explodes and chaos ensues around Linnekar's burning car, the scaffolding of the derricks is present in the background, enclosing the scene in a ring of tall dark structures with pumps slowly moving up and down. Later, as Miguel/Mike Vargas and American district attorney Schwartz drive to Quinlan's farm, a long shot reveals low-rise housing that is densely interlaced with oil pumps and machinery. As the narrative crosses back and forth over the border, the diegetic space is rendered more unstable and in-between. Not only does the film frequently lack clear signals as to which side of the border its locations are, the cinematic terrain too falls between this fictional border town and the heart of California's oil fields.

Susan Vargas is swallowed into the story of the film as she is trapped by the Grandi gang, drugged and framed for murder. It is no coincidence that the harassment she endures is enacted in two hotels and a motel. In their introduction to the volume *Moving Pictures/Stopping Places*, David B. Clarke, Valerie Crawford Pfannhauser, and Marcus A. Doel define hotels, motels, and hostels as "stopping places," which are characterized by their status as spaces "between belonging and being out of place."[56] As locations that are somehow out of place and disconnected, *Touch of Evil*'s hotels are off the map just like the town itself; Susan Vargas is unable to reach out for help and no one comes to her rescue. Despite frequent discussions and telephone conversations with Miguel/Mike, she is prevented from explaining to him the unwanted attentions she has been receiving. Even after waking up, undressed and drugged with Joe Grandi's bulbous head leering over her, when she screams for help from a balcony, Miguel/Mike is unable to hear and drives straight past.

Susan's entrapment is also indicated spatially as the Grandi gang begins their assault on her in the motel. The camera closes in on her face as dark figures circle around, filling the frame as her body becomes consumed within their shadows. Jann Matlock has argued that the Vargas's "need to sleep in hotels" forms a "kind of allegory for their inability to find a place where they belong."[57] However, it is only Susan Vargas who actually spends any time in these "unhomely" spaces, while Mike Vargas seems quite at home actively pursuing the police investigation and traversing both sides of the border.[58] In contrast, Susan is the one who remains out of place and unbelonging. Consigned to her hotel and motel rooms, she occupies a space outside of American society without any recourse to help, which recalls the kind of position held by the undocumented bracero workers in the United States in *Border Incident*.

The other key static character in the narrative is Quinlan, whose movements become more and more restricted over the course of the film as he loses knowledge and power. For Quinlan, stasis leads to decay and ultimately to his demise, and this process is played out most obviously on his body. His corpulence is constantly emphasized through low angle shots that highlight his weight as he moves slowly and painfully, leaning on his stick for support. The cigars, candy, and hooch, which he is constantly consuming, also attest to the corruption of his body as well as his actions. The film's press pamphlet capitalizes on the sheer hideousness of his decaying body, describing the character as "a grotesque, bloated figure, dragging his game leg like a great, wounded toad."[59] In the film's final scenes, Quinlan's body is at its most corrupt, mirroring his final betrayal of Menzies. During this altercation, sweat drips from his flabby face and spit flies across the screen. Quinlan is leaking, putrefying, and sure enough his body is finally dumped in the canal to fester in the rancid water.

Concerns over obesity and weight problems emerged as a major health concern in the United States during the 1950s. Reports from as early as 1952 cite obesity as the foremost nutritional problem in the country, affecting up to a quarter of adults.[60] A government committee on aging problems found that citizens were "eating their way into the grave," and press reporting around obesity highlighted the connections between the disease and death, claiming that "obesity is striking [people] down, impairing their productivity, restricting their enjoyment of life and killing them before their time."[61] Not only connecting Quinlan to his impending death, in the film his excessive obesity also invokes restriction, immobility, and impairment. It is exactly this decline in his ability to move around and command the filmic space that eventually sees his demise.

Like Quinlan, the whole border town is strikingly marked by decay throughout the film. The walls of buildings are covered with layer upon layer of advertisements, all partially stripped back and torn, creating a visual palimpsest of rotting posters, none of which are legible. The streets of the town are strewn with litter that floats across the screen in nearly every shot, and the canal, which features in film's final scenes, is a landscape of detritus. This waterway is filled with tires, oil drums, broken beds, moldering mattresses, crumbling couches, torn clothing, and waste paper (see figure 8.1). After he shoots Menzies, Quinlan momentarily takes a seat on a decomposing armchair. The rotten throne speaks to his stasis and powerlessness; his immobility leads to his lack of knowledge and ultimate defeat. In this border

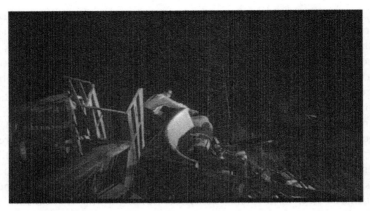

Figure 8.1   The detritus of American capitalist society suffocates the border town of *Touch of Evil*.

town, those who can easily traverse the boundary pass through safely but those without such freedom of movement become trapped.

The fact that *Touch of Evil*'s decaying spaces are filled with the rotting products of American consumer culture is significant. As a period of high consumption, the 1950s saw huge increases in advertising and spending, with economic growth of 200 percent per capita between 1947 and 1956.[62] According to Randall Bennett Woods, during the 1950s "consumption became a virtual obsession," with home ownership increasing by 50 percent between 1945 and 1960 and car ownership reaching almost 100 percent by the end of the decade. Woods explains that "spending on advertising increased 400% and almost tripled the amount spent on education."[63] In this period, American culture was changing from one that denounced waste as "immoral" to one in which "planned obsolescence" was normal.[64]

The consumer revolution of the 1950s was hailed as a great American success. Published in 1958, Louis O. Keslo and Mortimer J. Adler's *The Capitalist Manifesto* argues that "it is our industrial power and capital wealth, together with our institutions of political liberty and justice, that make America the place where the capitalist revolution must first take place."[65] Another report describes the United States as "uniquely dynamic [with] the highest standards of living closest to a democratic, classless society [which] has come about through a fantastic increase in productivity made possible through greater mechanization."[66] The celebratory tone of these edicts is not matched in the appearance of the products and advertisements that populate *Touch of Evil*'s border town. Hoardings and posters are decomposing, ripped, and torn, while all manner of household items lie discarded in the canal at the end of the movie. The border town is out of place, a space neither of the United States nor of Mexico, unstable in its shifting national terrain but trapped and entrapping at the same time. Lacking a clear national location, Los Robles is a non-space, frozen in time and decaying. Like its hotels, the "unhomeliness" of the town is such that ordinary household objects become grotesque and rotten.[67] Quinlan's armchair in the canal becomes the ultimate symbol of unhomeliness, stasis, and decay.

Conclusion

As it ends, *Touch of Evil* may resolve its two investigations but many questions remain unanswered. Both a corrupt cop and a good cop end up dead, and the man framed by Quinlan for murder apparently also confesses to the crime. Vargas's leading role seems to present a positive Mexican hero but his awkward accent and obvious makeup is a constant reminder that this Mexican is played by an American movie star. *Touch of Evil* presents a profound lack of clarity over who is in control and who has moral authority, alongside the constant ambiguities in its national territory. This chapter has sought to track these issues of regulation through the film following the dual axes of movement and stasis. Crucial in representations of the border, movement enables characters to cross boundaries freely and easily, to tour and travel, and to have experiences that constitute identity. Conversely, stasis leads to a loss of identity, disappearance, decay, and death. Where characters are unable to traverse the border, they remain stuck, outside of national belonging and eventually disappear.

In *Touch of Evil*, the most freedom of movement is granted to Miguel/Mike Vargas, the ethnically mobile and athletically itinerant hero. In contrast, Quinlan, the corrupt villain of the piece, descends steadily into fixity as his corpulence prevents him from moving easily and his body begins to putrefy and decay. The filmic space is regulated, mapped, and controlled by the film's ever-moving camera as it charts the course of the narrative. In this dramatization of the way in which movement and control of space is connected to knowledge and power, *Touch of Evil* directly recalls cinema's traveling heritage and the prolific early form of the travelogue. With its roving, mobile camera, space is controlled and mapped, an image without borders that encompasses and lays claim to that which it surveys. The camera's journeys back and forth across and around the border present the border town spaces for possession by film viewers, just as the traveling shots of *It's All True* sought to reveal the landscapes of Mexico and Brazil.

Although its representation of the border town and Mexico cannot escape the camera and Vargas's imperialist vision, the film presents the United States and Mexico as equally implicated in corruption and crime. The undecidability of Los Robles's national terrain is suggestive of a division between the two countries that is entirely symbolic and insignificant. Unable to escape the imperialist edge of US architectures of pan-American cooperation, *Touch of Evil* nevertheless offers a cold war vision of the United States and Mexico as equals and as equally responsible for tackling crime and corruption enacted by individuals and institutions alike. Understood as part of a cycle of 1950s border films rather than an isolated Wellesian masterpiece, *Touch of Evil's* narratives of mobility and staticity concur with the key concerns of these movies. Dramatizing the country's border and relationship with Mexico, these films examine the United States' place in the world and in cold war struggles. Debates around US intervention and Soviet expansion are played out in the discourses of colonialism that pervade the films' concern with the regulation of the border.

Conclusion

Border Film and Border Studies

Borderlands Cinema and Chicana/o Studies

While this book focuses on the period 1949–58 and what has been termed the peak cold war period, the US-Mexico border has been an important cinematic location since the earliest days of cinema and continues to feature regularly in films today. Academic interest in representations of the border has risen sharply since the publication of Gloria Anzaldúa's 1987 work *Borderlands/La Frontera* and the burgeoning of Chicana/o studies. This area of scholarly work is concerned with the position of Mexicans, Mexican-Americans, Latin Americans, and people of Latin American origin in the United States. It theorizes and establishes "the formation of hybrid cultures and identities that complicate dominant US notions of citizenship."[1]

Anzaldúa articulates this Chicana/o project in geographic terms in *Borderlands/La Frontera* where she envisages the creation of a new third space or border culture at the boundary.[2] Claudia Sadowski-Smith argues that Anzaldúa's work uses divisions of race, gender, and sexuality to construct a hybrid identity and a Chicana subjectivity: "To theorize a space in which these divisions can be overcome, *Borderlands/La Frontera* forges the now famous notion of a mestiza borderlands consciousness."[3] This hybrid *mestiza* consciousness is figured spatially, evoked not only through Anzaldúa's third border country but also through other theorists' invocation of the territory of Atzlán, mythic homeland of Chicanas and Chicanos.[4] Rosa Linda Fregoso and Angie Chabram-Dernersesian explain the importance of Atzlán for Chicano and subsequently Chicana/o studies: "Chicano identity was framed in Aztlán. And, Aztlán provided a basis for a return to the roots, for a return to an identity before domination and subjugation—a voyage back to pre-Colombian times."[5]

Alejandro Lugo concurs that the international boundary is theo-
retically crucial for Chicana/o scholarship, contending that "the
border region, as well as border theory and analysis, can erode
the hegemony of the privileged center by denationalizing and
deterritorializing the nation-state and culture theory."[6] Equally, for
Chabram-Dernersesian, the borderlands become a crucial "resource
for addressing a colonial condition in a supposedly postcolonial
world."[7] The spatial emphases in Chicana/o figurations of identity,
homelands, and theory thus make it an important framework for
analyzing US and Mexican culture in the borderlands and beyond
in the future. Fregoso's *The Bronze Screen* and collections *Chicano
Cinema* (edited by Gary Keller) and *Chicanos and Film* (edited
by Chon Noriega) provide insightful analyses of the growth of
Chicano and Chicana cinema.[8] Chicana/o studies has also turned
its attention specifically to the representation of the US-Mexico
border in recent American and Mexican cinema, for example, in
Lysa Rivera's provocative work on science-fiction literature and film
in the borderlands.[9]

Investigating the geographies of Chicana/o identities in recent
cinematic depictions of the borderlands is an important area of
work for the future. So too will be work on Latin American and
mestizo identities, Chicana feminism, and issues of class, which
have often been overlooked in studies of Hollywood cinema. While
these critical approaches have informed and provided frameworks
for my analyses of the films in this book, because of the historical
nature of the study, I have been more focused on attempting to
reconstruct what Hollywood films featuring the US-Mexico border of the 1950s can tell us about this period in history. Because
of limitations of space, I have been unable to consider the dialogue
between American and Mexican cinema and the many fascinating
Mexican border films produced during the mid-twentieth century
and beyond. Future research could fruitfully explore representations of the border in American, Mexican, and pan-American productions. For instance, the vision of the border and its relationship
to the migrant experience offered in the Mexican movie *Espaldas
Mojadas* (Galindo, 1953) is strikingly different from that presented
in the American movies of the same period. *Espaldas Mojadas* was
not released in the United States until two years after it was made
because censors initially decided its treatment of the theme of
undocumented migration and emphasis on the hardships faced by
Mexicans was inappropriate for American audiences, an intriguing
starting point for research in this area.[10]

The Future of the Cinematic Border

In this book I have contended that the way in which the border functions in my case study films is specific to the peak cold war period. Therefore, we might assume that in different eras the cinematic border operates in different ways. I have argued that representations of the border during the Cold War served not to engage with, debate, or raise awareness of border policies but as an arena where the United States' place in the wider world was negotiated. Representations of the border in American culture today may also be more closely concerned with the United States' global positioning, which is a significant implication given today's critical situation on the borderline itself. The US-Mexico border certainly remains a popular cinematic location and appears across a wide variety of genres into the twenty-first century. The boundary is also fast becoming a significant televisual location as well. Films and television shows featuring the border such as *Traffic* (Soderbergh, 2001), *The Three Burials of Melquiades Estrada* (Lee Jones, 2005), *Babel* (Iñárritu, 2006), *No Country for Old Men* (Coen and Coen, 2006), *Breaking Bad* (Gilligan, 2008–13), *Sin Nombre* (Fukunaga, 2009), *Monsters* (Edwards, 2010), and *The Bridge* (Reid, Stein, and Stiehm, 2013–), operate across many different generic traditions and therefore analyzing them through the spaces of the border may provide different ways of thinking about the relationship between media form, genre, and American culture.

For example, *Monsters* presents a startling vision of the US-Mexico border within its imagined future landscape that sees aliens invading the American continent. The borderlands have become an "infected" zone because of the alien presence and the US-Mexico border serves to protect the United States from invasion. Rising out of the rainforest, the border wall has overtaken the landscape and stands enormously tall, solid, and military gray (see figure C.1). This image of the border cannot help but recall the fortification of the "real" border today. The 1980s saw the commencement of the fortification of the border as a physical boundary and the erection of the first parts of the wall. Today the border wall, with a height of 17 feet, covers around 700 miles of the total 3,000 miles of the border. The magnitude and fortification of this cinematic border draws a clear parallel with continuing US government efforts to seal the border against aliens of the migrant variety.

Many of the films analyzed in this book seem to prefigure contemporary concerns and crises at the borderline today, such as racial profiling at identity checkpoints, the dangers faced by migrants

Figure C.1   *Monsters* imagines the US-Mexico border of the future.

crossing the borderlands, undocumented immigrant rights within the United States, and the rise of cartels and narcoviolence. *Border River*'s (Sherman, 1954) interrogation of US economic and territorial interests in Mexico is clearly echoed in modern day concerns about the dominance of international interests south of the border since the inauguration of the North American Free Trade Agreement (NAFTA) in 1994. Reflecting on 20 years of the trade agreement, Laura Carlsen contends that NAFTA "cut a path of destruction through Mexico," leaving 20 million Mexicans in food poverty as "transnational industrial corridors" have torn through the landscape bringing pollution, poorer working conditions through the growth of maquiladoras, and the closure of local businesses.[11] As Michael Dear and Gustavo Leclerc have argued, through NAFTA, "the spaces of the borderland became concrete manifestations of the emerging globalspace."[12] At the US-Mexico border, this globalspace is increasingly one where business, land, and workers are controlled by transnational corporations. In the border maquiladoras, factories where Mexican workers put together products for export to the United States, a system has developed that is entirely dependent on the low wages and poor conditions of the Mexican workers.

The spatial entrapment and disappearance of *Border Incident*'s undocumented Mexican migrants also has clear echoes in the plight facing undocumented migrants attempting to cross the US-Mexico border today. David K. Androff and Kyoko Y. Tavassoli estimate that the boundary has seen over five thousand migrant deaths since 1994.[13]

They argue that current strategies seeking to prevent undocumented migration through deterrence have not succeeded in reducing migrant numbers but rather have only resulted in more deaths. Androff and Tavassoli charge immigration policies with "compromis[ing] civil rights and social justice. Border security policy should be reformed to prevent the unnecessary deaths of migrants."[14] As security along the borderline is hardened in many urban areas, migrants are forced to attempt to cross the boundary through ever more dangerous terrain, where they are at the mercy of harsh elements as well as criminals. Many of those trying to cross simply disappear, lost in this unforgiving landscape. The organization Humane Borders/Fronteras Compasivas has developed a free open geographic information system that maps migrant deaths in the borderlands with the aim of raising awareness of migrant deaths and easing the suffering of their families. Since most border-crossing deaths are caused by dehydration, Humane Borders has also established a network of clean water stations across the borderlands, which are maintained by volunteers. Maps of the water stations are also provided free to migrants with the sole aim to "take death out of the immigration equation."[15]

Finally, *The Tijuana Story*'s (Kardos, 1957) shocking tale of a journalist's murder by criminal gangs has startling resonances with the situation facing journalists working in Tijuana today. Human Rights Watch reports that in Mexico "at least 85 journalists were killed between 2000 and August 2013, and 20 more were disappeared between 2005 and April 2013."[16] In its analysis of journalist murders in Mexico, the Committee to Protect Journalists claims that 80 percent of those killed wrote on crime.[17] Holding clear echoes of *El Imparcial*, a small Tijuanan weekly called *Zeta*, launched by Jesús Blancornelas, regularly publishes exposés about police and government corruption and complicity in drugs trafficking. Two journalists at the newspaper have been murdered since 1988 but it continues to publish critical stories and determinately remains, as its motto declares, "libre como el viento" (free like the wind).[18]

Understanding the relationship between the border and film in the United States continues to be a critical task, and not just because of the important role that Hollywood has historically played in shaping cultural understandings of the boundary. In 2009 the Texas Border Sheriff's Coalition launched "Virtual Community Watch," a public-private partnership that claimed to "empower the public to proactively participate in fighting border crime."[19] Virtual Community Watch was formed of a network of cameras and sensors along the Texas-Mexico border that fed live video streaming to a website, enabling

Internet users to monitor the area and report suspicious activity to the Border Patrol. The Virtual Community Watch website enabled people all around the world to sign up as "virtual deputies" and to watch live feed from cameras in a variety of locations on the border. Viewers also have the option to watch archived films of thwarted attempts to cross the international boundary. Initially condemned as a measure that would "invite extremists to participate in a virtual immigrant hunt," the scheme continued until its suspension in 2014, with the Border Patrol attesting that it helped to deter crime and concerned civil liberties groups claiming it incited vigilantism.[20] Although this official scheme is not currently operational, other websites such as http://secureborderintel.org/ continue to enable Internet users to watch videos shot from secret cameras positioned along the border.[21]

The use of film at the border today is thus contributing to the limiting of mobility around and across the boundary. As global users watch for border crossers remotely, these video systems further participate in the fixing and delimiting of potential migrants and immigrants, as huge tracts of the boundary come under constant surveillance, mapped out by the cameras. The statement by former Texas state senator Eliot Shapleigh quoted in the paragraph above paints an image of an extremist witch hunt where migrants and immigrants are hunted down and caught by virtual pursuers who possess an almost omniscient mobility through the vast network of cameras. This use of filmic technology at the border certainly replays the tensions around ideas of movement and stasis, which thread through all of the case studies examined in this book and which participate in the representation of border crossings through romance, revolution, and regulation.

However, film is also becoming an important strand of migrant protection, as campaign group CAMBIO (Campaign for an Accountable, Moral and Balanced Immigration Overhaul) calls for all Border Patrol agents to be equipped with lapel cameras to monitor their actions and deter abuse.[22] Film is becoming inextricably entwined with the ways in which border crossing is policed today. Therefore, it becomes crucial that we understand the ways in which the US-Mexico border and film have been connected throughout their histories. Because this book has contended that film is one of the key spaces in which the United States imagines itself, the history of cinematic engagement with the borderline is therefore vital to understandings of the way in which the border operates in American culture today.

Appendix A: Indicative List of Cold War Border Films

Bandido. Richard Fleischer. 1956. Bandido Productions/United Artists Corp. Mexico and US.

Big Steal, The. Don Siegel. 1949. RKO Radio Pictures, Inc./RKO Radio Pictures, Inc. US.

Black Whip, The. Charles Maquis Warren. 1956. Regal Films, Inc./Twentieth Century Fox Film Corp. US.

Border Bandits. Lambert Hillyer. 1946. Great Western Productions, Inc./ Monogram Distributing Corp. US.

Border City Rustlers. Frank McDonald. 1952. William F. Broidy Pictures Corp.; Newhall Productions/Allied Artists Pictures. US.

Border Fence. H. W. Keir and Norman Sheldon. 1951. Astor Pictures Corp./ Astor Pictures Corp. US.

Border Incident. Anthony Mann. 1949. Metro-Goldwyn-Mayer Corp/ Loew's, Inc. US.

Border Outlaws. Richard Talmadge. 1950. Jack Schwarz Productions, Inc.; United International, Inc./Eagle-Lion Films, Inc. US.

Border Rangers. William Berke. 1950. Lippert Productions, Inc./Lippert Pictures, Inc. US.

Border River. George Sherman. 1954. Universal-International Pictures Co., Inc./Universal Pictures Co., Inc. US.

Border Treasure. George Archainbaud. 1950. RKO Radio Pictures, Inc./ RKO Radio Pictures, Inc. US.

Borderline. William A. Seiter. 1950. Borderline Productions Corp./Universal Pictures Co., Inc. US.

Bottom of the Bottle, The. Henry Hathaway. 1955. Twentieth Century Fox Film Corp./Twentieth Century Fox Film Corp. US.

Branded. Rudolph Maté. 1951. Paramount Pictures Corp./Paramount Pictures Corp. US.

Canyon Ambush. Lewis D. Collins. 1952. Slivermine Productions/ Monogram Pictures Corp. US.

Cowboy. Delmer Daves. 1958. Phoenix Pictures Corp./Columbia Pictures Corp. US.

Fast and the Furious, The. John Ireland. 1954. Pablo Alto Productions, Inc./
American Releasing Corp.; State Rights. US.
Federal Agent at Large. George Blair. 1950. Republic Pictures Corp./
Republic Pictures Corp. US.
Federal Man. Robert Tansey. 1950. Jack Schwarz Productions, Inc./Eagle-
Lion Films, Inc. US.
Fort Apache. John Ford. 1948. Argosy Pictures Corp./RKO Radio Pictures,
Inc. US.
Four Guns to the Border. Richard Carlson. 1954. Universal-International
Pictures Co., Inc./Universal Pictures Co., Inc. US.
Fugitive, The. John Ford. 1947. Argosy Pictures Corp./RKO Radio Pictures,
Inc. US.
Gun Crazy. Joseph H. Lewis. 1950. King Bros. Productions, Inc./United
Artists Corp. US.
Gunfire at Indian Gap. Joseph Kane. 1957. Ventura Productions, Inc./
Republic Pictures Corp. US.
His Kind of Woman. John Farrow. 1951. RKO Radio Pictures, Inc.; A John
Farrow Production/RKO Radio Pictures, Inc. US.
King of the Bandits. Christy Cabanne. 1947. Monogram Productions, Inc./
Monogram Distributing Corp. US.
Man of the West. Anthony Mann. 1958. Ashton Productions, Inc./United
Artists Corp. US.
Out of the Past. Jacques Tourneur. 1947. RKO Radio Pictures, Inc./RKO
Radio Pictures, Inc. US.
Over the Border. Wallace W. Fox. 1950. Monogram Productions, Inc./
Monogram Distributing Corp. US.
Pals of the Golden West. William Winey. 1951. Republic Pictures Corp./
Republic Pictures Corp. US.
Rancho Notorious. Fritz Lang. 1952. Fidelity Pictures, Inc./RKO Radio
Pictures, Inc. US.
Red River. Howard Hawks. 1946. Monterey Productions, Inc./United
Artists Corp. US.
Ride the Pink Horse. Robert Montgomery. 1947. Universal-International
Pictures Co., Inc./Universal Pictures Co., Inc. US.
Rio Bravo. Howard Hawks. 1959. Armada Productions, Inc./Warner Bros.
Pictures, Inc. US.
Rio Grande. John Ford. 1950. Argosy Pictures Corp./Republic Pictures
Corp. US.
Rio Grande Patrol. Lesley Selander. 1950. RKO Radio Pictures, Inc./RKO
Radio Pictures, Inc. US.
River's Edge, The. Allan Dwan. 1957. Elmcrest Productions, Inc./Twentieth
Century Fox Film Corp. US.
Salt of the Earth. Herbert Biberman. 1954. The International Union of
Mine, Mill and Smelter Workers; Independent Productions Corp./IPC
Distributors, Inc.; Independent Productions Corp. US.

San Antone. Joe Kane. 1952. Republic Pictures Corp./Republic Pictures
   Corp. US.
Searchers, The. John Ford. 1956. C. V. Whitney Pictures, Inc./Warner Bros.
   Pictures, Inc. US.
Surrender. Allan Dwan. 1950. Republic Pictures Corp./Republic Pictures
   Corp. US.
They Came to Cordura. Robert Rossen. 1959. Goetz Pictures, Inc.; Baroda
   Productions, Inc.; A William Goetz Production/Columbia Pictures
   Corp. US.
Tijuana Story, The. Leslie Kardos. 1957. Clover Productions, Inc./Columbia
   Pictures Corp. US.
Touch of Evil. Orson Welles. 1958. Universal-International Pictures Co.,
   Inc./Universal Pictures Co., Inc. US.
Treasure of Pancho Villa, The. George Sherman. 1955. Edmund Grainger
   Productions, Inc.; RKO Radio Pictures, Inc./RKO Radio Pictures, Inc.
   Mexico and US.
Treasure of the Sierra Madre, The. John Huston. 1948. Warner Bros. Pictures,
   Inc./Warner Bros. Pictures, Inc. US.
Trigger, Jr. William Witney. 1950. Republic Pictures Corp./Republic
   Pictures Corp. US.
Under Mexicali Stars. George Blair. 1950. Republic Pictures Corp./Republic
   Pictures Corp. US.
Vera Cruz. Robert Aldrich. 1954. Flora Productions; Hecht-Lancaster
   Productions/United Artists Corp. Mexico and US.
Villa!! James Clark. 1958. Twentieth Century Fox Film Corp./Twentieth
   Century Fox Film Corp. Mexico and US.
Viva Zapata! Elia Kazan. 1952. Twentieth Century Fox Film Corp./
   Twentieth Century Fox Film Corp. US.
Wayward Bus, The. Victor Vicas. 1957. Twentieth Century Fox Film Corp./
   Twentieth Century Fox Film Corp. US.
Wetbacks. Hank McCune. 1956. Banner Pictures, Inc.; Pacific Coast Pictures/
   Gibraltar Motion Picture Distributors, Inc.; Realart Film Exchange. US.
Where Danger Lives. John Farrow. 1950. RKO Radio Pictures, Inc.;
   Westwood Productions, Inc./RKO Radio Pictures, Inc. US.
Woman They Almost Lynched. Allan Dwan. 1953. Republic Pictures Corp./
   Republic Pictures Corp. US.

Notes

Introduction   Screening the Spaces of the US-Mexico Border

1. See Appendix A for an indicative list of border films from this period.

2. The chronology of the Cold War has been much debated among historians, with some arguing that it lasted in total from 1945 to 1991. However, I use "cold war period" to refer to what M. Keith Booker terms the "long 1950s" and Alan Nadel calls the "peak cold war," covering the period of approximately 1946 to 1964, and centering on the 1950s. As Booker argues, this periodization encompasses the development of the Cold War from its initial outbreak up until the period when "nuclear and anti-Soviet paranoia in the United States began noticeably to decline." M. Keith Booker, *Monsters, Mushroom Clouds, and the Cold War: American Science Fiction and the Roots of Postmodernism, 1946–1964* (Westport, CT, and London: Greenwood Press, 2001), 3; and Alan Nadel, *Containment Culture: American Narrative, Postmodernism and the Atomic Age* (Durham, NC, and London: Duke University Press, 1995), 4. For a definition of the long Cold War, see, for example, David S. Painter, *The Cold War: An International History* (London: Routledge, 1999), 1.

3. The vast majority of critical work on Hollywood cinema and American culture, more generally during the Cold War, focuses on specific genres. See, for example, Mark Jancovich, *Rational Fears: American Horror in the 1950s* (Manchester: Manchester University Press, 1996); Cynthia Hendershot, *Paranoia, the Bomb and 1950s Science Fiction Films* (Bowling Green, OH: Bowling Green State University Popular Press, 1999); David Seed, *American Science Fiction and the Cold War: Literature and Film* (Edinburgh: Edinburgh University Press, 1999); and Stanley Corkin, *Cowboys as Cold Warriors: The Western and U.S. History* (Philadelphia, PA: Temple University Press, 2004). Notable exceptions include Elaine Tyler May, *Homeward Bound: American Families in the Cold War Era* (New York: Basic Books, 1988) and Nadel, *Containment Culture*, works which cut across generic frameworks.

4. Yi-Fu Tuan, *Topophilia: A Study of Environmental Perception, Attitudes, and Values* (New York: Columbia University Press, 1990), 2.
5. Tuan, *Topophilia*, 1.
6. Michel Foucault, "Questions on Geography," in *Power/Knowledge: Selected Interviews and Other Writings, 1972–1977*, ed. and trans. Colin Gordon (New York: Pantheon, 1980), 77.
7. Foucault, "Of Other Spaces," *Diacritics* 16 (1) (1986): 22.
8. For example, Jane Tompkins and Deborah Carmichael's books center on cinematic space and the Western, while Vivan Sobchack, Rob Kitchen, and James Kneale have considered space in science fiction. Jane Tompkins, *West of Everything: The Inner Life of Westerns* (New York and Oxford: Oxford University Press, 1992); Deborah A. Carmichael, ed., *The Landscape of Hollywood Westerns: Ecocriticism in an American Film Genre* (Salt Lake City: University of Utah Press, 2006); Vivian Sobchack, *Screening the Space: The American Science Fiction Film* (New York: Ungar, 1987); and Rob Kitchin and James Kneale, eds., *Lost in Space: Geographies of Science Fiction* (London: Continuum, 2002).
9. Pamela Robertson Wojcik, *The Apartment Plot: Urban Living in American Film and Popular Culture, 1945–1975* (Durham, NC: Duke University Press, 2010), 8.
10. Booker, *Monsters*, 16.
11. Peter Lev, *The Fifties: Transforming the Screen, 1950–1959* (Berkley and London: University of California Press, 2003), 63.
12. Franco Moretti, *Graphs, Maps, Trees* (London and New York: Verso, 2007), 3.
13. Homi K. Bhabha, *The Location of Culture* (London and New York: Routledge, 1994), 38–9.
14. For insightful histories of the border that detail such changes, see, for example, David Lorey, *The U.S.-Mexican Border in the Twentieth Century: A History of Economic and Social Transformation* (Wilmington, DE: Scholarly Resources, 1999); Samuel Truett and Elliott Young, eds., *Continental Crossroads: Remapping U.S.-Mexico Borderlands History* (Durham, NC: Duke University Press, 2004); and Joseph Nevins, *Operation Gatekeeper and Beyond: The War on "Illegals" and the Remaking of the U.S.-Mexico Boundary*, 2nd ed. (New York and London: Routledge, 2010). More specifically on the border and migration, see Kitty Calavita, *Inside the State: The Bracero Program, Immigration, and the INS* (New York and London: Routledge, 1992); Patrick Ettinger, *Imaginary Lines: Border Enforcement and the Origins of Undocumented Immigration, 1882–1930* (Austin: University of Texas Press, 2009); and Raul A. Fernandez and Gilbert G. Gonzalez, *A Century of Chicano History: Empire, Nations and Migration* (New York and London: Routledge, 2003).
15. A note on terminology: I use "undocumented" to describe migrants without official permission to stay or work in the United

States throughout the book. Today's popular lexicon of "illegal aliens" and "illegals" is both pejorative and inaccurate; as Kevin Johnson argues, the term "illegal" "fails to distinguish between types of undocumented persons in the United States." Given the specific historical context and the fact that US immigration agencies often turned a blind eye to such undocumented migration during this period (see chapter 3), the illegality of this kind of border crossing is itself questionable. I further differentiate between "migrant" and "immigrant" deliberately. "Migrant" is used to describe people intending to stay temporarily or periodically in the United States, as was the case for many Mexican workers crossing the border during the 1950s. "Immigrant" is used to refer to those with the intention of staying permanently in the country. Kevin R. Johnson, *The "Huddled Masses" Myth: Immigration and Civil Rights* (Philadelphia, PA: Temple University Press, 2004), 156. For authors who take a different stand on these terminological issues see, for example, Linda Newton, *Illegal, Alien, or Immigrant: The Politics of Immigration Reform* (New York: New York University Press, 2008); and Frank D. Bean and Marta Tienda, *The Hispanic Population of the United States* (New York: Russell Sage Foundation, 1987).

16. John A. Garcia, "The Chicano Movement: Its Legacy for Politics and Policy," in *Chicanas/Chicanos at the Crossroads: Social, Economic, and Political Change*, ed. David R. Maciel and Isidro D. Ortiz (Tucson: University of Arizona Press, 1996), 83–107.

17. Lorey, *U.S.-Mexican Border*, 121.

18. See Timothy J. Dunn, *The Militarization of the U.S.-Mexico Border 1978–1992: Low-Intensity Conflict Doctrine Comes Home* (Austin: Center for Mexican American Studies, University of Texas, 1996).

19. For useful accounts of situation on the borderline into the twenty-first century, see, for example, Kathleen Staudt and Irasema Coronado, *Fronteras No Más: Towards Social Justice at the U.S.-Mexico Border* (New York: Palgrave Macmillan, 2002); Andrew Grant Wood, ed., *On the Border: Society and Culture between the United States and Mexico* (Lanham, MD, and Oxford: SR Books, 2004); Alejandro Lugo, *Fragmented Lives, Assembled Parts: Culture, Capitalism, and Conquest at the U.S.-Mexico Border* (Austin: University of Texas Press, 2008); David Spener and Kathleen Staudt, eds., *The U.S.-Mexico Border: Transcending Divisions, Contesting Identities* (Boulder, CO, and London: Lynne Rienner, 1998); Pablo Vila, *Border Identifications: Narratives of Religion, Gender, and Class on the U.S.-Mexico Border* (Austin: University of Texas Press, 2005); Ed Vulliamy, *Amexica: War along the Borderline* (London: Vintage, 2011); and Melissa W. Wright, "Necropolitics, Narcopolitics, and Femicide: Gendered Violence on the Mexico-U.S. Border," *Signs* 36 (3) (2011): 707–31.

20. David R. Maciel, *El Norte: The U.S.-Mexican Border in Contemporary Cinema* (San Diego, CA: Institute for Regional Studies of the Californias, San Diego State University, 1990), 83.

21. Camilla Fojas, *Border Bandits: Hollywood on the Southern Frontier* (Austin: University of Texas Press, 2008), 2.

22. Carlos E. Cortés, "To View a Neighbor: The Hollywood Textbook on Mexico," in *Images of Mexico in the United States*, ed. John Coatsworth and Carlos Rico (San Diego: Center for U.S.-Mexican Studies, University of California, 1989), 95.

23. See, for example, Edward Renehan, *The Monroe Doctrine: The Cornerstone of American Foreign Policy* (New York: Chelsea House, 2007).

24. "Telegram from the Department of State to the Mission at the United Nations," November 1, 1960, in *United Nations and General International Matters*, ed. John P. Glennon, vol. 2 of *Foreign Relations of the United States, 1958–1960* (Washington, DC: United States Government Printing Office, 1991), 430.

25. "Telegram," 431, 430.

26. Mark Philip Bradley, "Decolonization, the Global South, and the Cold War, 1919–1962," in *The Cambridge History of the Cold War, Volume 1: Origins*, ed. Melvyn P. Leffler and Odd Arne Westad (Cambridge: Cambridge University Press, 2010), 473.

27. Christian G. Appy, "Eisenhower's Guatemalan Doodle, or How to Draw, Deny, and Take Credit for a Third World Coup," in *Cold War Constructions: The Political Culture of United States Imperialism, 1945–1966*, ed. Christian G. Appy (Amherst: University of Massachusetts Press, 2000), 186.

28. Richard Slotkin, *Gunfighter Nation: The Myth of the Frontier in Twentieth-Century America* (New York: Atheneum, 1992), 407.

29. John A. Britton, *Revolution and Ideology: Images of the Mexican Revolution in the United States* (Lexington: University of Kentucky Press, 1995), 8.

30. William Pietz, "The 'Post-Colonialism' of Cold War Discourse," *Social Text* 19–20 (1988): 55. See also Booker, *Monsters*, 8–9 and M. Keith Booker, *Colonial Power, Colonial Texts: India in the Modern British Novel* (Ann Arbor: University of Michigan, 1997).

31. Pietz, "Cold War Discourse," 58.

32. Pietz, "Cold War Discourse," 70.

33. Daniel Bell, *The End of Ideology: On the Exhaustion of Political Ideas in the Fifties*, revised ed. (New York: Free Press, 1962), 404–6.

34. Pietz, "Cold War Discourse," 71.

35. John Urry, *The Tourist Gaze: Leisure and Travel in Contemporary Societies*, 2nd ed. (London: Sage, 2002), 2.

36. Bronwyn Morkham and Russell Staiff, "The Cinematic Tourist: Perception and Subjectivity," in *The Tourist as a Metaphor of the Social World*, ed. Graham M. S. Dann (New York: CABI, 2002), 311, n. 1.

37. Giuliana Bruno, *Atlas of Emotion: Journeys in Art, Architecture and Film* (New York and London: Verso, 2002).

38. Edward Said, *Culture and Imperialism* (repr., London: Vintage, 1994 [1993]), 93.

39. Cole Harris, "How Did Colonialism Dispossess? Comments from an Edge of Empire," *Annals of the Association of American Geographers* 94 (1) (2004): 175.

40. Bhabha, *Location of Culture*, 66.

41. Said, *Culture and Imperialism*, 8.

42. Said, *Culture and Imperialism*, 8. Emphasis in original.

43. Genre is, of course, a much-debated and contentious term in film scholarship, and a structuring framework that this study seeks to avoid. I understand genres to be, as Rick Altman has contended, "not just discursive but, because they are mechanisms for co-ordinating diverse users, multi-discursive. Instead of utilizing a single master language...a genre may appropriately be considered multi-coded," comprising different, overlapping definitions and assignations according to different historical periods and different users. Rick Altman, *Film/Genre* (London: British Film Institute, 1999), 208. Genre debates are discussed in more detail in chapters 4 and 5.

44. "Western genre films" will hereafter be abbreviated as "Western(s)" in the text.

45. See Christopher Frayling, *Spaghetti Westerns: Cowboys and Europeans from Karl May to Sergio Leone* (repr., London and New York: I. B. Tauris, 1998 [1981]), 222; Corkin, *Cowboys as Cold Warriors* and Corkin, "Cowboys and Free Markets: Post-World War II Westerns and U.S. Hegemony," *Cinema Journal* 39 (3) (2000): 66–91.

46. Corkin, *Cowboys*, 20.

47. Frayling, *Spaghetti Westerns*, 222.

48. Frederick Jackson Turner, "The Significance of the Frontier in American History," 1893, reprinted in *The Early Writings of Frederick Jackson Turner*, ed. Everett E. Edwards (Madison: University of Wisconsin Press, 1938), 185–229.

49. For other studies of the West and the Western that focus on frontier mythology see, for example, Peter C. Rollins and John E. O'Connor, eds., *Hollywood's West: The American Frontier in Film, Television and History* (Lexington: University Press of Kentucky, 2005); Jennifer L. McMahon and B. Steve Csaki, eds., *The Philosophy of the Western* (Lexington: University Press of Kentucky, 2010); Robert G. Athearn, *The Mythic West in Twentieth Century America* (Lawrence: University Press of Kansas, 1986); Chris Bruce, *Myth of the West* (New York: Rizzoli, 1990); Richard A. Maynard, *The American West on Film: Myth and Reality* (Rochelle Park, NJ: Hayden, 1974). For interpretations that question the relationship between the West and the frontier, see Patricia Nelson Limerick, "The Adventures of the Frontier in the Twentieth Century," in *The Frontier in American Culture: Essays*

by Richard White and Patricia Nelson Limerick, ed. James Grossman (Berkley and London: University of California Press, 1994), 67–102; Gary J. Hausladen, ed., *Western Places, American Myths: How We Think about the West* (Reno: University of Nevada Press, 2003); and William G. Robbins, *Colony and Empire: The Capitalist Transformation of the American West* (Lawrence: University Press of Kansas, 1994).

50. Peter Stanfield, *Hollywood, Westerns and the 1930s: The Lost Trail* (Exeter: Exeter University Press, 2001), 8.

51. Stanfield, *Hollywood, Westerns*, 8–9.

52. A non-exhaustive list of other useful titles on cold war culture includes Appy, *Cold War Constructions*; Tom Engelhardt, *The End of Victory Culture: Cold War America and the Disillusioning of a Generation* (Amherst: University of Massachusetts Press, 2007); Woody Haut, *Pulp Fiction: Hardboiled Fiction and the Cold War* (London: Serpent's Tail, 1995); Richard M. Fried, *The Russians Are Coming! The Russians Are Coming!: Pageantry and Patriotism in Cold-War America* (New York and Oxford: Oxford University Press, 1998); Lary May, ed., *Recasting America: Culture and Politics in the Age of Cold War* (Chicago and London: University of Chicago Press, 1989); Stephen J. Whitfield, *The Culture of the Cold War* (Baltimore, MD, and London: John Hopkins University Press, 1996); and Frances Stonor Saunders, *Who Paid the Piper? The CIA and the Cultural Cold War* (London: Granta, 1999).

53. Ronald Radosh and Allis Radosh, *Red Star over Hollywood: The Film Colony's Long Romance with the Left* (San Francisco: Encounter Books, 2005), 207; Lary May, *The Big Tomorrow: Hollywood and the Politics of the American Way* (Chicago: University of Chicago Press, 2000), 2.

54. Drew Casper, *Postwar Hollywood, 1946–1962* (Malden, MA, and Oxford, UK: Blackwell, 2007), 5.

55. In addition to the works mentioned in the text, see also Paul Buhle and David Wagner, *A Very Dangerous Citizen: Abraham Lincoln Polonsky and the Hollywood Left* (Berkley and London: University of California Press, 2001); Bob Hertzberg, *The Left Side of the Screen: Communist and Left-Wing Ideology in Hollywood, 1929–2009* (Jefferson, NC, and London: McFarland and Co., Inc., Publishers, 2011); Frank Krutnik et al eds., *"Un-American" Hollywood: Politics and Film in the Blacklist Era* (Piscataway, NJ: Rutgers University Press, 2007); and Larry Ceplair, "The Film Industry's Battle against Left-Wing Influences, from the Russian Revolution to the Blacklist," *Film History* 20 (4) (2008): 399–411. Specifically on the HUAC investigations in Hollywood, see Larry Ceplair and Steven Englund, *The Inquisition in Hollywood: Politics and the Film Community, 1930–1960* (repr., Berkley and London: University of California Press, 1983 [1980]); M. Keith Booker, *From Box Office*

to Ballot Box: The American Political Film (Westport, CT: Praeger, 2007); and John Joseph Gladchuk, Hollywood and Anticommunism: HUAC and the Evolution of the Red Menace, 1935–1950 (London: Routledge, 2007).

56. Paul Buhle and David Wagner, Radical Hollywood: The Untold Story behind America's Favorite Movies (New York: New Press, 2002), xvii.

57. Buhle and Wagner, Radical Hollywood, xvii.

58. Casper, Postwar Hollywood, 5.

59. Nadel, Containment Culture, 6.

60. John Fousek, To Lead the Free World: American Nationalism and the Cultural Roots of the Cold War, (Chapel Hill and London: The University of North Carolina Press, 2000), 2.

61. See May, Big Tomorrow, chapter 6.

62. Michael Denning, The Cultural Front: The Laboring of American Culture in the Twentieth Century (repr., London and New York: Verso, 2010 [1997]), xvi.

63. Fousek, Free World, 2.

64. Denning, Cultural Front, 12–13.

65. Rebecca M. Schreiber, Cold War Exiles in Mexico: U.S. Dissidents and the Culture of Resistance (Minneapolis and London: University of Minnesota Press, 2008), ix–xii.

66. Radosh and Radosh, Red Star, viii.

67. In this approach, I draw on the concept of mobility as developed particularly by Urry and Peter Adey. See John Urry, Mobilities (Cambridge, UK: Polity, 2007) and Peter Adey, Mobility (London: Routledge, 2010). Chapter 6 further elaborates on theories of mobility in relation to regulation. Of course, no cultural text can be reduced to a single simple political position, and it is certainly not the aim of this book to label particular films as left-wing, liberal, radical, or conservative. Rather, taking into consideration the complex and contradictory politics of these texts, I will question how multiple influences including filmmakers' stated personal political positions may have impacted on films and will track political tensions within representations of colonialism at the border. In doing so, I seek to emphasize the plurality and diversity of political reactions to American cold war policies that are articulated through the US-Mexico border. I make use of terms such as "left-wing" and "right-wing" but I do not seek to flatten the politics of these films or their filmmakers into simple binaries, but to emphasize the fact that each text presents a complex, contradictory, and different politics. Indeed, as Richard Pells has argued, during the 1950s, "the terms liberal and conservative had already begun to shed whatever precise political meanings they might have once possessed." In using this terminology I wish not only to evoke the historical slippage of such labels, but also to indicate the broad positioning of people and films discussed within the

political continuum and to emphasize the differences between their ideologies. Richard H. Pells, *The Liberal Mind in a Conservative Age: American Intellectuals in the 1940s and 1950s*, 2nd ed. (Middletown, CT: Wesleyan University Press, 1989), vii.

68. Peter Jackson, *Maps of Meaning: An Introduction to Cultural Geography* (repr., London and New York: Routledge, 2001 [1989]), 3. Emphasis in original.

69. See Bruno, *Atlas*, and Tom Conley, *Cartographic Cinema* (Minneapolis and London: University of Minnesota Press, 2007).

70. Bruno, *Atlas*, 16. One of the few texts written about the border that has a specifically spatial focus is Lawrence Arthur Herzog's *Where North Meets South: Cities, Space and Politics on the U.S.-Mexico Border* (Austin: University of Texas, 1990).

71. Conley, *Cartographic Cinema*, 1.

72. Conley, *Cartographic Cinema*, 2.

73. Edward Soja, *Thirdspace: Journeys to Los Angeles and Other Real-and-Imagined Places* (Cambridge, MA, and Oxford, UK: Blackwell Publishers, 1996), 3.

74. Soja, *Thirdspace*, 5.

75. Edward Said, *Orientalism* (repr., London: Penguin, 2003 [1978]).

76. For example, Dennis Porter argues that Said "fails to historicize adequately the texts he cites and summarizes, finding always the same triumphant discourse when frequently several are in conflict." Dennis Porter, "Orientalism and Its Problems," in *Colonial Discourse and Post-Colonial Theory: A Reader*, ed. Patrick Williams and Laura Chrisman (New York: Columbia University Press, 1994), 160. Bhabha too criticizes *Orientalism*, claiming that the book retains the binary opposition that separates knowledge and power that Said seeks to deconstruct. Bhabha, *Location of Culture*, 72.

77. Said, *Orientalism*, 22.

78. The idea of a nation as an "imagined political community" is borrowed from Benedict Anderson, *Imagined Communities: Reflections on the Origin and Spread of Nationalism* (London and New York: Verso, 1983), 6.

79. The newspaper primarily used is the *New York Times*. As one of the leading national newspapers in terms of both circulation figures and prestige, the *Times* held a highly influential position in the United States during this period. As Donald Shaw and Charles McKenzie argue, in addition to priding itself on publishing "all the news that is fit to print," the *Times* served the "normative role of establishing news agendas for both [its] communities and the nation—and for television networks and national magazines." Donald Shaw and Charles McKenzie, "American Daily Newspaper Evolution: Past, Present…and Future," in *The Function of Newspapers in Society: A Global Perspective*, ed. Shannon E. Martin and David A. Copeland (Westport, CT, and London: Praeger, 2003), 140.

80. Although I primarily use US publications, UK reviews and commentary are also sometimes consulted, as they offer easily accessible and insightful analyses of the films and reflect the increasing interconnectedness of US and UK culture and media environments at this time.

81. Jacques Derrida, *Of Grammatology*, trans. Gayatri Chakravorty Spivak (Baltimore, MD, and London: The John Hopkins University Press, 1976), see, for example, 24.

82. Although I do retain "America" to refer to Colonial America. Jeffrey Geiger, *American Documentary Film: Projecting the Nation* (Edinburgh: Edinburgh University Press, 2011), 1. As Geiger notes, alternative approaches to the use of "America" are also offered by Malini Johar Schueller, *U.S. Orientalisms: Race, Nation, and Gender in Literature, 1790–1890* (Ann Arbor: University of Michigan Press, 1998) and Mary A. Renda, *Taking Tahiti: Military Occupation and the Culture of U.S. Imperialism, 1915–1940* (Chapel Hill: University of North Carolina Press, 2001).

83. Gloria Anzaldúa, *Borderlands/La Frontera: The New Mestiza* (San Francisco: Aunt Lute Books, 1987). On the Chicano and Chicana/o movements see, for example, David R. Maciel and Isidro D. Ortiz, eds., *Chicanas/Chicanos at the Crossroads*; Angie Chabram-Dernersesian, ed., *The Chicana/o Cultural Studies Reader* (London: Routledge, 2006); Rodolfo F. Acuña, *The Making of Chicana/o Studies: In the Trenches of Academe* (New Brunswick, NJ, and London: Rutgers University Press, 2010); Adela de la Torre and Beatríz M. Pesquera, *Building with Our Hands: New Directions in Chicana Studies* (Berkley and London: University of California Press, 1993). Specifically on Chicano and Chicana/o studies and film, see Chon A. Noriega, ed., *Chicanos and Film: Representation and Resistance* (Minneapolis: University of Minnesota Press, 1992); Chon A. Noriega, ed., *Visible Nations: Latin American Cinema and Video* (Minneapolis: University of Minnesota Press, 2000); Frederick Luis Aldama, *Brown on Brown: Chicano/a Representations of Gender, Sexuality, and Ethnicity* (Austin: University of Texas Press, 2005); and Rosa Linda Fregoso, *The Bronze Screen: Chicana and Chicano Film Culture* (Minneapolis and London: University of Minnesota Press, 1993).

1 The Romance of Mexico: Tourists, Fugitives, and Escaping the United States

1. Patricia Jane Jasen, *Wild Things: Nature, Culture, and Tourism in Ontario, 1790–1914* (Toronto and Buffalo, NY: University of Toronto Press, 1995), 11.

2. Amanda Gilroy, "Introduction," in *Romantic Geographies: Discourses of Travel, 1775–1844*, ed. Amanda Gilroy (Manchester: Manchester University Press, 2000), 2.

3. George Dekker, *The Fictions of Romantic Tourism: Radcliffe, Scott and Mary Shelley* (Stanford, CA: Stanford University Press, 2005), 3.
4. John Urry, *The Tourist Gaze: Leisure and Travel in Contemporary Societies*, 2nd ed. (London: Sage, 2002), 2.
5. Dean MacCannell, *The Tourist: A New Theory of the Leisure Class* (repr., Berkeley and London: University of California Press, 1999 [1976]), 2.
6. The 1819 Adams-Onis treaty between Spain and the United States established that Texas, California, and New Mexico belonged to the Spanish Empire. This treaty was ratified in 1831, and in 1836 Texas won independence from Mexico, to be later annexed by the United States in 1845. Following the 1848 treaty of Guadalupe Hidalgo, which ended the US-Mexican war, Mexico was forced to sell around a third of its land to the United States. In 1853, the United States made a further purchase and together the area bought by the United States comprised all of the land known today as California, New Mexico, Nevada, Utah, Arizona, as well as parts of Wyoming and Colorado. Chapter 2 considers the history of the mapping of the borderline in more detail. See John Davenport, *The U.S.-Mexico Border: The Treaty of Guadalupe Hidalgo*, foreword by Senator George J. Mitchell (New York: Chelsea House Publishers, 2005).
7. Steven Bender, *Run for the Border: Vice and Virtue in U.S.-Mexico Border Crossings* (New York and London: New York University Press, 2012), 13.
8. For a clear assessment of the United States' changing relationship with Villa, see, John A. Britton, *Revolution and Ideology: Images of the Mexican Revolution in the United States* (Lexington: University of Kentucky Press, 1995), 177–8.
9. See Bender, *Run for the Border*, Chapter 1.
10. Bender, *Run for the Border*, 12.
11. Rupert Gresham, "Drive on to Mexico: More than Half Million Tourists Crossing the Border Annually," *New York Times*, April 15, 1951, 265.
12. Quotation taken from William G. Preston, "Pesos Go Farther at Story-Book Acapulco," *New York Times*, November 21, 1948, 15. See also Bernadine Bailey, "Acapulco—Resort City for Budgeteers, Too," *New York Times*, October 26, 1958, 37.
13. Edward Wood, "Motoring in Mexico: Three-Day Trip from Texas to Mexico City Opens Many New Vistas," *New York Times*, December 4, 1949, 24.
14. See, for example, "Hall, Fugitive Red, Seized in Mexico, Deported to U.S.," *New York Times*, October 10, 1951, 1. On the self-imposed exile of communists, socialists, and fellow travelers, see Rebecca M. Schreiber, *Cold War Exiles in Mexico: U.S. Dissidents and the Culture of Resistance* (Minneapolis and London: University of Minnesota Press, 2008).

15. Schreiber, *Cold War Exiles*, 166.
16. Schreiber, *Cold War Exiles*, ix.
17. Schreiber, *Cold War Exiles*, x.
18. Schreiber, *Cold War Exiles*, xi.
19. Britton, *Revolution and Ideology*, 8.
20. Schreiber, *Cold War Exiles*, 137.
21. Schreiber, *Cold War Exiles*, 138.
22. Mark Osteen, "Noir's Cars: Automobility and Amoral Space in American Film Noir," *Journal of Popular Film and Television* 35 (4) (2008): 184.
23. James R. Akerman, "Twentieth-Century American Road Maps and the Making of a National Motorized Space," in *Cartographies of Travel and Navigation*, ed. James R. Akerman (Chicago and London: University of Chicago Press, 2006), 152.
24. Akerman, "Twentieth-Century American Road Maps," 152.
25. Akerman, "Twentieth-Century American Road Maps," 154.
26. Giuliana Bruno, *Atlas of Emotion: Journeys in Art, Architecture and Film* (New York and London: Verso, 2002), 176. Much work has been undertaken on the connections between movies, motorcars, and modernity more broadly. See, for example, Edward Dimendberg, *Film Noir and the Spaces of Modernity* (Cambridge, MA, and London: Harvard University Press, 2004) and Tom Gunning, "Modernity and Cinema: A Culture of Shocks and Flows," in *Cinema and Modernity*, ed. Murray Pomerance (New Brunswick, NJ: Rutgers University Press, 2006), 297–315. Akerman also discusses the influence of both railways and automobiles on American culture in "Twentieth-Century American Road Maps."
27. Pablo is devoid of a surname and his overtly typically Mexican forename further emphasizes the reductive and tokenistic role the character serves.
28. Akerman, "Twentieth-Century American Road Maps," 152.
29. Sheila Croucher, *The Other Side of the Fence: American Migrants in Mexico* (Austin: University of Texas Press, 2009), 6.

2 Mapping Borders and Identity: Representation, Transformation, and Ethnicity

1. Amanda Gilroy, "Introduction," in *Romantic Geographies: Discourses of Travel, 1775–1844*, ed. Amanda Gilroy (Manchester: Manchester University Press, 2000), 2.
2. "Treaty of Guadalupe Hidalgo," in *Treaties and Other International Agreements of the United States of America, 1776–1949*, vol. 9, ed. Charles Bevans (Washington, DC: US Department of State, 1972), 794.
3. For an account of the writing and implementation of the treaty, see Richard Griswold Del Castillo, "The Treaty of Guadalupe Hidalgo,"

in *U.S.-Mexico Borderlands: Historical and Contemporary Perspectives*, ed. Oscar J. Martínez (Wilmington, DE: Scholarly Resources, 1996), 2–9.

4. David Lorey, *The U.S.-Mexican Border in the Twentieth Century: A History of Economic and Social Transformation* (Wilmington, DE: Scholarly Resources, 1999), 154.

5. Jean Baudrillard, *Simulacra and Simulation*, trans. Sheila Faria Glaser (repr., Ann Arbor: University of Michigan Press, 1994 [1981]), 1.

6. John Pickles, *A History of Spaces: Cartographic Reason, Mapping and the Geo-Coded World* (London: Routledge, 2004), 93.

7. "Treaty of Guadalupe Hidalgo," *Treaties and Other International Agreements*, 794.

8. Jeffrey Peters, *Mapping Discord: Allegorical Cartography in Early Modern French Writing* (Newark: University of Delaware Press, 2004), 41.

9. Claire F. Fox, *The Fence and the River: Culture and Politics at the U.S.-Mexico Border* (Minneapolis and London: University of Minnesota Press, 1999), 50.

10. Fox, *Fence and River*, 78.

11. Giuliana Bruno, *Atlas of Emotion: Journeys in Art, Architecture and Film* (New York and London: Verso, 2002), 271.

12. Camilla Fojas, *Border Bandits: Hollywood on the Southern Frontier* (Austin: University of Texas Press, 2008), 184.

13. Fojas, *Border Bandits*, 184.

14. *Borderline* press pack, British Film Institute National Archive, 1950, n.p.

15. Paul Smethurst, *Travel Writing and the Natural World: 1768–1840* (Basingstoke: Palgrave MacMillan, 2013), 184.

16. Smethurst, *Travel Writing*, 184.

17. John Torpey, *The Invention of the Passport: Surveillance, Citizenship and the State* (Cambridge: Cambridge University Press, 2000), 1.

18. Annette Kuhn, *The Power of the Image: Essays on Representation and Sexuality* (London: Routledge, 1985), 52.

19. Ray Hagen, "Claire Trevor: Brass with Class," in *Killer Tomatoes: Fifteen Tough Film Dames*, by Ray Hagen and Laura Wagner (Jefferson, NC, and London: McFarland and Co., Inc., Publishers, 2004), 222.

20. This understanding of the relationship between actors and characters is informed by Paul McDonald's approach in *Hollywood Stardom* (Malden: Wiley Blackwell, 2013) and his conflation of actor and character names as a means of demonstrating the important impact of star personas and brands on characters. See, for example, his analysis of Tom Hanks's star brand, 65–83.

21. I use the term "Chicano" to refer historically to Mexicans or people of Mexican or mixed Mexican origin living in the United States rather than today's more commonly accepted term "Mexican American"

because it was the language used during the 1950s, the period that also saw the emergence of the Chicano movement. In this way, I seek also to begin to understand what this particular ethnic label meant at this point in time. I am not using Chicana/o here, because with its masculine (o) ending, Chicano deliberately retains the gender imbalance that female Mexicans and Mexican Americans faced at this time. On the emergence and use of these different labels, see Jacqueline M. Martinez, *Phenomenology of Chicana Experience and Identity: Communication and Transformation in Praxis* (Lanham, MD, and Oxford, UK: Rowman and Littlefield, 2000), 33–58.

22. Victoria Sturtevant, "Spitfire: Lupe Vélez and the Ambivalent Pleasures of Ethnic Masquerade," *The Velvet Light Trap* 55 (2005): 23–4.
23. Quinn won the Academy Award for Best Supporting Actor for his role in border film *Viva Zapata!* just years earlier in 1952. He would win this award a second time in 1956 for *Lust for Life*.
24. See Richard Rees, *Shades of Difference: A History of Ethnicity in America* (Lanham, MD, and Plymouth: Rowman and Littlefield Publishers, 2007), chapter 3 in particular.
25. Lester D. Friedman, "Celluloid Palimpsests: An Overview of Ethnicity and the American Film," in *Unspeakable Images: Ethnicity and the American Cinema*, ed. Lester D. Friedman (Urbana: University of Illinois Press, 1991), 24.
26. Friedman, *Unspeakable Images*, 27.
27. Matthew Frye Jacobson, *Whiteness of a Different Colour: European Immigrants and the Alchemy of Race* (Cambridge, MA, and London: Harvard University Press, 1999), 176, 6.
28. Diane Negra, *Off-White Hollywood: American Culture and Ethnic Female Stardom* (London and New York: Routledge, 2001), 6.
29. Clara E. Rodriguez, *Heroes, Lovers and Others: The Story of Latinos in Hollywood* (Washington, DC: Smithsonian Books, 2004), 110–11.
30. Sturtevant, "Spitfire," 21.
31. Mary Beltrán and Camilla Fojas, "Mixed Race in Hollywood Film and Media Culture," in *Mixed Race Hollywood*, ed. Mary Beltrán and Camilla Fojas (New York and London: New York University Press, 2008), 3.
32. Gary Gerstle, *American Crucible: Race and Nation in the Twentieth Century* (Princeton, NJ: Princeton University Press, 2001), 4.
33. Gerstle, *American Crucible*, 8.
34. As Gerstle points out, this 1790 law "limit[ed] naturalization to 'free white persons'" and although it was modified in 1870 it was not abolished until the 1950s. *American Crucible*, 8, 4.
35. Rodriguez, *Heroes*, 137–8.
36. William Anthony Nericcio, *Tex[t]-Mex: Seductive Hallucinations of the "Mexican" in America* (Austin: University of Texas Press, 2007), 93.

37. Francisco Arturo Rosales, *Chicano! The History of the Mexican American Civil Rights Movement* (Houston: Arte Público Press, 1997), 252.

38. For a history of Mexican experiences of assimilation in the United States, see Edward E. Telles and Vilma Ortiz, *Generations of Exclusion: Mexican Americans, Assimilation, and Race* (New York: Russell Sage Foundation, 2008).

39. Dale Adams, "Saludos Amigos: Hollywood and FDR's Good Neighbor Policy," *Quarterly Review of Film and Video* 24 (3) (2007): 291.

40. Ian Roxborough, "Mexico," in *Latin America between the Second World War and the Cold War, 1944–1948*, ed. Leslie Bethell and Ian Roxborough (Cambridge: Cambridge University Press, 1992), 190–216.

41. Alfred Charles Richard Jr., *Censorship and Hollywood's Hispanic Image: An Interpretive Filmography, 1936–1955* (Westport, CT: Greenwood Press, 1993), xxix.

42. Richard, *Censorship*, xvi.

43. Richard, *Censorship*, xvii.

44. Richard, *Censorship*, xxi.

45. Richard, *Censorship*, 410.

46. Richard, *Censorship*, 410.

47. See Emilio García Riera, *México Visto Por el Cine Extranjero 4: 1941/1969: Filmografía* (Guadalajara: Universidad de Guadalajara, 1988), 60.

48. See the US Customs and Border Patrol website for more details, http://www.cbp.gov/.

49. People Helping People in the Border Zone, "Community Report: Campaign Documents Systemic Racial Discrimination at Arizona Border Patrol Checkpoint," accessed February 20, 2015, http://phparivaca.org/?p=567. See also Mary Romero, "Racial Profiling and Immigration Law Enforcement: Rounding up of Usual Suspects in the Latino Community," *Critical Sociology* 32 (2–3) (2006): 447–73.

3   Danger, Disappearance, and the Exotic: American Travelers and Mexican Migrants

1. The title of the film and the use of the term "Wetbacks" in press and academic writing of the cold war period demonstrate the prevalence of this label at this time. It is a highly pejorative term that refers to those who have crossed into the United States from Mexico through the Rio Grande.

2. *Wetbacks* press pack, British Film Institute National Archive, 1956, n.p.

3. David Lorey, *The U.S.-Mexican Border in the Twentieth Century: A History of Economic and Social Transformation* (Wilmington, DE: Scholarly Resources, 1999), 121.

4. Kitty Calavita, *Inside the State: The Bracero Program, Immigration, and the INS* (New York and London: Routledge, 1992), 32.

5. Calavita, *Inside the State*, 37.

6. Lorey, *U.S.-Mexican Border*, 122.

7. Lorey, *U.S.-Mexican Border*, 121.

8. Joseph Nevins, *Operation Gatekeeper and Beyond: The War on "Illegals" and the Remaking of the U.S.-Mexico Boundary*, 2nd ed. (New York and London: Routledge, 2010), 38.

9. Manuel G. Gonzales, *Mexicanos: A History of Mexicans in the United States*, 2nd ed. (Bloomington: Indiana University Press, 2009), 180.

10. John A. Garcia, "The Chicano Movement: Its Legacy for Politics and Policy," in *Chicanas/Chicanos at the Crossroads: Social, Economic, and Political Change*, ed. David R. Maciel and Isidro D. Ortiz (Tucson: University of Arizona Press, 1996), 87.

11. See, for example, "Flaws Are Noted in 'Wetback' Curb: Traffic Only a 'Trickle,' but Abuses Persist on Farms, Texas Unions Assert," *New York Times*, August 28, 1955, 55.

12. "Flaws Are Noted," 55.

13. Calavita, *Inside the State*, 47.

14. Eleanor M. Hadley, "A Critical Analysis of the Wetback Problem," *Law and Contemporary Problems* 21 (2) (1956): 334–57.

15. Gladwin Hill, "Wetback Ousting by Airlift Revived: Action by Congress Remedies Shortage of Funds," *New York Times*, June 13, 1952, 11; Hadley, "Critical Analysis of the Wetback Problem," 334; "Wetback Bill Approved: House Judiciary Committee Will Report Search Measure," *New York Times*, January 25, 1952, 9; and "Wetback Action Planned: Mexican President Asserts New Lands Will Be Cultivated," *New York Times*, September 2, 1953, 18.

16. "Drive on Wetbacks Termed a Success," *New York Times*, March 10, 1955, 29.

17. Gladwin Hill, "Wetback Invasion Is Broadening Despite All U.S. Counter-Moves," *New York Times*, Top of Form February 11, 1952, 12; and Gladwin Hill, "Wetback Influx Moves Westward: Two States Have Record Job Rush by Mexicans," *New York Times*, October 9, 1953, 40.

18. GI Forum of Texas and Texas State Federation of Labor, *What Price Wetbacks?* (Austin: GI Forum of Texas, 1953), 6, quoted in Hadley, "Critical Analysis of the Wetback Problem," 335.

19. See Dina Berger and Andrew Grant Wood, eds., *Holiday in Mexico: Critical Reflections on Tourism and Tourist Encounters* (Durham, NC: Duke University Press, 2010), particularly Andrew Sackett's chapter, "Fun in Acapulco? The Politics of Development on the Mexican Riviera," 161–82.

20. Rebecca Torres and Janet Henshall Momsen, "Gringolandia: Cancún and the American Tourist," in *Adventures into Mexico: American Tourism beyond the Border*, ed. Nicholas Dagen Bloom (Lanham,

MD, and Oxford, UK: Rowman and Littlefield Publishers, Inc., 2006), 59. Chapter 7 of this book explores the role of Hollywood stars in glamorizing such Mexican resorts.

21. *Wetbacks* press pack.
22. Rev. of *Wetbacks*, *Harrison's Reports*, March 3, 1956, 34.
23. Rev. of *Wetbacks*, *Kinematograph Weekly*, January 9, 1958, 30.
24. Rev. of *Wetbacks*, *Variety*, March 7, 1956, 6.
25. "McCune Revises Setup; Sets 'Wetbacks' Feature," *The Hollywood Reporter*, May 3, 1955, 5.
26. Jeffrey Geiger, "Imagined Islands: 'White Shadows in the South Seas' and Cultural Ambivalence," *Cinema Journal* 41 (3) (2002): 107.
27. Betts argues that the "purifying gaze of the Hollywood lens strove to construct the South Pacific as an illusionary island." Raymond F. Betts, "The Illusionary Island: Hollywood's Pacific Place," *East-West Film Journal* 5 (2) (1991): 41.
28. Geiger, "Imagined Islands," 110.
29. Edward Said, *Culture and Imperialism* (repr., London: Vintage, 1994 [1993]), 271.
30. Cole Harris, "How Did Colonialism Dispossess? Comments from an Edge of Empire," *Annals of the Association of American Geographers* 94 (1) (2004): 175.
31. DeSoto Brown, "Beautiful, Romantic Hawaii: How the Fantasy Image Came to Be," *Journal of Decorative and Propaganda Arts* 20 (1994): 252–71.
32. As Brown explains, "The soon-to-be-famous ukulele (originally a Portuguese instrument) was joined by the guitar, tuned in a special manner and often played with a metal bar that produced a unique sliding sound. This came to be known as the steel guitar, and for millions of people all over the world only its tones qualify as 'Hawaiian music.'" "Beautiful, Romantic Hawaii," 253.
33. Stewart Brewer, *Borders and Bridges: A History of U.S.-Latin American Relations* (Westport, CT, and London: Praeger Security international, 2006), 112.
34. Brewer, *Borders and Bridges*, 115.
35. Brewer, *Borders and Bridges*, 115.
36. Brewer, *Borders and Bridges*, 115. It is important to note that the US government was using a very broad definition of communism at this time and that many of these Latin American movements were similar in ideology and ethos to the policies of United States' own New Deal era.
37. George Kennan, "Latin America as a Problem in U.S. Foreign Policy," in *Neighborly Adversaries: Readings in U.S.-Latin American Relations*, 2nd ed., ed. Michael J. LaRosa and Frank O. Mora (Lanham, MD: Rowman and Littlefield Publishers, 2007), 123–34.

38. Jonathan Auerbach, *Dark Borders: Film Noir and American Citizenship* (Durham, NC: Duke University Press, 2011), 187.
39. Auerbach, *Dark Borders*, 187–8.
40. M. Keith Booker, *Monsters, Mushroom Clouds, and the Cold War: American Science Fiction and the Roots of Postmodernism, 1946–1964* (Westport, CT, and London: Greenwood Press, 2001), 127.
41. Calavita, *Inside the State*, 78.
42. "184 Subversives in Deported List: Report for Five Years Made by Immigration Service—5,261 Criminals Ousted," *New York Times*, January 3, 1955, 8. The Alien Registration Act of June 22, 1940, had already established "protocols for the registration and deportation of noncitizens with radical affiliations." Auerbach, *Dark Borders*, 35.
43. Alfred Charles Richard Jr., *Censorship and Hollywood's Hispanic Image: An Interpretive Filmography, 1936–1955* (Westport, CT: Greenwood Press, 1993), xxxix–xl.
44. Richard, *Censorship*, xxxix–xl.
45. For a detailed history of Breen and the PCA, see Thomas Doherty, *Hollywood's Censor: Joseph I. Breen & the Production Code Administration* (New York and Chichester: Columbia University Press, 2007).
46. Emilio García Riera, *México Visto por el Cine Extranjero 3: 1941/1969* (Guadalajara: Universidad de Guadalajara, 1988), 65.
47. American Film Institute Catalogue, "Wetbacks," accessed August 20, 2013, http://afi.chadwyck.co.uk/home.
48. Bruce Newman, "Lloyd Bridges: Hollywood Family Man," *TV Guide*, April 11, 1998, 28. See also "The Life Story of Lloyd Bridges," *Pictureshow*, March 28, 1953, 12.
49. Jeremy Byman, *Showdown at High Noon: Witch-hunts, Critics, and the End of the Western* (Lanham, MD, and Oxford: Scarecrow Press, 2004), 92.
50. Byman, *Showdown*, 92.
51. On the extent of US involvement and influence in Latin American during this period, see, for example, Hal Brands, *Latin America's Cold War* (Cambridge, MA: Harvard University Press, 2010), 10–11. This idea is something that will be returned to in the later chapters of the book.
52. "Telegram from the Department of State to the Mission at the United Nations," November 1, 1960, in *United Nations and General International Matters*, ed. John P. Glennon, vol. 2 of *Foreign Relations of the United States, 1958–1960* (Washington, DC: United States Government Printing Office, 1991), 430.
53. "Telegram," 430.
54. Fernanda Santos and Rebekah Zemansky, "Death Rate Climbs as Migrants Take Bigger Risks to Cross Tighter Borders," *New York Times*, May 21, 2013, A14.

4 The Revolutionary Politics of Mexico: Individualism, Communitarianism, and Landscape

1. Carlos E. Cortés, "To View a Neighbor: The Hollywood Textbook on Mexico," in *Images of Mexico in the United States*, ed. John Coatsworth and Carlos Rico (San Diego: Center for U.S.-Mexican Studies, University of California, 1989), 96–7.
2. Tim Girven, "Hollywood's Heterotopia: US Cinema, the Mexican Border and the Making of Tijuana," *Travesia: Journal of Latin American Cultural Studies* 3 (1–2) (1994): 101.
3. Early films about Mexico such as *The Mexican Revolutionist* (George Melford, 1912), *Life of Villa* (Christy Cabanne, 1912), *Barbarous Mexico* (Irving G. Ries, 1913), and *'Cross the Mexican Line* (Wallace Reid, 1914) focus on the revolution.
4. See note 48 to the introduction to this book for a selection of studies of the Western genre that focus on frontier mythology.
5. Michael Coyne, *The Crowded Prairie: American National Identity in the Hollywood Western* (London: I. B. Tauris, 1997), 11.
6. Peter Stanfield, *Hollywood, Westerns and the 1930s: The Lost Trail* (Exeter: Exeter University Press, 2001), 8.
7. Camilla Fojas, *Border Bandits: Hollywood on the Southern Frontier* (Austin: University of Texas Press, 2008), 69.
8. Fojas, *Border Bandits*, 69.
9. Jack Moffitt, "Hecht-Lancaster, Hill and Aldrich Turn out a Natural," Rev. of *Vera Cruz*, *The Hollywood Reporter*, December 22, 1954, 3.
10. Bosley Crowther, Rev. of *Vera Cruz*, *New York Times*, December 27, 1954, 22.
11. Fojas, *Border Bandits*, 68.
12. Jane Tompkins, *West of Everything: The Inner Life of Westerns* (New York and Oxford: Oxford University Press, 1993), 70.
13. Tompkins, *West of Everything*, 76.
14. According to a newspaper article about the production, much of the filming was indeed undertaken in Mexico City and the nearby Cuernavaca valley. See Flora Lewis, "Cameras Capture 'Vera Cruz' in Cuernavaca," *New York Times*, April 11, 1954, X5.
15. George L. Cowgill, "State and Society at Teotihuacan, Mexico," *Annual Review of Anthropology* 26 (1997): 130–5.
16. See, for example, Coyne, *Crowded Prairie*; Peter C. Rollins and John E. O'Connor and, eds., *Hollywood's West: The American Frontier in Film, Television and History* (Lexington: University Press of Kentucky, 2005); John H. Lenihan, *Showdown: Confronting Modern America in the Western Film* (Urbana: University of Illinois Press, 1985); Will Wright, *The Wild West: The Mythical Cowboy and Social Theory* (London: Sage, 2001).
17. Frederick Elkin, "The Psychological Appeal of the Hollywood Western," *Journal of Educational Sociology* 24 (2) (1950): 74; Henry

NOTES 175

Nash Smith, *Virgin Land: The American West as Symbol and Myth*, 20th anniversary ed. (Cambridge, MA, and London: Harvard University Press, 1970), 81.
18. Stanley Corkin, "Cowboys and Free Markets: Post-World War II Westerns and U.S. Hegemony," *Cinema Journal* 39 (3) (2000): 79.
19. Morris Ankrum's character is referred to as General Aguilar throughout the press pack rather than General Ramírez as in the film itself, indicating the name was changed during filming, perhaps to a more recognizably "Mexican" name for US audiences.
20. *Vera Cruz* press pack, British Film Institute National Archive, 1954, 1.
21. John Kenneth Galbraith, *The Affluent Society* (Cambridge, MA: The Riverside Press, 1958), 201.
22. Galbraith, *Affluent Society*, 48, 63.
23. Richard Slotkin, *Gunfighter Nation: The Myth of the Frontier in Twentieth-Century America* (New York: Atheneum, 1992), 421; Paul Vanderwood, "An American Cold Warrior: Viva Zapata!," in *American History/American Film: Interpreting the Hollywood Image*, ed. John E. O'Connor and Martin A. Jackson (New York: Frederick Ungar Publishing Co., 1979), 186.
24. Noël Carroll, "Toward a Theory of Point-of-View Editing: Communication, Emotion, and the Movies," *Poetics Today* 14 (1) (1993): 126. Carroll further argues that this type of shot is deployed for the "communication of emotion" and works to align audiences with characters in film.
25. Fojas, *Border Bandits*, 69.
26. Philip French, *Westerns: Aspects of a Movie Genre and Westerns Revisited* (Manchester: Carcanet Press Limited, 2005), 69.
27. Jeffrey Belnap, "Diego Rivera's Greater America Pan-American Patronage, Indigenism, and H.P.," *Cultural Critique* 63 (2006): 62.
28. Belnap, "Diego Rivera," 65. Most famously, Rivera refused to remove an image of Lenin from his Rockefeller Institute project, which resulted in the complete destruction of the mural.
29. Edward Said, *Orientalism* (repr., London: Penguin, 2003 [1978]), 21.
30. Said, *Orientalism*, 3.
31. Gary Fishgall, *Against Type: The Biography of Burt Lancaster* (New York and London: Scribner, 1995), 123.
32. Edwin T. Arnold and Eugene L. Miller, *The Films and Career of Robert Aldrich* (Knoxville: University of Tennessee Press, 1986), 31.
33. Lewis, "Cameras Capture," X5.
34. Fishgall, *Against Type*, 135.
35. Arnold and Miller, *Films and Career*, 2.
36. Tino Balio, *United Artists: The Company That Changed the Film Industry* (Madison and London: University of Wisconsin Press, 1987), 3.
37. Quoted in Edwin T. Arnold and Eugene L. Miller, eds., *Robert Aldrich: Interviews* (Jackson: University Press of Mississippi, 2004), xii.

38. Arnold and Miller, *Films and Career*, 1.
39. Fishgall, *Against Type*, 68.
40. Quoted in Fishgall, *Against Type*, 102.
41. Larry Swindell, *The Last Hero: A Biography of Gary Cooper* (Garden City, NY: Doubleday and Co., Inc., 1980), 275.
42. Bernard F. Dick, *Radical Innocence: A Critical Study of the Hollywood Ten* (Lexington: University Press of Kentucky, 1989), 2.
43. Tony Williams, *Body and Soul: The Cinematic Vision of Robert Aldrich* (Lanham, MD, and Oxford: Scarecrow Press, Inc., 2004), 174.
44. Rebecca M. Schreiber, *Cold War Exiles in Mexico: U.S. Dissidents and the Culture of Resistance* (Minneapolis and London: University of Minnesota Press, 2008), xii.

5 Territory, Colonialism, and Gender at the American Frontier

1. André Bazin, *What Is Cinema?* Vol. 2, trans. Hugh Gray (repr., Berkeley, Los Angeles, and London: University of California Press, 2005 [1971]), 147.
2. Scott Simmon, *The Invention of the Western Film: A Cultural History of the Genre's First Half-Century* (Cambridge: Cambridge University Press, 2003), 45.
3. Lee Clark Mitchell, *Westerns: Making the Man in Fiction and Film* (Chicago and London: University of Chicago Press, 1996), 3.
4. Henry Nash Smith, *Virgin Land: The American West as Symbol and Myth*, 20th anniversary ed. (Cambridge, MA, and London: Harvard University Press, 1970), 3.
5. Thomas J. McCormick, *America's Half-Century: United States Foreign Policy in the Cold War* (Baltimore, MD, and London: John Hopkins University Press, 1989), 48.
6. John Kenneth Galbraith, *The Affluent Society* (Cambridge, MA: The Riverside Press, 1958), 48.
7. Linda Hall and Don Coerver, *Revolution on the Border: The United States and Mexico, 1910–1920* (Albuquerque: University of New Mexico Press, 1988), 12.
8. John A. Britton, *Revolution and Ideology: Images of the Mexican Revolution in the United States* (Lexington: University of Kentucky Press, 1995), 6.
9. The premise is based loosely on historical events as the Mexican government did establish free zones along the borderline in the late nineteenth century. Writing in 1892, Mexican minister to the United States, M. Romero tried to assuage US antagonisms about these measures. M. Romero, "The Free Zone in Mexico," *The North American Review* 154 (425) (1892): 459–71.
10. Camilla Fojas, *Border Bandits: Hollywood on the Southern Frontier* (Austin: University of Texas Press, 2008), 29.

11. Britton, *Revolution and Ideology*, 8. The revolution also posed occasional security threats to the United States, for example, Pancho Villa's 1916 incursion into Columbus, New Mexico.
12. Fox goes on to explain, "In the 1911 battle of Juárez, for example, four US spectators were killed, and nine were wounded." Claire F. Fox, *The Fence and the River: Culture and Politics at the U.S.-Mexico Border* (Minneapolis and London: University of Minnesota Press, 1999), 81.
13. Fox, *Fence and the River*, 81.
14. Alan Nadel, *Containment Culture: American Narrative, Postmodernism and the Atomic Age* (Durham, NC, and London: Duke University Press, 1995).
15. John Lewis Gaddis, *Strategies of Containment: A Critical Appraisal of American National Security Policy during the Cold War* (New York and Oxford: Oxford University Press, 2005), 41–4.
16. Elaine Tyler May, *Homeward Bound: American Families in the Cold War Era* (New York: Basic Books, 1988), 22.
17. May, *Homeward Bound*, 23–4.
18. See, for example, Odd Arne Westad, "The Cold War and the International History of the Twentieth Century," in *The Cambridge History of the Cold War, Volume 1: Origins*, ed. Melvyn P. Leffler and Odd Arne Westad (Cambridge: Cambridge University Press, 2010), 8–11.
19. Britton, *Revolution and Ideology*, 8.
20. Kitty Calavita, *Inside the State: The Bracero Program, Immigration, and the INS* (New York and London: Routledge, 1992), 49.
21. Greg Grandin, *The Last Colonial Massacre: Latin America in the Cold War* (Chicago and London: University of Chicago Press, 2004), 1–18.
22. See J. Brian Harley, *The New Nature of Maps: Essays in the History of Cartography*, ed. Paul Laxton with an Introduction by J. H. Andrews (Baltimore, MD, and London: John Hopkins University Press, 2001); Tom Conley, *The Self-Made Map: Cartographic Writing in Early Modern France* (Minneapolis and London: University of Minnesota Press, 1996); *Cartographic Cinema* (Minneapolis and London: University of Minnesota Press, 2007); and Karen Piper, *Cartographic Fictions: Maps, Race and Identity* (New Brunswick, NJ: Rutgers University Press, 2002).
23. Harley, "Texts and Contexts in the Interpretation of Early Maps," in *New Nature of Maps*, 35.
24. Cole Harris, "How Did Colonialism Dispossess? Comments from an Edge of Empire," *Annals of the Association of American Geographers* 94 (1) (2004): 175. See also chapter 3 of this book for a discussion of the overwriting of landscape and colonialism.
25. Harris, "How Did Colonialism Dispossess?," 175.
26. Piper, *Cartographic Fictions*, 11.

27. Piper, *Cartographic Fictions*, 10.

28. Joan Blaeu, *Le Grand Atlas*, vol. 1, 1667, Library of Congress Atlas Collection, Washington, DC. The frontispiece is based on a Peter Paul Rubens painting.

29. Caterina Albano, "Visible Bodies: Cartography and Anatomy," in *Literature, Mapping, and the Politics of Space in Early Modern Britain*, ed. Andrew Gordon and Bernhard Klein (Cambridge: Cambridge University Press, 2001), 101.

30. For example, French has argued that there are just "two kinds of women" in traditional Westerns: "On the one hand there is the unsullied pioneer heroine: virtuous wife, rancher's virginal daughter, schoolteacher, etc.; on the other hand there is the saloon girl with her entourage of dancers." Philip French, *Westerns: Aspects of a Movie Genre and Westerns Revisited* (Manchester: Carcanet Press Limited, 2005), 38.

31. Laura Mulvey, "Afterthoughts on 'Visual Pleasure and Narrative Cinema' Inspired by King Vidor's *Duel in the Sun* (1946)," in *Visual and Other Pleasures*, by Laura Mulvey (Basingstoke: Macmillan, 1989), 35–6.

32. Like the actors described in chapter 2, De Carlo played a startling array of different ethnicities on screen. Her Hollywood break-through came in 1945 when she played an Austrian seductress in *Salome, Where She Danced* (Lamont, 1945). Following this success she went on to play a French dancer in *Song of Scheherazade* (Reisch, 1947), a Persian princess in *The Desert Hawk* (de Cordova, 1950), a half-Polynesian in *Hurricane Smith* (Hopper, 1952), and a Mexican maid in *Sombrero* (Foster, 1953).

33. Charles Ramirez Berg, *Latino Images in Film: Stereotypes, Subversion, and Resistance* (Austin: University of Texas Press, 2002), 66.

34. Clara E. Rodriguez, *Heroes, Lovers and Others: The Story of Latinos in Hollywood* (Washington, DC: Smithsonian Books, 2004), 104.

35. Peter Stanfield, *Hollywood, Westerns and the 1930s: The Lost Trail* (Exeter: Exeter University Press, 2001), 30. Further, in other films of the period where American men travel south of the border, although they may desire Mexican women, they only form relationships with Americans. In *Out of the Past* (Tourneur, 1947), *Borderline* (Seiter, 1950), *His Kind of Woman* (Farrow, 1951), and *The Treasure of Pancho Villa* (Sherman, 1955), the male Americans in Mexico always meet and fall in love with American women, despite admiring Mexican women along the way.

36. Stanfield, *Westerns*, 38. For examples of studies of the Westerns focused on masculinity, see Mitchell, *Westerns*, and Roderick McGillis, *He Was Some Kind of a Man: Masculinities in the B Western* (Waterloo, ON: Wilfrid Laurier University Press, 2009).

37. Rev. of *Border River*, *Today's Cinema*, February 1, 1954, 14; Rev. of *Border River*, *Variety*, January 6, 1954, 3; and Rev. of *Border River*, *The Hollywood Reporter*, January 4, 1954, 3.

38. Alfred Charles Richard Jr., *Censorship and Hollywood's Hispanic Image: An Interpretive Filmography, 1936–1955* (Westport, CT: Greenwood Press, 1993), 479.

39. Quoted in Jimmie Hicks, "Joel McCrea," *Films in Review* 42 (11–12) (1991): 392–404.

40. Quoted in Hicks, "Joel McCrea," 392–404.

41. See also Robert Nott, *Last of the Cowboy Heroes: The Westerns of Randolph Scott, Joel McCrea, and Andy Murphy*, foreword by Butt Boetticher (Jefferson, NC: McFarland and Co., Inc., Publishers, 2000).

42. Nott, *Last of the Cowboy Heroes*, 30.

43. Interview with Joel McCrea, May 24, 1970, in Will Rogers, *Will Rogers Scrapbook*, ed. Bryan B. Sterling (New York: Grosset and Dunlap, 1976), 117. Quoted in Lary May, *The Big Tomorrow: Hollywood and the Politics of the American Way* (Chicago: University of Chicago Press, 2000), 46.

44. May, *Big Tomorrow*, 28.

6 Ethnicity, Imperialism, and the Law: Policing Identities at the Border

1. Headlines taken from the *New York Times*, March 27, 1951, 31; April 16, 1953, 31; and March 27, 1950, 1.

2. See chapter 3 for more detail on the history of Mexican migration to the United States.

3. John Urry, *Mobilities* (Cambridge, UK: Polity Press, 2007), 186.

4. Urry, *Mobilities*, 205.

5. Peter Adey, *Mobility* (London: Routledge, 2010), 88–9.

6. Ernesto Galarza, *Merchants of Labor: The Mexican Bracero Story: An Account of the Managed Migration of Mexican Farm Workers in California, 1942–1960* (repr., New York: McNally and Loftin, 1972 [1964]), 16.

7. Mai M. Ngai, *Impossible Subjects: Illegal Aliens and the Making of Modern America* (Princeton, NJ, and Woodstock: Woodstock University Press, 2004), 95.

8. Ngai, *Impossible Subjects*, 4.

9. As described in previous chapters, the American-Mexican war ended with Mexico being forced to cede almost a third of its territory to the United States in 1848, including all of the land now known as California where the action on the US side of the border takes place in the film.

10. Jonathan Auerbach, "Noir Citizenship: Anthony Mann's *Border Incident*," *Cinema Journal* 47 (4) (2008): 112. Emphasis in original.

11. Jonathan Auerbach, *Dark Borders: Film Noir and American Citizenship* (Durham, NC: Duke University Press, 2011), 124.

12. Auerbach, *Dark Borders*, 4. Emphases in original.

13. Auerbach, "Noir Citizenship," 107.

14. Tom Conley, "Border Incidence," *Symploke* 15 (1–2) (2007): 112.

15. Geiger has examined aerial views in American cinema in the postwar period, arguing that they articulate a form of American nationalism. Following this idea, for *Border Incident*, the aerial view is bound up with a celebration of institutions through the precise, geometric visions of American farmland, at the expense of the trapped Mexican workers. Jeffrey Geiger, "Adrenaline Views: Rethinking Aerial Affect" (paper presented at the School of Film, Television and Media research seminar series, University of East Anglia, UK, April 29, 2013).

16. Christian Parenti, *The Soft Cage: Surveillance in America from Slavery to the War on Terror* (New York: Basic Books, 2003), 42; 39.

17. Parenti, *Soft Cage*, 19.

18. Simon Cole, *Suspect Identities: A History of Fingerprinting and Criminal Identification* (Cambridge, MA, and London: Harvard University Press, 2001), 121.

19. *Border Incident* press pack, British Film Institute National Archive, 1949, 5. Capitalization in original.

20. Piyasiri Wickramasekara, "Globalisation, International Labour Migration and the Rights of Migrant Workers," in *Globalisation and Migration: New Issues, New Politics*, ed. Ronaldo Munck (London: Routledge, 2013), 28.

21. The White House Office of the Press Secretary, "Fact Sheet: Immigration Accountability Executive Action," November 20, 2014, accessed February 20, 2015, http://www.whitehouse.gov/the-press-office/2014/11/20/fact-sheet-immigration-accountability-executive-action.

22. Charles J. Lazarus, Rev. of *Border Incident*, *Motion Picture Herald Product Digest*, August 27, 1949, 4730; Bosley Crowther, "Border Incident, Adventure Film about U.S. Immigration Service, Opens at Globe," Rev. of *Border Incident*, *New York Times*, November 21, 1949, 29; Rev. of *Border Incident*, *Variety*, August 31, 1949, 8; "Grim Adventures on Mexican Border," Rev. of *Border Incident*, *The Hollywood Reporter*, August 26, 1949, 4.

23. Christopher Wicking and Barrie Pattison, "Interviews with Anthony Mann," *Screen* 10 (4–5) (1969): 37.

24. William Luhr, "Experiment in Terror: Dystopian Modernism, the Police Procedural, and the Space of Anxiety," in *Cinema and Modernity*, ed. Murray Pomerance (New Brunswick, NJ: Rutgers University Press, 2006), 176.

25. Will Straw, "Documentary Realism and the Postwar Left," in *"Un-American" Hollywood: Politics and Film in the Blacklist Era*, eds. Frank Krutnik et al. (New Brunswick, NJ, and London: Rutgers University Press, 2007), 139.

26. Martin Rubin, *Thrillers* (Cambridge: Cambridge University Press, 1999), 243.

27. Straw, "Documentary Realism," 139.

28. Again, this actor/character formulation is borrowed from Paul McDonald, *Hollywood Stardom* (Malden: Wiley Blackwell, 2013).
29. Frank Krutnik, *In a Lonely Street: Film Noir, Genre, Masculinity* (London: Routledge, 1991), 204.
30. Dale Adams, "Saludos Amigos: Hollywood and FDR's Good Neighbor Policy," *Quarterly Review of Film and Video* 24 (3) (2007): 289–95. *It's All True* and Hollywood's role in enlisting Latin American support during the Second World War is discussed in more detail in chapter 8.
31. Brian O'Neill, "The Demands of Authenticity: Addison Durland and Hollywood's Latin Images during World War II," in *Classic Hollywood, Classic Whiteness*, ed. Daniel Bernardi (Minneapolis and London: University of Minneapolis Press, 2001), 359.
32. Adams, "Saludos Amigos," 291.
33. Raymond Del Castillo, "The End of the Latin Lover?" *Picturegoer*, August 2, 1947, 11.
34. Alfred Charles Richard Jr., *Censorship and Hollywood's Hispanic Image: An Interpretive Filmography, 1936–1955* (Westport, CT: Greenwood Press, 1993), xxi.
35. Richard, *Censorship*, 392.
36. Richard, *Censorship*, xxix.
37. As an interesting counterpoint to this book's discussion of the ways in which the United States imagines its place in the world, Joyce Chaplin argues that historical acts of circumnavigation of the globe had a profound effect on the American relationship not only to the rest of the world but also to the physical planet. Joyce E. Chaplin, "Planetary Power? The United States and the History of around the World Travel," *Journal of American Studies* 47 (2013): 1–21.
38. Clara E. Rodriguez, *Heroes, Lovers and Others: The Story of Latinos in Hollywood* (Washington, DC: Smithsonian Books, 2004), 110.
39. Rodriguez, *Heroes*, 110–11.
40. Rodriguez, *Heroes*, 111–12.
41. Rodriguez, *Heroes*, 178–9.
42. Rodriguez, *Heroes*, 112.
43. *Border Incident* press pack, 2–3.
44. *Border Incident* press pack, 3.
45. Del Castillo, "End of the Latin Lover," 11.
46. Del Castillo, "End of the Latin Lover," 11.
47. Charles M. Tatum, *Chicano Popular Culture: Que Hable el Pueblo* (Tucson: University of Arizona Press), 58.
48. Ricardo Montalban with Bob Thomas, *Reflections: A Life in Two Worlds* (Garden City, NY: Doubleday and Co., Inc., 1980), 151. Emphasis in original.
49. Victoria Thomas, *Hollywood's Latin Lovers: Latino, Italian and French Men Who Make the Screen Smolder* (Santa Monica, CA: Angel City Press, 1998), 68–70.

50. Auerbach, *Dark Borders*, 126.
51. Thomas Schatz, *Boom and Bust: American Cinema in the 1940s* (Berkley and Los Angeles: University of California Press, 1999), 382.
52. Schatz, *Boom and Bust*, 382.
53. Auerbach, "Noir Citizenship," 117, n. 3.
54. Torvay plays Miguel in *Borderline* (Seiter, 1950) and Bedoya plays Captain Vargas in *Border River* (Sherman, 1954). Both Torvay and Moss also had important roles in *The Treasure of the Sierra Madre* (Huston, 1948) while Moss would go on to play a key part in *Viva Zapata!* (Kazan, 1952).
55. Rev. of *Border Incident*, *Variety*, 8; Crowther, "Border Incident," 29.

7　Border Cities as Contested Space: Postcolonial Resistance in Tijuana

1. John A. Price, *Tijuana: Urbanization in a Border Culture* (Notre Dame and London: University of Notre Dame Press, 1973), 49; Paul Coates, "Tijuana's Vigilantes Swing into Action," *Los Angeles Mirror*, April 13, 1960, cited by Larry Harnisch in "Larry Harnisch Reflects on Los Angeles History," *LA Times Blogs*, April 13, 2010, accessed May 22, 2013, http://latimesblogs.latimes.com/thedailymirror/2010/04/paul-v-coates-confidential-file-april-13-1960.html, n.p.
2. Paul Vanderwood, *Satan's Playground: Mobsters and Movie Stars at America's Greatest Gaming Resort* (Durham, NC: Duke University Press, 2010), 72.
3. Vanderwood, *Satan's Playground*, 72.
4. Tim Girven, "Hollywood's Heterotopia: US Cinema, the Mexican Border and the Making of Tijuana," *Travesia: Journal of Latin American Cultural Studies* 3 (1–2) (1994): 120.
5. Josh Kun and Fiamma Montezemolo, "Introduction: The Factory of Dreams," in *Tijuana Dreaming: Life and Art at the Global Border*, ed. Josh Kun and Fiamma Montezemolo (Durham, NC, and London: Duke University Press, 2012), 3.
6. Humberto Félix Berumen, "Snapshots from and about a City Named Tijuana," in Kun and Montezemolo, 30.
7. Santiago Vaquera-Vásquez, "Postcards from the Border: In Tijuana, Revolución Is an Avenue," in Kun and Montezemolo, 131.
8. Berumen, "Snapshots," 28.
9. Berumen, "Snapshots," 29.
10. Berumen, "Snapshots," 31.
11. Quoted in Girven, "Hollywood's Heterotopia," 93.
12. Girven, "Hollywood's Heterotopia," 116.
13. Films about Tijuana from this period include *Riders Up*, *The Sunset Derby* (Rogell, 1927), *True to the Navy* (Tuttle, 1930), and *In Caliente* (Bacon, 1935). See Girven, "Hollywood's Heterotopia," 120.

14. Girven, "Hollywood's Heterotopia," 115.
15. Girven, "Hollywood's Heterotopia," 114.
16. Kenneth Anger, *Hollywood Babylon*, Vol. 1 (London: Arrow, 1986), 65.
17. See reproductions of advertisements for Agua Caliente featuring Hollywood stars, top political figures and businessmen in Vanderwood, *Satan's Playground*, 31–2.
18. Price, *Tijuana*, 44.
19. Price, *Tijuana*, 41.
20. Jennifer Insley, "Redefining Sodom: A Latter-Day Vision of Tijuana," *Mexican Studies/Estudios Mexicanos* 20 (1) (2004): 102.
21. Diana Palaversich, "La Ciudad Que Recorro. Un *Flâneur* en Tijuana," *Literatura Mexicana* 13 (2) (2002): 215.
22. Margaret M. Greer, Walter D. Mignolo, and Maureen Quilligan, "Introduction," in *Rereading the Black Legend: The Discourses of Religious and Racial Difference in the Renaissance Empires*, ed. Margaret M. Greer, Walter D. Mignolo, and Maureen Quilligan (Chicago: University of Chicago Press, 2007), 1.
23. Rafaela Castro, *Chicano Folklore: A Guide to the Folktales, Traditions, Rituals and Religious Practices of Mexican-Americans* (Oxford: Oxford University Press, 2000), 138.
24. Berumen, "Snapshots," 32.
25. Following Joanne Sharp, I understand postcolonialism to be a "critical approach to analysing colonialism and one that seeks to offer alternate accounts of the world," as opposed to post-colonialism, a temporal and geographic term denoting countries that were formerly colonies. Joanne P. Sharp, *Geographies of Postcolonialism: Spaces of Power and Representation* (Los Angeles and London: Sage, 2009), 4.
26. Jane Jacobs, *Edge of Empire: Postcolonialism and the City* (London: Routledge, 1996), 4.
27. Jacobs, *Edge of Empire*, 4.
28. Giuliana Bruno, *Atlas of Emotion: Journeys in Art, Architecture and Film* (New York and London: Verso, 2002), 178.
29. Eloy Méndez Sáinz and Jeff Banister, "Transitional Architecture or Espacios de Paso y Simulacro," *Journal of the Southwest* 45 (1–2) (2003): 167.
30. Michael Dear and Gustavo Leclerc, "Tijuana Desenmarcada," *Wide Angle* 20 (3) (1998): 211.
31. "Katzman-Kardos Pic Documented Expose," Rev. of *The Tijuana Story*, *The Hollywood Reporter*, October 9, 1957, 3; Rev. of *The Tijuana Story*, *Variety*, October 9, 1957, 6.
32. Rev. of *The Tijuana Story*, *Kinematograph Weekly*, November 7, 1957, 47.
33. Rev. of *The Tijuana Story*, *Variety*, 6.
34. J. Brian Harley, "Maps, Knowledge and Power," in *The New Nature of Maps: Essays in the History of Cartography*, ed. Paul Laxton with

an Introduction by J. H. Andrews (Baltimore and London: John Hopkins University Press, 2001), 52–81.

35. John Steinbeck, *The Grapes of Wrath* (repr., London: Penguin, 1992 [1939]), 439. The 1940 John Ford film plays with the radical sentiments of the novel in interesting ways in relation to the New Deal. See, for example, Vivian Sobchack, "*The Grapes of Wrath* (1940): Thematic Emphasis through Visual Style," *American Quarterly* 31 (5) (1979): 596–615.

36. Yannis Tzioumakis, *American Independent Cinema: An Introduction* (Edinburgh: Edinburgh University Press, 2006), 146.

37. Wheeler Winston Dixon, *Lost in the Fifties: Recovering Phantom Hollywood* (Carbondale: Southern Illinois University Press, 2005), 56.

38. Dixon, *Lost in the Fifties*, 46.

39. "Meet Jungle Sam," *Life*, March 23, 1953, 79; and Dixon, *Lost in the Fifties*, 46. As a comparison, Twentieth Century Fox spent an average of between $1.4 and $2 million on films in the 1950s. See Joel Waldo Finler, *The Hollywood Story* (London: Wallflower Press, 2003), 49.

40. "Meet Jungle Sam," 82.

41. Dixon, *Lost in the Fifties*, 46.

42. Dixon, *Lost in the Fifties*, 65.

43. Will Straw, "Urban Confidential: The Lurid City of the 1950s," in *The Cinematic City*, ed. David B. Clarke (London: Routledge, 1997), 110.

44. Straw, "Urban Confidential," 111.

45. Rev. of *The Houston Story*, *Monthly Film Bulletin* 23 (264): 91.

46. Kun, "The Kidnapped City," in Kun and Montezemolo, 367.

47. Coates, "Tijuana's Vigilantes."

48. Rev. of *The Tijuana Story*, *Monthly Film Bulletin* 24 (276) (1957): 153.

49. "Katzman-Kardos Pic," 3.

50. "Katzman-Kardos Pic," 3.

51. Rev. of *The Tijuana Story*, *Variety*, 6.

52. "Mexican Editor Is Slain by Unidentified Gunmen," *New York Times*, July 28, 1956, 35.

53. Will Straw, "Documentary Realism and the Postwar Left," in *"Un-American" Hollywood: Politics and Film in the Blacklist Era*, eds. Frank Krutnik et al. (New Brunswick, NJ, and London: Rutgers University Press, 2007), 139, 135.

54. Jeffrey Ruoff, "Introduction: The Filmic Fourth Dimension: Cinema as Audiovisual Vehicle," in *Virtual Voyages: Cinema and Travel*, ed. Jeffrey Ruoff (Durham, NC: Duke University Press, 2006), 11.

55. Alfred Bendixen and Judith Hamera, "Introduction: New Worlds and Old Lands—the Travel Book and the Construction of American Identity," in *The Cambridge Companion to American Travel Writing*, ed. Alfred Bendixen and Judith Hamera (Cambridge: Cambridge University Press, 2009), 1.

56. John Fousek, *To Lead the Free World: American Nationalism and the Cultural Roots of the Cold War*, (Chapel Hill and London: The University of North Carolina Press, 2000), 2.
57. Fousek, *Free World*, 2.
58. Christian G. Appy, "Introduction: Struggling for the World," in *Cold War Constructions: The Political Culture of United States Imperialism, 1945–1966*, ed. Christian G. Appy (Amherst: University of Massachusetts Press, 2000), 2.
59. Appy, "Introduction," 2.
60. Daniel Bell, *The End of Ideology: On the Exhaustion of Political Ideas in the Fifties*, revised ed. (New York: Free Press, 1962), 404–6.

8 Imperial Journeys and Traveling Shots: Regulation, Power, and Mobility

1. Orson Welles, "Memo to Universal," in *This Is Orson Welles*, by Orson Welles and Peter Bogdanovich, ed. Jonathan Rosenbaum, revised ed. (New York: Da Capo Press, 1998), 499.
2. I use both forenames as Vargas is referred to by both his Mexican name and the Anglicized version at different moments in the film. The solidus is used to denote a sense of Vargas's ethnic fluidity, which will be discussed below.
3. The sheer number of books on Welles's life and films attest to the persistence with which his movies are viewed as personal achievements contributing to his genius. In addition to the Bazin, Truffaut, and Naremore works cited in the paragraph, see Comito's volume and any of a number of review articles written in response to the release of a new version of the movie in 1998, which is described on the fiftieth anniversary DVD box set as the "definitive cut of the film...restored to Orson Welles' vision based on his detailed 58-page memo to the studio."
4. François Truffaut, Rev. of *Touch of Evil*, trans. Leonard Mayhew, in *Touch of Evil: Orson Welles Director*, ed. Terry Comito (New Brunswick, NJ: Rutgers, 1985), 229.
5. André Bazin, *Orson Welles: A Critical View*, trans. Jonathan Rosenbaum, foreword by François Truffaut (London: Elm Tree Books, 1978), 123.
6. James Naremore, *The Magic of Orson Welles* (New York: Oxford University Press, 1978), 205.
7. Brooke Rollins, "Some Kind of a Man: Orson Welles as *Touch of Evil*'s Masculine Auteur," *The Velvet Light Trap* 57 (2006): 34.
8. Howard Thompson, "Orson Welles Is Triple Threat in Thriller," Rev. of *Touch of Evil, New York Times*, May 22, 1958, 25; Jack Moffitt, "Zugsmith Depiction of Dope Ring Dizzy," Rev. of *Touch of Evil, The Hollywood Reporter*, March 17, 1958, 3.
9. The fiftieth anniversary DVD box set includes all three versions of the film: the 1958 theatrical version, a preview version created prior

to the theatrical version and discovered by Universal in 1976, and a restored version edited by Walter Murch, released in 1998 and recut according to Welles's memo.

10. As Pease has argued, critical readings of *Touch of Evil* tend to reinterpret its contexts and bring new disciplinary knowledges to bear on it that overwrite previous analyses. Stephen Heath interpreted the film through the lens of psychoanalysis with a focus on sexuality. Later, Bhabha situated the film within the framework of postcolonialism. And subsequently Denning argued that the film's most important context is Welles's involvement with Mexican American activism. In his own analysis, Pease goes on to add yet another framework, arguing that contemporary debates around Mexican immigration to the United States must be taken into consideration. See Donald Pease, "Borderline Justice/States of Emergency: Orson Welles' Touch of Evil." *The New Centennial Review* 1 (2001): 75–105; Stephen Heath, "Film and System: Terms of Analysis," *Screen* 16 (1–2) (1975): 7–77; Homi K. Bhabha, *The Location of Culture* (London and New York: Routledge, 1994), 66–79; Michael Denning, *The Cultural Front: The Laboring of American Culture in the Twentieth Century* (repr., London and New York: Verso, 2010 [1997]), 362–402; Tony Grajeda, "'A Question of the Ear': Listening to *Touch of Evil*," in *Lowering the Boom: Critical Studies in Film Sound*, ed. Jay Beck and Tony Grajeda (Urbana: University of Illinois Press, 2008), 201–17; and Luz Calvo, "'Lemme Stay, I Want to Watch': Ambivalence in Borderlands Cinema," in *Latino/a Popular Culture*, ed. Michelle Habell-Pallán and Mary Romero (New York and London: New York University Press, 2002), 73–81.
11. Heath, "Film and System," 8.
12. Terry Comito, "Welles's Labyrinths: An Introduction to *Touch of Evil*," in *Touch of Evil*, 9.
13. Naremore, *Magic of Orson Welles*, 189.
14. Comito, "Welles's Labyrinths," 11.
15. William Anthony Nericcio, *Tex[t]-Mex: Seductive Hallucinations of the "Mexican" in America* (Austin: University of Texas Press, 2007), 62.
16. Bhabha, *Location of Culture*, 69.
17. Bhabha, *Location of Culture*, 70–1.
18. Denning, *Cultural Front*, 42; Pease, "Borderline Justice," 87.
19. Denning, *Cultural Front*, 376.
20. Denning, *Cultural Front*, 376.
21. Irwin F. Gellman, *Good Neighbor Diplomacy: United States Politics in Latin America, 1933–1945* (Baltimore, MD: John Hopkins University Press, 1979), 148. The fact that 18 Latin American countries had banned *Confessions of a Nazi Spy* (Litvak, 1939) and almost all Latin American countries banned *The Great Dictator* (Chaplin, 1940), two of Hollywood's most virulently antifascist movies, was

testament to the CIAA's perceived need to bolster relations within the hemisphere. See Dale Adams, "Saludos Amigos: Hollywood and FDR's Good Neighbor Policy," *Quarterly Review of Film and Video* 24 (3) (2007): 290.

22. Catherine Benamou, *It's All True: Orson Welles' Pan-American Odyssey* (Berkley and London: University of California Press, 2007), 46.

23. Marguerite Rippy, *Orson Welles and the Unfinished RKO Projects: A Postmodern Perspective* (Carbondale: Southern Illinois University Press, 2009), 110.

24. Denning, *Cultural Front*, 397.

25. Benamou, *It's All True*, 37–8.

26. Denning, *Cultural Front*, 398.

27. Brady indicates that Welles chose to shoot *The Lady from Shanghai* in Mexico because it might give him opportunity to do further work on "Bonito," suggesting this element of the film was of particular import to Welles. Frank Brady, *Citizen Welles: A Biography of Orson Welles* (repr., London: Hodder and Stoughton, 1990 [1989]), 395.

28. Jeffrey Ruoff, "Introduction: The Filmic Fourth Dimension: Cinema as Audiovisual Vehicle," in *Virtual Voyages: Cinema and Travel*, ed. Jeffrey Ruoff (Durham, NC: Duke University Press, 2006), 11.

29. Ruoff, "Introduction," 2–4.

30. Tom Gunning, "'The Whole World within Reach': Travel Images without Borders," in *Virtual Voyages*, 27. On travel and "touristic consciousness," see also Lynne Kirby, *Parallel Tracks: The Railroad and Silent Cinema* (Durham, NC: Duke University Press, 1997).

31. Gunning, "The Whole World," 30.

32. Gunning, "The Whole World," 25.

33. Gunning, "The Whole World," 36.

34. Denning, *Cultural Front*, 374.

35. John Houseman, "The Birth of the Mercury Theatre," *Educational Theatre Journal* 24 (1) (1972): 34.

36. Denning, *Cultural Front*, 5–6.

37. Denning, *Cultural Front*, 362.

38. Denning, *Cultural Front*, 363; 373.

39. Of course, Welles already had an acrimonious relationship with the Heart press ever since he loosely based *Citizen Kane* on the life of William Randolph Hearst. See, for example, Denning, *Cultural Front*, 386.

40. Peter Wollen, "Foreign Relations: Welles and Touch of Evil," *Sight and Sound* 6 (10) (1996): 22.

41. Denning, *Cultural Front*, 373.

42. Denning, *Cultural Front*, 400; Wollen, "Foreign Relations," 23.

43. Thompson, "Orson Welles Is Triple Threat," 25.

44. Moffitt, "Zugsmith Depiction," 3.

45. Gunning, "The Whole World," 36.

46. Bhabha, *Location of Culture*, 70–1.

47. See also Mercedes McCambridge's performance as a Mexican member of the Grandi gang. Joseph Calleia of Maltese origins does play an American cop however, demonstrating the easy assimilation of western European immigrants in the United States.

48. Nericcio, *Tex[t]-Mex*, 78.

49. *Touch of Evil* press pack, British Film Institute National Archive, 1958, n.p.

50. Her name too is unfixable and shifting, as indicated by reviews and scholarship on the film that use "Tana" and "Tanya" interchangeably. According to the American Film Institute Catalogue entry for the film, the name used in the film is Tana. Accessed May 22, 2013, http://afi.chadwyck.co.uk/home.

51. Jill Leeper, "Crossing Musical Borders: The Soundtrack for *Touch of Evil*," in *Soundtrack Available: Essays on Film and Popular Music*, ed. Pamela Robertson Wojcik and Arthur Knight (Durham, NC, and London: Duke University Press, 2001), 236.

52. Brady, *Citizen Welles*, 502.

53. Bhabha, *Location of Culture*, 66.

54. Welles and Bogdanovich, *This Is Orson Welles*, 310.

55. Brady claims that this choice of location was suggested to Welles by Aldous Huxley. Brady, *Citizen Welles*, 501.

56. David B. Clarke, Valerie Crawford Pfannhauser, and Marcus A. Doel, "Checking In," in *Moving Pictures/Stopping Places: Hotels and Motels on Film*, ed. David B. Clarke, Valerie Crawford Pfannhauser, and Marcus A. Doel (Lanham, MD, and Plymouth: Lexington Books, 2009), 1. On the wider relationship between hotels and the city see Donald McNeil, "The Hotel and the City," *Progress in Human Geography* 32 (3) (2008): 383–98.

57. Jann Matlock, "Vacancies: Hotels, Reception Desks and Identity in American Cinema, 1929–1964," in *Moving Pictures/Stopping Places*, 117.

58. Matlock, "Vacancies," 117.

59. The press kit makes a selling point of Welles's transformation for the role, with publicity stories explaining that the "false stomach and hump on his back [give] the character more than one-fourth again the weight Orson carries in real life." Another publicity piece titled, "Welles—'My Weightiest Role,'" muses that "on anyone else, the false nose and the padding necessary for the part would be merely absurd." *Touch of Evil* press pack.

60. Bess Furman, "Obesity Is Termed No. 1 Nutritional Ill," *New York Times*, December 9, 1952, 45.

61. "Obesity Peril Stressed," *New York Times*, February 27, 1953, 25.

62. Randall Bennett Woods, *Quest For Identity: America since 1945* (Cambridge: Cambridge University Press, 2005), 126.

63. Woods, *Quest*, 127.

64. Woods, *Quest*, 127.
65. Louis O. Keslo and Mortimer J. Adler, *The Capitalist Manifesto* (New York: Random House, 1958), 4.
66. "People's Capitalism," *New York Times*, June 11, 1957, 34.
67. See Matlock, "Vacancies," 117, for a discussion of homeliness and unhomeliness in relation to hotels and motels.

Conclusion   Border Film and Border Studies

1. Claudia Sadowski-Smith, *Border Fictions: Globalization, Empire, and Writing at the Boundaries of the United States* (Charlottesville and London: University of Virginia Press, 2008), 27.
2. Gloria Anzaldúa, *Borderlands/La Frontera: The New Mestiza* (San Francisco: Aunt Lute Books, 1987), see in particular 2–3.
3. Sadowski-Smith, *Border Fictions*, 28–9.
4. Rosa Linda Fregoso and Angie Chabram-Dernersesian, "Chicana/o Cultural Representations: Reframing Alternative Critical Discourses," in *The Chicana/o Cultural Studies Reader*, ed. Angie Chabram-Dernersesian (London: Routledge, 2006), 27.
5. Fregoso and Chabram-Dernersesian, "Chicana/o Cultural Representations," 27.
6. Alejandro Lugo, *Fragmented Lives, Assembled Parts: Culture, Capitalism, and Conquest at the U.S.-Mexico Border* (Austin: University of Texas Press, 2008), 214.
7. Chabram-Dernersesian, "Introduction: Locating Chicana/o Cultural studies: Contentious Dialogues and Alternative Legacies," in *The Chicana/o Cultural Studies Reader*, 7.
8. Rosa Linda Fregoso, *The Bronze Screen: Chicana and Chicano Film Culture* (Minneapolis and London: University of Minnesota Press, 1993); Gary Keller, ed., *Chicano Cinema: Research, Reviews and Resources* (Tempe, AZ: Bilingual Review Press, 1993); and Chon A. Noriega, ed., *Chicanos and Film: Representation and Resistance* (Minneapolis: University of Minnesota Press, 1992).
9. Lysa Rivera, "Future Histories and Cyborg Labor: Reading Borderlands Science Fiction after NAFTA," *Science Fiction Studies* 39 (3) (2012): 415–36.
10. Emilio García Riera, *México Visto por el Cine Extranjero 3: 1941/1969* (Guadalajara: Universidad de Guadalajara, 1988), 64.
11. Laura Carlsen, "Under Nafta, Mexico Suffered, and the United States Felt Its Pain," *New York Times*, November 24, 2013, accessed February 20, 2015, http://www.nytimes.com/roomfordebate/2013/11/24/what-weve-learned-from-nafta/under-nafta-mexico-suffered-and-the-united-states-felt-its-pain.
12. Michael Dear and Gustavo Leclerc, "Tijuana Desenmarcada," *Wide Angle* 20 (3) (1998): 213.

13. David K. Androff and Kyoko Y. Tavassoli, "Deaths in the Desert: The Human Rights Crisis on the U.S.-Mexico Border," *Social Work* 57 (2) (2012): 165–73.
14. Androff and Tavassoli, "Deaths in the Desert," 171.
15. Humane Borders/Fronteras Compasivas, accessed February 20, 2015, http://www.humaneborders.org/. The website has full details of the organization's programs alongside its important migrant death and water station maps.
16. Human Rights Watch, "Mexico," *World Report 2014*, accessed July 12, 2014, http://www.hrw.org/world-report/2014/country-chapters/mexico?page=2.
17. Committee to Protect Journalists, "30 Journalists Killed in Mexico since 1992/Motive Confirmed," accessed July 12, 2014, http://www.cpj.org/killed/americas/mexico/.
18. Semanario Zeta, accessed July 12, 2014, http://zetatijuana.com/.
19. Texas Border Patrol, Blueservo.net Program, accessed July 23, 2013, http://www.blueservo.net/; accessed July 17, 2015, http://wayback.archive-it.org/all/20130423005812/http://www.blueservo.com/. The Blueservo.net program is currently suspended apparently due to financial constraints, despite appeals by the Texas Border Sheriffs Coalition to have it reinstated. See Frank Gaffney Jr., "No-Brainer: The 'BlueServo' Solution to Border Insecurity," *Centre for Security Policy*, July 23, 2014, accessed February 20, 2015, http://www.centerforsecuritypolicy.org/2014/07/23/no-brainer-the-blueservo-solution-to-border-insecurity/. An archived version of the site is available to view via the internet archive: https://web.archive.org/web/20130930122101/http://www.blueservo.net/.
20. Eliot Shapleigh, quoted in Claire Prentice, "Armchair Deputies Enlisted to Patrol US-Mexico Border," *BBC News*, December 26, 2009, accessed July 23, 2013, http://news.bbc.co.uk/1/hi/world/americas/8412603.stm.
21. Secure Border Intelligence, "Hidden Cameras on the Border," accessed July 23, 2013, http://secureborderintel.org/.
22. See CAMBIO, "CAMBIO Believes the Following Elements Are Essential to Responsible Enforcement Activity in the Border Region," accessed July 23, 2013, http://cambio-us.org/.

Filmography

Across the Bridge. Ken Annakin. 1957. The Rank Organisation/Rank Film Distributors of America. UK.

And Starring Pancho Villa as Himself. Bruce Beresford. 2003. City Entertainment; Green Moon Productions; The Mark Gordon Co./HBO Films.

Apache. Robert Aldrich. 1954. Norma Productions, Inc.; Hecht-Lancaster Productions/United Artists Corp. US.

Attila. Pietra Francisci. 1958. Compagnie Cinématographique de France; Lux Film; Procucciones Pont-de Laurentiis/Lux Film. Italy and France.

Babel. Alejandro González Iñárritu. 2006. Paramount Vantage; Anonymous Content; Central Films; Zeta Film/Paramount Pictures Corp. France, US, and Mexico.

Bandido. Richard Fleischer. 1956. Bandido Productions/United Artists Corp. Mexico and US.

Bandits of Corsica. Ray Nazarro. 1953. Global/United Artists Corp. US.

Barbarous Mexico. Irving G. Ries. 1913. America's Feature Film Co. US.

Border Incident. Anthony Mann. 1949. Metro-Goldwyn-Mayer Corp./Loew's, Inc. US.

Border Raiders, The. Stuart Paton. 1918. Diando Film Corp./Pathé Exchange, Inc. US.

Border River. George Sherman. 1954. Universal-International Pictures Co., Inc./Universal Pictures Co., Inc. US.

Borderline. William A. Seiter. 1950. Borderline Productions Corp./Universal Pictures Co., Inc. US.

Bordertown. Archie Mayo. 1935. Warner Bros. Productions Corp./The Vitaphone Corp.; Warner Bros. Pictures, Inc. US.

Breaking Bad. Vince Gilligan. 2008–13. High Bridge Productions; Gran Via Productions; Sony Pictures Television/American Movie Classics. US.

Bridge, The. Elwood Reid, Björn Stein, and Meredith Stiehm. 2013–. FX Productions; Shine America/FX Network. US.

Cattle Drive. Kurt Neumann. 1951. Universal-International Pictures Co., Inc./Universal Pictures Co., Inc. US.

Citizen Kane. Orson Welles. 1941. RKO Radio Pictures, Inc.; Mercury Productions/RKO Radio Pictures, Inc. US.

City of Bad Men. Harmon Jones. 1953. Twentieth Century Fox Film Corp./ Twentieth Century Fox Film Corp. US.

Confessions of a Nazi Spy. Anatole Litvak. 1939. Warner Bros. Pictures, Inc./ Warner Bros. Pictures, Inc. US.

Conqueror, The. Dick Powell. 1956. RKO Radio Pictures, Inc./RKO Radio Pictures, Inc. US.

'Cross the Mexican Line. Wallace Reid. 1914. Nestor Film Co./Universal Film Mfg. Co. US.

Desert Hawk, The. Frederick de Cordova. 1950. Universal International Pictures/Universal Pictures. US.

Don't Knock the Rock. Fred Sears. 1956. Clover Productions, Inc./Columbia Pictures Corp. US.

Double Indemnity. Billy Wilder. 1944. Paramount Pictures, Inc./Paramount Pictures, Inc. US.

Duel in the Sun. King Vidor. 1946. Vanguard Films, Inc./Selznick Releasing Organization. US.

Espaldas Mojadas [Wetbacks]. Alejandro Galindo. 1953. ATA Films; Atlas Films/Distribuidora Mexicana de Películas S. A. Mexico.

Fast and the Furious, The. John Ireland. 1954. Pablo Alto Productions, Inc./ American Releasing Corp.; State Rights. US.

Federal Man. Robert Tansey. 1950. Jack Schwarz Productions, Inc./Eagle-Lion Films, Inc. US.

Fiesta. Richard Thorpe. 1947. Metro-Goldwyn-Mayer Corp./Loew's, Inc. US.

Fugitive, The. John Ford. 1947. Argosy Pictures Corp./RKO Radio Pictures, Inc. US.

Golden Earrings. Mitchell Leisen. 1947. Paramount Pictures, Inc.; A Mitchell Leisen Production/Paramount Pictures, Inc. US.

Grapes of Wrath, The. John Ford. 1940. Twentieth Century Fox Film Corp.; A Darry F. Zanuck Production/Twentieth Century Fox Film Corp. US.

Great Dictator, The. Charles Chaplin. 1940. Charles Chaplin Film Corp./ United Artists Corp. US.

Gun Crazy. Joseph H. Lewis. 1950. King Bros. Productions, Inc./United Artists Corp. US.

High Noon. Fred Zimmerman. 1952. Stanley Kramer Productions, Inc./ United Artists Corp. US.

His Kind of Woman. John Farrow. 1951. RKO Radio Pictures, Inc.; A John Farrow Production/RKO Radio Pictures, Inc. US.

Houston Story, The. William Castle. 1955. Clover Productions, Inc./ Columbia Pictures Corp. US.

Hurricane Smith. Jerry Hopper. 1952. Nat Holt and Co.; Paramount Pictures Corp./Paramount Pictures Corp. US.

In Caliente. Lloyd Bacon. 1935. First National Productions Corp./First National Pictures, Inc.; The Vitaphone Corp. US.

Invasion of the Body Snatchers. Don Siegel. 1956. Walter Wanger Pictures, Inc./Allied Artists Pictures Corp. US.

It's All True. Orson Welles. 1942–3. RKO Radio Pictures, Inc.; Mercury Productions, Inc. US.

It's All True: Based on an Unfinished Film by Orson Welles. Richard Wilson, Myron Meisel, Bill Krohn, and Orson Welles. 1993. Les Films Balenciaga/ Paramount Pictures Corp. France, Brazil, and US.

Juarez. William Dieterle. 1939. Warner Bros. Pictures, Inc./Warner Bros. Pictures, Inc. US.

Kissing Bandit, The. Laslo Benedek. 1949. Metro-Goldwyn-Mayer Corp./ Loew's, Inc. US.

La Strada. Federico Fellini. 1954. Ponti-De Laurentiis Cinematografica/ Dino De Laurentiis Distribuzione. Italy.

La Terra Trema [The Earth Trembles]. Luchino Visconti. 1948. Universalia/ Mario de Vecchi. Italy.

Lady from Shanghai, The. Orson Welles. 1947. Columbia Pictures Corp./ Columbia Pictures Corp. US.

Last of the Fast Guns. George Sherman. 1958. Universal-International Pictures Co., Inc./Universal Pictures Co., Inc. Mexico and US.

Life at Stake, A. Paul Guilfoyle. 1954. Hank McCune Productions; Telecraft Productions, Inc./Gibraltar Motion Picture Distributors, Inc. US.

Life of Villa. Christy Cabanne. 1912. Biograph Co./Biograph Co. US.

Lone Hand, The. George Sherman. 1953. Universal-International Pictures Co., Inc./Universal Pictures Co., Inc. US.

Lust for Life. Vincente Minelli. 1956. Metro-Goldwyn-Mayer Corp./Metro-Goldwyn-Mayer Corp. US.

Magic Carpet, The. Lew Landers. 1951. The Katzman Corporation; Esskay Pictures Corporation/Columbia Pictures. US.

Magnificent Ambersons, The. Orson Welles. 1942. RKO Radio Pictures, Inc.; Mercury Productions/RKO Radio Pictures, Inc. US.

Major Dundee. Sam Peckinpah. 1965. Colombia Pictures Corp.; Jerry Bresler Productions/Columbia Pictures. US.

Mexicali Rose. George Sherman. 1939. Republic Pictures Corp./Republic Pictures Corp. US.

Mexican Revolutionist, The. George Melford. 1912. Kalem Co./General Film Co. US.

Miami Exposé. Fred Sears. 1956. Clover Productions, Inc./Columbia Pictures Corp. US.

Mixed Blood. Charles Swickard. 1916. Universal Film Mfg. Co.; Red Feather Photoplays/Universal Film Mfg. Co. US.

Monsters. Gareth Edwards. 2010. Vertigo Films/Magnet Releasing; Vertigo Films. UK.

My Darling Clementine. John Ford. 1948. Twentieth Century Fox Film Corp./Twentieth Century Fox Film Corp. US.

No Country for Old Men. Ethan and Joel Coen. 2006. Scott Rudin Productions; Mike Zoss Productions/Miramax Film Corp; Paramount Vantage. US.

Nosotros [Us]. Fernando Rivera. 1945. Producciones México/Producciones México. Mexico.

On an Island with You. Richard Thorpe. 1948. Metro-Goldwyn-Mayer Corp./Loew's, Inc. US.

Out of the Past. Jacques Tourneur. 1947. RKO Radio Pictures, Inc./RKO Radio Pictures, Inc. US.

Postman Always Rings Twice, The. Tay Garnett. 1946. Metro-Goldwyn-Mayer Corp./Loew's, Inc. US.

Professionals, The. Richard Brooks. 1966. Pax Enterprises/Columbia Pictures. US.

¡Que Viva México! Sergei Eisenstein. 1933. Mexican Picture Trust/Principal Distributing Corp. Mexico and US.

Rancho Notorious. Fritz Lang. 1952. Fidelity Pictures, Inc./RKO Radio Pictures, Inc. US.

Rear Window. Alfred Hitchcock. 1954. Paramount Pictures, Inc.; Patron Inc./Paramount Pictures, Inc. US.

Red River. Howard Hawks. 1946. Monterey Productions, Inc./United Artists Corp. US.

Redes [The Wave]. Emilio Gómez Muriel, Paul Stroud, and Fred Zinneman. 1935. Azteca Films; Secretaría de Educación Pública/Garrison Film Distributors Inc. Mexico.

Riders Up. Irving Cummings. 1924. Universal Pictures. US.

Rio Bravo. Howard Hawks. 1959. Warner Bros. Pictures, Inc./Warner Bros. Pictures, Inc. US.

River's Edge, The. Allan Dwan. 1957. Elmcrest Productions, Inc./Twentieth Century Fox Film Corp. US.

Rock around the Clock. Fred Sears. 1956. Clover Productions, Inc./Columbia Pictures Corp. US.

Saddle Tramp. Hugo Fregonese. 1950. Universal-International Pictures Co., Inc./Universal Pictures Co., Inc. US.

Salome, Where She Danced. Charles Lamont. 1945. Universal Pictures Co., Inc./Universal Pictures Co., Inc. US.

Salt of the Earth. Herbert Biberman. 1954. The International Union of Mine, Mill and Smelter Workers; Independent Productions Corp./IPC Distributors, Inc.; Independent Productions Corp. US.

Saludos Amigos. Wilfred Jackson, Bill Roberts, Jack Kinney, and Ham Luske. 1942. Walt Disney Productions/RKO Radio Pictures, Inc. US.

Savage Innocents, The. Nicholas Ray. 1961. Gray Films; Joseph Janni; Appia Films; Magic Film; Play Art; Société Nouvelle Pathé Cinéma/J. Arthur Rank Film Distributors. France, Italy, and UK.

Sea Hunt. James Buxbaum. 1958–61. United Artists Television/United Artists Television. US.

Sin Nombre. Cary Fukunaga. 2009. Primary Productions; Canana Films/ Focus Features. Mexico, UK, and US.

Sombrero. Norman Foster. 1953. Metro-Goldwyn-Mayer Corp./Loew's, Inc. US.

Song of Scheherazade. Walter Reisch. 1947. Universal-International Pictures Co., Inc./Universal Pictures Co., Inc. US.

South of the Border. George Sherman. 1939. Republic Pictures Corp./ Republic Pictures Corp. US.

Stage Fright. Alfred Hitchcock. 1950. Warner Bros. Pictures, Inc./Warner Bros. Pictures, Inc. UK and US.

Stagecoach. John Ford. 1939. Walter Wanger Productions, Inc./United Artists Corp. US.

Stranger, The. Orson Welles. 1946. International Pictures, Inc. /RKO Radio Pictures, Inc. US.

Sunset Derby, The. Albert Rogell. 1927. First National Pictures. US.

T-Men. Anthony Mann. 1948. Edward Small Productions, Inc./Eagle-Lion Films, Inc. US.

They Came to Cordura. Robert Rossen. 1959. Goetz Pictures, Inc.; Baroda Productions, Inc.; A William Goetz Production/Columbia Pictures Corp. US.

Three Burials of Melquiades Estrada, The. Tommy Lee Jones. 2005. Javelina Film Co.; EuropaCorp/Sony Pictures Classics. France and US.

Tijuana Story, The. Leslie Kardos. 1957. Clover Productions, Inc./Columbia Pictures Corp. US.

Touch of Evil. Orson Welles. 1958. Universal-International Pictures Co., Inc./Universal Pictures Co., Inc. US.

Traffic. Steven Soderbergh. 2001. Initial Entertainment Group; Bedford Falls/USA Films. US.

Treasure of Pancho Villa, The. George Sherman. 1955. Edmund Grainger Productions, Inc.; RKO Radio Pictures, Inc./RKO Radio Pictures, Inc. Mexico and US.

Treasure of the Sierra Madre, The. John Huston. 1948. Warner Bros. Pictures, Inc./Warner Bros. Pictures, Inc. US.

True to the Navy. Frank Tuttle. 1930. Paramount Publix Corp./Paramount Public Corp. US.

Unconquered. Cecil B. DeMille. 1948. Paramount Pictures, Inc./Paramount Pictures, Inc. US.

Vera Cruz. Robert Aldrich. 1954. Flora Productions; Hecht-Lancaster Productions/United Artists Corp. Mexico and US.

Villa!! James Clark. 1958. Twentieth Century-Fox Film Corp./Twentieth Century-Fox Film Corp. Mexico and US.

Viva Villa. Jack Conway. 1934. Metro-Goldwyn-Mayer Corp./Loew's, Inc. US.

Viva Zapata! Elia Kazan. 1952. Twentieth Century Fox Film Corp./ Twentieth Century Fox Film Corp. US.

Wetbacks. Hank McCune. 1956. Banner Pictures, Inc.; Pacific Coast Pictures/ Gibraltar Motion Picture Distributors, Inc.; Realart Film Exchange. US.

Where Danger Lives. John Farrow. 1950. RKO Radio Pictures, Inc.; Westwood Productions, Inc./RKO Radio Pictures, Inc. US.

White Shadows in the South Seas. W. S. Van Dyke. 1928. Cosmopolitan Productions/Metro-Goldwyn-Mayer Distributing Corp. US.

Bibliography

"184 Subversives in Deported List: Report for Five Years Made by Immigration Service—5,261 Criminals Ousted." *New York Times*, January 3, 1955, 8.

Acuña, Rodolfo F. *The Making of Chicana/o Studies: In the Trenches of Academe*. New Brunswick, NJ, and London: Rutgers University Press, 2010.

Adams, Dale. "Saludos Amigos: Hollywood and FDR's Good Neighbor Policy." *Quarterly Review of Film and Video* 24 (3) (2007): 289–95.

Adams, Rachel. *Continental Divides: Remapping the Cultures of North America*. Chicago and London: University of Chicago Press, 2009.

Adey, Peter. *Mobility*. London: Routledge, 2010.

Akerman, James R., ed. *Cartographies of Travel and Navigation*. Chicago and London: University of Chicago Press, 2006.

———. "Twentieth-Century American Road Maps and the Making of a National Motorized Space." In *Cartographies of Travel and Navigation*, edited by James R. Akerman, 151–206. Chicago and London: University of Chicago Press, 2006.

Albano, Caterina. "Visible Bodies: Cartography and Anatomy." In *Literature, Mapping, and the Politics of Space in Early Modern Britain*, edited by Andrew Gordon and Bernhard Klein, 89–106. Cambridge: Cambridge University Press, 2001.

Aldama, Frederick Luis. *Brown on Brown: Chicano/a Representations of Gender, Sexuality, and Ethnicity*. Austin: University of Texas Press, 2005.

Altman, Rick. *Film/Genre*. London: British Film Institute, 1999.

———. "A Semantic/Syntactic Approach to Film Genre." *Cinema Journal* 23 (3) (1984): 6–18.

American Film Institute Catalogue. "Touch of Evil." Accessed May 22, 2013. http://afi.chadwyck.co.uk/home.

———. "Wetbacks." Accessed August 20, 2013. http://afi.chadwyck.co.uk/home.

Anderson, Benedict. *Imagined Communities: Reflections on the Origin and Spread of Nationalism*. London and New York: Verso, 1983.

Andreas, Peter. *Border Games: Policing the U.S.-Mexico Divide.* Ithaca, NY, and London: Cornell University Press, 2009.

Androff, David K., and Kyoko Y. Tavassoli. "Deaths in the Desert: The Human Rights Crisis on the U.S.-Mexico Border." *Social Work* 57 (2) (2012): 165–73.

Anger, Kenneth. *Hollywood Babylon.* Vol. 1. London: Arrow, 1986.

Anzaldúa, Gloria. *Borderlands/La Frontera: The New Mestiza.* San Francisco: Aunt Lute Books, 1987.

Appy, Christian G., ed. *Cold War Constructions: The Political Culture of United States Imperialism, 1945–1966.* Amherst: University of Massachusetts Press, 2000.

———. "Eisenhower's Guatemalan Doodle, or How to Draw, Deny, and Take Credit for a Third World Coup." In *Cold War Constructions: The Political Culture of United States Imperialism, 1945–1966,* edited by Christian G. Appy, 183–216. Amherst: University of Massachusetts Press, 2000.

———. "Introduction: Struggling for the World." In *Cold War Constructions: The Political Culture of United States Imperialism, 1945–1966,* edited by Christian G. Appy, 1–10. Amherst: University of Massachusetts Press, 2000.

Arnold, Edwin T., and Eugene L. Miller. *The Films and Career of Robert Aldrich.* Knoxville: University of Tennessee Press, 1986.

———, eds. *Robert Aldrich: Interviews.* Jackson: University Press of Mississippi, 2004.

Athearn, Robert G. *The Mythic West in Twentieth Century America.* Lawrence: University Press of Kansas, 1986.

Auerbach, Jonathan. *Dark Borders: Film Noir and American Citizenship.* Durham, NC: Duke University Press, 2011.

———. "Noir Citizenship: Anthony Mann's *Border Incident.*" *Cinema Journal* 47 (4) (2008): 102–20.

Bailey, Bernadine. "Acapulco—Resort City for Budgeteers, Too." *New York Times,* October 26, 1958, 37.

Balio, Tino. *United Artists: The Company That Changed the Film Industry.* Madison and London: University of Wisconsin Press, 1987.

Barthes, Roland. *Mythologies.* 1957. Translated by Annette Lavers. Reprint, London: Vintage, 2009.

Baudrillard, Jean. *Simulacra and Simulation.* Translated by Sheila Faria Glaser. Reprint, Ann Arbor: University of Michigan Press, 1994 [1981].

Bazin, André. *Orson Welles: A Critical View.* Translated by Jonathan Rosenbaum, foreword by François Truffaut. London: Elm Tree Books, 1978.

———. *What Is Cinema?* Vol. 2. 1971. Translated by Hugh Gray. Reprint, Berkeley, Los Angeles, and London: University of California Press, 2005.

Bean, Frank D., and Marta Tienda. *The Hispanic Population of the United States.* New York: Russell Sage Foundation, 1987.

Beckham, Jack. "Border Policy/Border Cinema: Placing *Touch of Evil*, *The Border*, and *Traffic* in the American Imagination." *Journal of Popular Film and Television* 33 (3) (2005): 130–41.

Bell, Daniel. *The End of Ideology: On the Exhaustion of Political Ideas in the Fifties*. Revised ed. New York: Free Press, 1962.

Belnap, Jeffrey. "Diego Rivera's Greater America Pan-American Patronage, Indigenism, and H.P." *Cultural Critique* 63 (2006): 61–98.

Beltrán, Mary, and Camilla Fojas. "Mixed Race in Hollywood Film and Media Culture." In *Mixed Race Hollywood*, edited by Mary Beltrán and Camilla Fojas, 1–22. New York and London: New York University Press, 2008.

———, eds. *Mixed Race Hollywood*. New York and London: New York University Press, 2008.

Benamou, Catherine. *It's All True: Orson Welles' Pan-American Odyssey*. Berkley and London: University of California Press, 2007.

Bender, Steven. *Run for the Border: Vice and Virtue in U.S.-Mexico Border Crossings*. New York and London: New York University Press, 2012.

Bendixen, Alfred, and Judith Hamera, eds. *The Cambridge Companion to American Travel Writing*. Cambridge: Cambridge University Press, 2009.

———. "Introduction: New Worlds and Old Lands—the Travel Book and the Construction of American Identity." In *The Cambridge Companion to American Travel Writing*, edited by Alfred Bendixen and Judith Hamera, 1–10. Cambridge: Cambridge University Press, 2009.

Berg, Charles Ramirez. *Latino Images in Film: Stereotypes, Subversion, and Resistance*. Austin: University of Texas Press, 2002.

Berger, Dina, and Andrew Grant Wood, eds. *Holiday in Mexico: Critical Reflections on Tourism and Tourist Encounters*. Durham, NC: Duke University Press, 2010.

Bernardi Daniel, ed. *Classic Hollywood, Classic Whiteness*. Minneapolis, MN, and London: University of Minneapolis Press, 2001.

———. *The Persistence of Whiteness: Race and Contemporary Hollywood Cinema*. London: Routledge, 2008.

Berumen, Humberto Félix. "Snapshots from and about a City Named Tijuana." In *Tijuana Dreaming: Life and Art at the Global Border*, edited by Josh Kun and Fiamma Montezemolo, 25–46. Durham, NC, and London: Duke University Press, 2012.

Bethell, Leslie, and Ian Roxborough, eds. *Latin America between the Second World War and the Cold War, 1944–1948*. Cambridge: Cambridge University Press, 1992.

Betts, Raymond F. "The Illusionary Island: Hollywood's Pacific Place." *East-West Film Journal* 5 (2) (1991): 30–45.

Bhabha, Homi K. *The Location of Culture*. London and New York: Routledge, 1994.

Blaeu, Joan. *Le Grand Atlas*. Vol. 1. 1667. Library of Congress Atlas Collection, Washington, DC.

Bogdanovich, Peter. *Who the Devil Made It: Conversations with Robert Aldrich, George Cukor, Allan Dwan, Howard Hawks, Alfred Hitchcock, Chuck Jones, Fritz Lang, Joseph H. Lewis, Sidney Lumet, Leo McCarey, Otto Preminger, Don Siegel, Josef von Sternberg, Frank Teshlin, Edgar G. Ulmer, Raoul Walsh.* New York: Ballantine Books, 1998.

Booker, M. Keith. *Colonial Power, Colonial Texts: India in the Modern British Novel.* Ann Arbor: University of Michigan, 1997.

———. *From Box Office to Ballot Box: The American Political Film.* Westport, CT: Praeger, 2007.

———. *Monsters, Mushroom Clouds, and the Cold War: American Science Fiction and the Roots of Postmodernism, 1946–1964.* Westport, CT, and London: Greenwood Press, 2001.

Border Incident press pack. British Film Institute National Archive. 1949.

"Border River." *Motion Picture Herald Product Digest,* June 13, 1953, 28.

Borderline press pack. British Film Institute National Archive. 1950.

Bradley, Mark Philip. "Decolonization, the Global South, and the Cold War, 1919–1962." In *The Cambridge History of the Cold War, Volume 1: Origins,* edited by Melvyn P. Leffler and Odd Arne Westad, 464–85. Cambridge: Cambridge University Press, 2010.

Brady, Frank. *Citizen Welles: A Biography of Orson Welles.* 1989. Reprint, London: Hodder and Stoughton, 1990.

Brands, Hal. *Latin America's Cold War.* Cambridge, MA: Harvard University Press, 2010.

Brewer, Stewart. *Borders and Bridges: A History of U.S.-Latin American Relations.* Westport, CT, and London: Praeger Security international, 2006.

Britton, John A. *Revolution and Ideology: Images of the Mexican Revolution in the United States.* Lexington: University of Kentucky Press, 1995.

Brown, DeSoto. "Beautiful, Romantic Hawaii: How the Fantasy Image Came to Be." *Journal of Decorative and Propaganda Arts* 20 (1994): 252–71.

Brown, Wendy. *Walled States, Waning Sovereignty.* New York: Zone, 2010.

Bruce, Chris. *Myth of the West.* New York: Rizzoli, 1990.

Bruno, Giuliana. *Atlas of Emotion: Journeys in Art, Architecture and Film.* New York and London: Verso, 2002.

———. "Bodily Architectures." *Assemblage* 19 (1992): 106–11.

———. *Public Intimacy: Architecture and the Visual Arts.* Cambridge, MA, and London: The MIT Press, 2007.

Buhle, Paul, and Dave Wagner. *Radical Hollywood: The Untold Story behind America's Favorite Movies.* New York: New Press, 2002.

———. *A Very Dangerous Citizen: Abraham Lincoln Polonsky and the Hollywood Left.* Berkley and London: University of California Press, 2001.

Buscombe, Edward, ed. *The BFI Companion to the Western.* Revised ed. London: Deutsch/British Film Institute, 1993.

———. "Border Control." *Sight and Sound* 13 (10) (2003): 22–4.

Byman, Jeremy. *Showdown at High Noon: Witch-hunts, Critics, and the End of the Western.* Lanham, MD, and Oxford, UK: Scarecrow Press, 2004.

Calavita, Kitty. *Inside the State: The Bracero Program, Immigration, and the INS.* New York and London: Routledge, 1992.

Calvo, Luz. "'Lemme Stay, I Want to Watch': Ambivalence in Borderlands Cinema." In *Latino/a Popular Culture*, edited by Michelle Habell-Pallán and Mary Romero, 73–81. New York and London: New York University Press, 2002.

Campaign for an Accountable, Moral, and Balanced Immgration Overhaul (CAMBIO). "CAMBIO Believes the Following Elements are Essential to Responsible Enforcement Activity in the Border Region." Accessed July 23, 2013. http://cambio-us.org/.

Carlsen, Laura. "Under Nafta, Mexico Suffered, and the United States Felt Its Pain." *New York Times*, November 24, 2013. Accessed February 20, 2015. http://www.nytimes.com/roomfordebate/2013/11/24/what-weve-learned-from-nafta/under-nafta-mexico-suffered-and-the-united-states-felt-its-pain.

Carmichael, Deborah A., ed. *The Landscape of Hollywood Westerns: Ecocriticism in an American Film Genre.* Salt Lake City: University of Utah Press, 2006.

Carroll, Noël. "Toward a Theory of Point-of-View Editing: Communication, Emotion, and the Movies." *Poetics Today* 14 (1) (1993): 123–41.

Casper, Drew. *Postwar Hollywood, 1946–1962.* Malden, MA, and Oxford, UK: Blackwell, 2007.

Castro, Rafaela. *Chicano Folklore: A Guide to the Folktales, Traditions, Rituals and Religious Practices of Mexican-Americans.* Oxford: Oxford University Press, 2000.

Cawelti, John G. *The Six-Gun Mystique.* Bowling Green, OH: Bowling Green University Popular Press, 1971.

———. *The Six-Gun Mystique Sequel.* Bowling Green, OH: Bowling Green University Popular Press, 1999.

Ceplair, Larry. "The Film Industry's Battle against Left-Wing Influences, from the Russian Revolution to the Blacklist." *Film History* 20 (4) (2008): 399–411.

Ceplair, Larry, and Steven Englund. *The Inquisition in Hollywood: Politics and the Film Community, 1930–1960.* Reprint, Berkley and London: University of California Press: 1983 [1980].

Chabram-Dernersesian, Angie, ed. *The Chicana/o Cultural Studies Reader.* London: Routledge, 2006.

———. "Introduction: Locating Chicana/o Cultural Studies: Contentious Dialogues and Alternative Legacies." In *The Chicana/o Cultural Studies Reader*, edited by Angie Chabram-Dernersesian, 3–25. London: Routledge, 2006.

Chaplin, Joyce E. "Planetary Power? The United States and the History of around the World Travel." *Journal of American Studies* 47 (2013): 1–21.

Chopra-Gant, Mike. *Hollywood Genres and Postwar America: Masculinity, Family and Nation in Popular Movies and Film Noir.* London: I. B. Tauris, 2006.

Christensen, Terry. *Reel Politics: American Political Movies from Birth of a Nation to Platoon.* Oxford, UK: Basil Blackwell, 1987.

Clarke, David B., ed. *The Cinematic City.* London: Routledge, 1997.

Clarke, David B., Valerie Crawford Pfannhauser, and Marcus A. Doel. "Checking In." In *Moving Pictures/Stopping Places: Hotels and Motels on Film,* edited by David B. Clarke, Valerie Crawford Pfannhauser, and Marcus A. Doel, 1–12. Lanham, MD, and Plymouth: Lexington Books, 2009.

———, eds. *Moving Pictures/Stopping Places: Hotels and Motels on Film.* Lanham, MD, and Plymouth: Lexington Books, 2009.

Cline, Howard F. *The United States and Mexico.* 1953. Revised ed. Cambridge, MA: Harvard University Press, 1963.

Coates, Paul. "Moral Rap Hits Beverly Pictures of Wild Aadland Party." *Los Angeles Mirror,* April 13, 1960. Cited by Larry Harnisch in "Larry Harnisch Reflects on Los Angeles History." *LA Times Blogs,* April 13, 2010. Accessed May 22, 2013. http://latimesblogs.latimes.com/thedailymirror/2010/04/paul-v-coates-confidential-file-april-13-1960.html.

Coatsworth, John H., and Carlos Rico, eds. *Images of Mexico in the United States.* San Diego: Center for U.S.-Mexican Studies, University of California, 1989.

Cole, Simon. *Suspect Identities: A History of Fingerprinting and Criminal Identification.* Cambridge, MA, and London: Harvard University Press, 2001.

Combs, James, ed. *Movies and Politics: The Dynamic Relationship.* New York and London: Garland Publishing, 1993.

———. "Understanding the Politics of Movies." In *Movies and Politics: The Dynamic Relationship,* edited by James Combs, 3–25. New York and London: Garland Publishing, 1993.

Comito, Terry, ed. *Touch of Evil: Orson Welles, Director.* New Brunswick: Rutgers University Press, 1985.

———. "Welles's Labyrinths: An Introduction to *Touch of Evil.*" In *Touch of Evil: Orson Welles, Director,* edited by Terry Comito, 3–33. New Brunswick, NJ: Rutgers University Press, 1985.

Committee to Protect Journalists. "30 Journalists Killed in Mexico since 1992/Motive Confirmed." Accessed July 12, 2014. http://www.cpj.org/killed/americas/mexico/.

Conley, Tom. "Border Incidence." *Symploke* 15 (1–2) (2007): 100–14.

———. *Cartographic Cinema.* Minneapolis and London: University of Minnesota Press, 2007.

———. *The Self-Made Map: Cartographic Writing in Early Modern France.* Minneapolis and London: University of Minnesota Press, 1996.

Conrad, Joseph. *Heart of Darkness and Other Tales*. Edited with an introduction and notes by Cedric Watts. Oxford: Oxford University Press,
2002 [1899].

Corkin, Stanley. "Cowboys and Free Markets: Post-World War II Westerns
and U.S. Hegemony." *Cinema Journal* 39 (3) (2000): 66–91.

———. *Cowboys as Cold Warriors: The Western and U.S. History*. Philadelphia,
PA: Temple University Press, 2004.

Cortés, Carlos E. "To View a Neighbor: The Hollywood Textbook
on Mexico." In *Images of Mexico in the United States*, edited by John
Coatsworth and Carlos Rico, 91–118. San Diego: Center for U.S.-
Mexican Studies, University of California, 1989.

Cowgill, George L. "State and Society at Teotihuacan, Mexico." *Annual
Review of Anthropology* 26 (1997): 129–61.

Coyne, Michael. *The Crowded Prairie: American National Identity in the
Hollywood Western*. London: I. B. Tauris, 1997.

Crampton, Jeremy W., and Stuart Elden, eds. *Space, Knowledge, and Power:
Foucault and Geography*. Aldershot: Ashgate, 2007.

Croucher, Sheila. *The Other Side of the Fence: American Migrants in Mexico*.
Austin: University of Texas Press, 2009.

Crowther, Bosley. "Border Incident, Adventure Film about U.S. Immigration
Service, Opens at Globe." Rev. of *Border Incident* (Anthony Mann, 1949).
New York Times, November 21, 1949, 29.

———. Rev. of *Vera Cruz* (Robert Aldrich, 1954). *New York Times*,
December 27, 1954, 22.

Cunningham, Michelle. *Mexico and the Foreign Policy of Napoleon III*.
Basingstoke: Palgrave, 2001.

Davenport, John. *The U.S.-Mexico Border: The Treaty of Guadalupe Hidalgo*.
Foreword by Senator George J. Mitchell. New York: Chelsea House
Publishers, 2005.

Davies, Philip, and Brian Neve, eds. *Cinema, Politics and Society in America*.
Manchester: Manchester University Press, 1981.

De la Garza, Armida. *Mexico on Film: National Identity and International
Relations*. Bury St Edmunds: Arena Books, 2006.

De la Garza, Rodolfo O., and Jesus Velasco, eds. *Bridging the Border:
Transforming Mexico-U.S. Relations*. Lanham, MD, and Oxford, UK:
Rowman and Littlefield Publishers, Inc., 1997.

De la Torre, Adela, and Beatríz M. Pesquera, eds. *Building with Our Hands:
New Directions in Chicana Studies*. Berkley and London: University of
California Press, 1993.

Dear, Michael, and Gustavo Leclerc. "Tijuana Desenmarcada." *Wide Angle*
20 (3) (1998): 210–21.

Dekker, George. *The Fictions of Romantic Tourism: Radcliffe, Scott and Mary
Shelley*. Stanford, CA: Stanford University Press, 2005.

Del Castillo, Raymond. "The End of the Latin Lover?" *Picturegoer*, August
2, 1947, 11.

Del Castillo, Richard Griswold. "The Treaty of Guadalupe Hidalgo." In *U.S.-Mexico Borderlands: Historical and Contemporary Perspectives*, edited by Oscar J. Martínez, 2–9. Wilmington, DE: Scholarly Resources, 1996.

Delgado, Richard, ed. *Critical Race Theory: The Cutting Edge*. Philadelphia, PA: Temple University Press, 1995.

Delgado, Richard, and Jean Stefancic, eds. *The Latino/a Condition: A Critical Reader*. New York and London: University Press, 1998.

Dell'Agnese, Ellena. "The US-Mexico Border in American Movies: A Political Geography Perspective." In *Cinema and Popular Geo-Politics*, edited by Marcus Power and Andrew Crampton, 12–28. London: Routledge, 2007.

Denning, Michael. *The Cultural Front: The Laboring of American Culture in the Twentieth Century*. Reprint, London and New York: Verso, 2010 [1997].

Derrida, Jacques. *Of Grammatology*. Translated by Gayatri Chakravorty Spivak. Baltimore, MD, and London: The John Hopkins University Press, 1976.

Dick, Bernard F. *Radical Innocence: A Critical Study of the Hollywood Ten*. Lexington: University Press of Kentucky, 1989.

Dimendberg, Edward. *Film Noir and the Spaces of Modernity*. Cambridge, MA, and London: Harvard University Press, 2004.

Dixon, Wheeler Winston. *Lost in the Fifties: Recovering Phantom Hollywood*. Carbondale: Southern Illinois University Press, 2005.

Doherty, Thomas. *Hollywood's Censor: Joseph I. Breen & the Production Code Administration*. New York and Chichester: Columbia University Press, 2007.

Dowdy, Andrew. *The Films of the Fifties: The American State of Mind*. New York: Morrow, 1975.

"Drive on Wetbacks Termed a Success." *New York Times*, March 10, 1955, 29.

Dunn, Timothy J. *The Militarization of the U.S.-Mexico Border 1978–1992: Low-Intensity Conflict Doctrine Comes Home*. Austin: Center for Mexican American Studies, University of Texas, 1996.

Elkin, Frederick. "The Psychological Appeal of the Hollywood Western." *Journal of Educational Sociology* 24 (2) (1950): 72–86.

Elsner, Jaⵥ, and Joan-Pau Rubiés, eds. *Voyages and Visions: Towards a Cultural History of Travel*. London: Reaktion Books, 1999.

Engelhardt, Tom. *The End of Victory Culture: Cold War America and the Disillusioning of a Generation*. Amherst: University of Massachusetts Press, 2007.

Ettinger, Patrick. *Imaginary Lines: Border Enforcement and the Origins of Undocumented Immigration, 1882–1930*. Austin: University of Texas Press, 2009.

Fanon, Frantz. *Black Skin, White Masks*. Translated by Charles Lam Markmann. Reprint, London: Pluto Press, 2008 [1952].

Fein, Seth. "Transcultured Anticommunism: Cold War Hollywood in Postwar Mexico." In *Visible Nations: Latin American Cinema and Video*, edited by Chon A. Noriega, 82–111. Minneapolis: University of Minnesota Press, 2000.

Fernandez, Raul A., and Gilbert G. Gonzalez. *A Century of Chicano History: Empire, Nations and Migration*. New York and London: Routledge, 2003.

Finler, Joel Waldo. *The Hollywood Story*. London: Wallflower Press, 2003.

Fishgall, Gary. *Against Type: The Biography of Burt Lancaster*. New York and London: Scribner, 1995.

"Flaws Are Noted in 'Wetback' Curb: Traffic Only a 'Trickle,' but Abuses Persist on Farms, Texas Unions Assert." *New York Times*, August 28, 1955, 55.

Fojas, Camilla. *Border Bandits: Hollywood on the Southern Frontier*. Austin: University of Texas Press, 2008.

———. "Bordersploitation: Hollywood Border Crossers and Buddy Cops." *Symploke* 15 (1–2) (2007): 80–9.

———. "Hollywood Border Cinema: Westerns with a Vengeance." *Journal of Popular Film and Television* 39 (2) (2011): 93–101.

Foucault, Michel. "Of Other Spaces." *Diacritics* 16 (1) (1986): 22–7.

———. "Questions on Geography." In *Power/Knowledge: Selected Interviews and Other Writings, 1972–1977*, edited and translated by Colin Gordon, 63–77. New York: Pantheon, 1980.

Fousek, John. *To Lead the Free World: American Nationalism and the Cultural Roots of the Cold War*. Chapel Hill and London: The University of North Carolina Press, 2000.

Fox, Claire F. *The Fence and the River: Culture and Politics at the U.S.-Mexico Border*. Minneapolis and London: University of Minnesota Press, 1999.

Frayling, Christopher. *Spaghetti Westerns: Cowboys and Europeans from Karl May to Sergio Leone*. Reprint, London and New York: I.B. Tauris, 1998 [1981].

Fregoso, Rosa Linda. *The Bronze Screen: Chicana and Chicano Film Culture*. Minneapolis and London: University of Minnesota Press, 1993.

Fregoso, Rosa Linda, and Angie Chabram-Dernersesian. "Chicana/o Cultural Representations: Reframing Alternative Critical Discourses." In *The Chicana/o Cultural Studies Reader*, edited by Angie Chabram-Dernersesian, 26–32. London: Routledge, 2006.

French, Philip. *Westerns: Aspects of a Movie Genre and Westerns Revisited*. Manchester: Carcanet Press Limited, 2005.

Fried, Richard M. *The Russians Are Coming! The Russians Are Coming!: Pageantry and Patriotism in Cold-War America*. New York and Oxford: Oxford University Press, 1998.

Friedman, Lester D. "Celluloid Palimpsests: An Overview of Ethnicity and the American Film." In *Unspeakable Images: Ethnicity and the American*

Cinema, edited by Lester D. Friedman, 11–38. Urbana: University of Illinois Press, 1991.

———, ed. *Unspeakable Images: Ethnicity and the American Cinema.* Urbana: University of Illinois Press, 1991.

Furman, Bess. "Obesity Is Termed No. 1 Nutritional Ill." *New York Times*, December 9, 1952, 45.

Gaddis, John Lewis. *Strategies of Containment: A Critical Appraisal of American National Security Policy during the Cold War.* New York and Oxford: Oxford University Press, 2005.

Gaffney, Frank Jr. "No-Brainer: The 'BlueServo' Solution to Border Insecurity." *Centre for Security Policy*, July 23, 2014. Accessed February 20, 2015. http://www.centerforsecuritypolicy.org/2014/07/23/no-brainer-the-blueservo-solution-to-border-insecurity/.

Galarza, Ernesto. *Merchants of Labor: The Mexican Bracero Story: An Account of the Managed Migration of Mexican Farm Workers in California, 1942–1960.* Reprint, New York: McNally and Loftin, 1972 [1964].

Galbraith, John Kenneth. *The Affluent Society.* Cambridge, MA: The Riverside Press, 1958.

Garcia, John A. "The Chicano Movement: Its Legacy for Politics and Policy." In *Chicanas/Chicanos at the Crossroads: Social, Economic, and Political Change*, edited by David R. Maciel and Isidro D. Ortiz, 83–107. Tucson: University of Arizona Press, 1996.

———. "'Yo Soy Mexicano...': Self-Identity and Sociodemographic Correlates." *Social Science Quarterly* 62 (1) (1981): 88–98.

Garcia Riera, Emilio. *México Visto por el Cine Extranjero 3: 1941/1969.* Guadalajara: Universidad de Guadalajara, 1988.

———. *México Visto Por el Cine Extranjero 4: 1941/1969: Filmografía.* Guadalajara: Universidad de Guadalajara, 1988.

Geiger, Jeffrey. "Adrenaline Views: Rethinking Aerial Affect." Paper presented at the School of Film, Television and Media research seminar series, University of East Anglia, UK, April 29, 2013.

———. *American Documentary Film: Projecting the Nation.* Edinburgh: Edinburgh University Press, 2011.

———. "Imagined Islands: 'White Shadows in the South Seas' and Cultural Ambivalence." *Cinema Journal* 41 (3) (2002): 98–121.

Gellman, Irwin F. *Good Neighbor Diplomacy: United States Politics in Latin America, 1933–1945.* Baltimore, MD: John Hopkins University Press, 1979.

Gerstle, Gary. *American Crucible: Race and Nation in the Twentieth Century.* Princeton, NJ: Princeton University Press, 2001.

Gilroy, Amanda. "Introduction." In *Romantic Geographies: Discourses of Travel, 1775–1844*, edited by Amanda Gilroy, 1–15. Manchester: Manchester University Press, 2000.

———, ed. *Romantic Geographies: Discourses of Travel, 1775–1844.* Manchester: Manchester University Press, 2000.

Girven, Tim. "Hollywood's Heterotopia: US Cinema, the Mexican Border and the Making of Tijuana." *Travesia: Journal of Latin American Cultural Studies* 3 (1–2) (1994): 93–133.

Gladchuk, John Joseph. *Hollywood and Anticommunism: HUAC and the Evolution of the Red Menace, 1935–1950*. London: Routledge, 2007.

Glennon, John P., ed. *United Nations and General International Matters*. Vol. 2 of *Foreign Relations of the United States, 1958–1960*. Washington, DC: United States Government Printing Office, 1991.

Gonzales, Manuel. *Mexicanos: A History of Mexicans in the United States*. 2nd ed. Bloomington: Indiana University Press, 1999.

Gonzalez, Michael J. *The Mexican Revolution, 1910–1940*. Albuquerque: University of New Mexico Press, 2002.

Grajeda, Tony. "'A Question of the Ear': Listening to *Touch of Evil*." In *Lowering the Boom: Critical Studies in Film Sound*, edited by Jay Beck and Tony Grajeda, 201–17. Urbana: University of Illinois Press, 2008.

Grandin, Greg. *The Last Colonial Massacre: Latin America in the Cold War*. Updated ed. Chicago and London: University of Chicago Press, 2004.

Greer, Margaret M., Walter D. Mignolo, and Maureen Quilligan. "Introduction." In *Rereading the Black Legend: The Discourses of Religious and Racial Difference in the Renaissance Empires*, edited by Margaret M. Greer, Walter D. Mignolo, and Maureen Quilligan, 1. Chicago: University of Chicago Press, 2007.

Gregory, Derek. *Geographical Imaginations*. Cambridge, MA, and Oxford, UK: Blackwell Publishers, 1994.

Gresham, Rupert. "Drive on to Mexico: More than Half Million Tourists Crossing the Border Annually." *New York Times*, April 15, 1951, 265.

"Grim Adventures on Mexican Border." Rev. of *Border Incident* (Anthony Mann, 1949). *The Hollywood Reporter*, August 26, 1949, 4.

Gunning, Tom. "Modernity and Cinema: A Culture of Shocks and Flows." In *Cinema and Modernity*, edited by Murray Pomerance, 297–315. New Brunswick, NJ: Rutgers University Press, 2006.

———. "'The Whole World within Reach': Travel Images without Borders." In *Virtual Voyages: Cinema and Travel*, edited by Jeffrey Ruoff, 25–41. Durham, NC: Duke University Press, 2006.

Habell-Pallán, Michelle, and Mary Romero, eds. *Latino/a Popular Culture*. New York and London: New York University Press, 2002.

Hadley, Eleanor M. "A Critical Analysis of the Wetback Problem." *Law and Contemporary Problems* 21 (2) (1956): 334–57.

Hagen, Ray. "Claire Trevor: Brass with Class." In *Killer Tomatoes: Fifteen Tough Film Dames*, by Ray Hagen and Laura Wagner, 222–35. Jefferson, NC, and London: McFarland and Co., Inc., Publishers, 2004.

Hagen, Ray, and Laura Wagner. *Killer Tomatoes: Fifteen Tough Film Dames*. Jefferson, NC, and London: McFarland and Co., Inc., Publishers, 2004.

"Hall, Fugitive Red, Seized in Mexico, Deported to U.S." *New York Times*, October, 10, 1951, 1.

Hall, Linda, and Don Coerver. *Revolution on the Border: The United States and Mexico, 1910–1920.* Albuquerque: University of New Mexico Press, 1988.

Hamnett, Brian. *Juárez.* London: Longman Group, 1994.

Harley, J. Brian. "Maps, Knowledge and Power." In *The New Nature of Maps: Essays in the History of Cartography*, edited by Paul Laxton, Introduction by J. H. Andrews, 52–81. Baltimore, MD, and London: John Hopkins University Press, 2001.

———. *The New Nature of Maps: Essays in the History of Cartography*, edited by Paul Laxton, Introduction by J. H. Andrews. Baltimore, MD, and London: John Hopkins University Press, 2001.

———. "Texts and Contexts in the Interpretation of Early Maps." In *The New Nature of Maps: Essays in the History of Cartography*, edited by Paul Laxton, Introduction by J. H. Andrews, 33–49. Baltimore, MD, and London: John Hopkins University Press, 2001.

Harris, Cole. "How Did Colonialism Dispossess? Comments from an Edge of Empire." *Annals of the Association of American Geographers* 94 (1) (2004): 165–82.

Hausladen, Gary, ed. *Western Places, American Myths: How We Think about the West.* Reno: University of Nevada Press, 2003.

Hauss, Charles. *Comparative Politics: Domestic Responses to Global Challenges.* 7th ed. Boston, MA: Wadsworth Cengage Learning, 2011.

Haut, Woody. *Pulp Fiction: Hardboiled Fiction and the Cold War.* London: Serpent's Tail, 1995.

Heath, Stephen. "Film and System: Terms of Analysis." *Screen* 16 (1–2) (1975): 7–77.

Hendershot, Cynthia. *I Was a Cold War Monster: Horror Films, Eroticism, and the Cold War Imagination.* Bowling Green, OH: Bowling Green State University Popular Press, 2001.

———. *Paranoia, the Bomb and 1950s Science Fiction Films.* Bowling Green, OH: Bowling Green State University Popular Press, 1999.

Hertzberg, Bob. *The Left Side of the Screen: Communist and Left-Wing Ideology in Hollywood, 1929–2009.* Jefferson, NC, and London: McFarland and Co., Inc., Publishers, 2011.

Herzog, Lawrence Arthur. *Where North Meets South: Cities, Space and Politics on the U.S.-Mexico Border.* Austin: University of Texas, 1990.

Heston, Charlton. *In the Arena: The Autobiography.* London: Harper Collins Publishers, 1995.

Hicks, Jimmie. "Joel McCrea." *Films in Review* 42 (11–12) (1991): 392–404.

Hill, Gladwin. "Mexicans Convert Border into a Sieve." *New York Times*, March 27, 1950, 1.

———. "Peons in the West Lowering Culture." *New York Times*, March 27, 1951, 31.

———. "Wetback Influx Moves Westward: Two States Have Record Job Rush by Mexicans." *New York Times*, October 9, 1953, 40.

————. "Wetback Invasion Is Broadening Despite All U.S. Counter-Moves." *New York Times*, February 11, 1952, 12.

————. "Wetback Ousting by Airlift Revived: Action by Congress Remedies Shortage of Funds." *New York Times*, June 13, 1952, 11.

————. "Wetbacks Cross at Two a Minute." *New York Times*, April 16, 1953, 31.

Hjort, Mette, and Scott Mackenzie. *Cinema and Nation*. London: Routledge, 2000.

Houseman, John. "The Birth of the Mercury Theatre." *Educational Theatre Journal* 24 (1) (1972): 33–47.

Human Rights Watch. "Mexico," *World Report 2014*. Accessed July 12, 2014. http://www.hrw.org/world-report/2014/country-chapters/mexico?page=2.

Humane Borders/Fronteras Compasivas. Accessed February 20, 2015. http://www.humaneborders.org/.

Iglesias, Norma Prieto. *La Visión de la Frontera a Través del Cine Mexicano*. Tijuana: Centros Estudios Fronterizos del Norte México, 1985.

Insley, Jennifer. "Redefining Sodom: A Latter-Day Vision of Tijuana." *Mexican Studies/Estudios Mexicanos* 20 (1) (2004): 99–122.

Ivers, J. D. Rev. of *Touch of Evil*. *Motion Picture Herald Product Digest*, March 22, 1958, 765.

Jackson, Peter. *Maps of Meaning: An Introduction to Cultural Geography*. Reprint, London and New York: Routledge, 2001 [1989].

Jacob, Christian. *The Sovereign Map: Theoretical Approaches in Cartography throughout History*. Translated by Tom Conley, edited by Edward H. Dahl. Chicago and London: The University of Chicago Press, 2006.

Jacobs, Jane. *Edge of Empire: Postcolonialism and the City*. London: Routledge, 1996.

Jacobson, Matthew Frye. *Whiteness of a Different Color: European Immigrants and the Alchemy of Race*. Cambridge, MA, and London: Harvard University Press, 1999.

Jancovich, Mark. *Rational Fears: American Horror in the 1950s*. Manchester: Manchester University Press, 1996.

Jasen, Patricia Jane. *Wild Things: Nature, Culture, and Tourism in Ontario, 1790–1914*. Toronto and Buffalo, NY: University of Toronto Press, 1995.

Jenkins, Steve. Rev. of *Where Danger Lives* (John Farrow, 1950). *Monthly Film Bulletin* 48 (571) (1981): 166–7.

Johnson, David E., and Scott Michaelsen, eds. *Border Theory: The Limits of Cultural Politics*. Minneapolis, MN, and London: University of Minnesota Press, 1997.

Johnson, Kevin R. *The "Huddled Masses" Myth: Immigration and Civil Rights*. Philadelphia, PA: Temple University Press, 2004.

Johnson, Kevin R., and Bernard Trujillo. *Immigration Law and the U.S.-Mexico Border: ¿Sí Se Puede?* Tucson: University of Arizona Press, 2011.

Kaplan, Caren. *Questions of Travel: Postmodern Discourses of Displacement*. Durham, NC, and London: Duke University Press, 1996.

Katz, Friedrich. *The Secret War in Mexico: Europe, the United States and the Mexican Revolution.* Chicago and London: University of Chicago Press, 1981.

"Katzman-Kardos Pic Documented Expose." Rev. of *The Tijuana Story* (Leslie Kardos, 1957). *The Hollywood Reporter*, October 9, 1957, 3.

Kaufmann, Florian K. *Mexican Labor Migrants and U.S. Immigration Policies: From Sojourner to Emigrant?* El Paso: LFB Scholarly Publishers, 2011.

Kazan, Elia. *Kazan on Kazan.* Edited by Jeff Young. London: Faber, 1997.

Keller, Gary, ed. *Chicano Cinema: Research, Reviews and Resources.* Tempe, AZ: Bilingual Review Press, 1993.

Kemp, Philip. "Burt Lancaster: Charmer Chameleon." *Sight and Sound* 18 (2008): 36–8.

Kennan, George. "Latin America as a Problem in U.S. Foreign Policy." In *Neighborly Adversaries: Readings in U.S.-Latin American Relations*, edited by Michael J. LaRosa and Frank O. Mora, 123–34. 2nd ed. Lanham, MD: Rowman and Littlefield Publishers, 2007.

Keslo, Louis O., and Mortimer J. Adler. *The Capitalist Manifesto.* New York: Random House, 1958.

Kirby, Lynne. *Parallel Tracks: The Railroad and Silent Cinema.* Durham, NC: Duke University Press, 1997.

Kitchin, Rob, and James Kneale, eds. *Lost in Space: Geographies of Science Fiction.* London: Continuum, 2002.

Krutnik, Frank. *In a Lonely Street: Film Noir, Genre, Masculinity.* London: Routledge, 1991.

Krutnik, Frank, Steve Neale, Brian Neve, and Peter Stanfield, eds. *"Un-American" Hollywood: Politics and Film in the Blacklist Era.* Piscataway, NJ: Rutgers University Press, 2007.

Kuhn, Annette. *The Power of the Image: Essays on Representation and Sexuality.* London: Routledge, 1985.

Kun, Josh. "The Kidnapped City." In *Tijuana Dreaming: Life and Art at the Global Border*, edited by Josh Kun and Fiamma Montezemolo, 355–69. Durham, NC, and London: Duke University Press, 2012.

Kun, Josh, and Fiamma Montezemolo. "Introduction: The Factory of Dreams." In *Tijuana Dreaming: Life and Art at the Global Border*, edited by Josh Kun and Fiamma Montezemolo, 1–20. Durham, NC, and London: Duke University Press, 2012.

Langford, Barry. *Film Genre: Hollywood and Beyond.* Edinburgh: Edinburgh University Press, 2006.

LaRosa, Michael J., and Frank O. Mora, eds. *Neighborly Adversaries: Readings in U.S.-Latin American Relations.* 2nd ed. Lanham, MD: Rowman and Littlefield Publishers, 2007.

Lazarus, Charles J. Rev. of *Border Incident* (Anthony Mann, 1949). *Motion Picture Herald Product Digest*, August 27, 1949, 4730.

Leeper, Jill. "Crossing Musical Borders: The Soundtrack for *Touch of Evil.*" In *Soundtrack Available: Essays on Film and Popular Music*, edited by

Pamela Robertson Wojcik and Arthur Knight, 226–43. Durham, NC, and London: Duke University Press, 2001.

Leffler, Melvyn P., and Odd Arne Westad, eds. *The Cambridge History of the Cold War, Volume 1: Origins.* Cambridge: Cambridge University Press, 2010.

Lenihan, John H. *Showdown: Confronting Modern America in the Western Film.* Urbana: University of Illinois Press, 1985.

Lev, Peter. *The Fifties: Transforming the Screen, 1950–1959.* Berkley and London: University of California Press, 2003.

Lewis, Flora. "Cameras Capture 'Vera Cruz' in Cuernavaca." *New York Times,* April 11, 1954, X5.

"The Life Story of Lloyd Bridges." *Pictureshow,* March 28, 1953, 12.

Limerick, Patricia Nelson. "The Adventures of the Frontier in the Twentieth Century." In *The Frontier in American Culture: Essays by Richard White and Patricia Nelson Limerick.* Edited by James Grossman, 67–102. Berkley and London: University of California Press, 1994.

Lodge, Jack. "Alfonso Bedoya." In *The BFI Companion to the Western,* edited by Edward Buscombe. Revised ed. London: Andre Deutsch/British Film Institute, 1993.

Lopez, Ana M. "Are All Latins from Manhattan? Hollywood, Ethnography and Cultural Colonialism." In *Mediating Two Worlds: Cinematic Encounters in the Americas,* edited by John King III, Ana M. Lopez, and Manuel Alvarado, 195–214. London: British Film Institute, 1993.

Lorey, David E. *The U.S.-Mexican Border in the Twentieth Century: A History of Economic and Social Transformation.* Wilmington, DE: Scholarly Resources, 1999.

Lugo, Alejandro. *Fragmented Lives, Assembled Parts: Culture, Capitalism, and Conquest at the U.S.-Mexico Border.* Austin: University of Texas Press, 2008.

Luhr, William. "Experiment in Terror: Dystopian Modernism, the Police Procedural, and the Space of Anxiety." In *Cinema and Modernity,* edited by Murray Pomerance, 175–93. New Brunswick, NJ: Rutgers University Press, 2006.

———. *Film Noir.* Chichester: Wiley-Blackwell, 2012.

Lyons, Donald. "Dances with Aldrich." *Film Comment* 27 (2) (1991): 72–6.

MacCannell, Dean. *The Tourist: A New Theory of the Leisure Class.* Reprint, Berkeley and London: University of California Press, 1999 [1976].

Maciel, David R. *El Norte: The U.S.-Mexican Border in Contemporary Cinema.* San Diego, CA: Institute for Regional Studies of the Californias, San Diego State University, 1990.

Maciel, David R., and Isidro D. Ortiz, eds. *Chicanas/Chicanos at the Crossroads: Social, Economic, and Political Change.* Tucson: University of Arizona Press, 1996.

Mack, Ruth P. "Trends in American Consumption and the Aspiration to Consume." *The American Economic Review* 46 (2) (1956): 55–68.

Madsen, Deborah L., ed. *Beyond the Borders: American Literature and Post-Colonial Theory*. London and Sterling, VA: Pluto Press, 2003.

Mann, Katrina. "'You're Next!': Postwar Hegemony Besieged in *Invasion of the Body Snatchers*." *Cinema Journal* 44 (1): 49–68.

Manzanas, Ana Maria, and Jesús Benito. *Cities, Borders, and Spaces in Intercultural American Literature and Film*. New York and London: Routledge, 2011.

Martinez, Jacqueline M. *Phenomenology of Chicana Experience and Identity: Communication and Transformation in Praxis*. Lanham, MD, and Oxford, UK: Rowman and Littlefield Publishers, 2000.

Martinez, Oscar J. *Border People: Life and Society in the U.S.-Mexico Borderlands*. Tucson and London: University of Arizona Press, 1994.

———, ed. *U.S.-Mexico Borderlands: Historical and Contemporary Perspectives*. Wilmington, DE: SR Books, 1996.

Massey, Doreen. *Space, Place and Gender*. Cambridge, UK: Polity Press, 1994.

Masterson, Whit. *Badge of Evil*. Reprint, London: Transworld Publishers, 1957 [1956].

Matlock, Jann. "Vacancies: Hotels, Reception Desks and Identity in American Cinema, 1929–1964." In *Moving Pictures/Stopping Places: Hotels and Motels on Film*, edited by David B. Clarke, Valerie Crawford Pfannhauser, and Marcus A. Doel. Lanham, MD, and Plymouth: Lexington Books, 2009.

May, Elaine Tyler. *Homeward Bound: American Families in the Cold War Era*. New York: Basic Books, 1988.

May, Lary. *The Big Tomorrow: Hollywood and the Politics of the American Way*. Chicago: University of Chicago Press, 2000.

———, ed. *Recasting America: Culture and Politics in the Age of Cold War*. Chicago and London: University of Chicago Press, 1989.

———. *Screening out the Past: The Birth of Mass Culture and the Motion Picture Industry*. New York: Oxford University Press, 1980.

Mayer, Geoff, and Brian McDonnell. *Encyclopedia of Film Noir*. Westport, CT: Greenwood, 2007.

Maynard, Richard A. *The American West on Film: Myth and Reality*. Rochelle Park, NJ: Hayden Book Co., Inc., 1974.

McCombe, Leonard. "The Drama of Mexico." *Life*, January 9, 1950, 54–67.

McCormick, Thomas J. *America's Half-Century: United States Foreign Policy in the Cold War*. Baltimore, MD, and London: John Hopkins University Press, 1989.

"McCune Revises Setup; Sets 'Wetbacks' Feature." *The Hollywood Reporter*, May 3, 1955, 5.

McDonald, Paul. *Hollywood Stardom*. Malden: Wiley-Blackwell, 2013.

McGillis, Roderick. *He Was Some Kind of a Man: Masculinities in the B Western*. Waterloo, ON: Wilfrid Laurier University Press, 2009.

McLynn, Frank. *Villa and Zapata: A Biography of the Mexican Revolution.* London: Jonathan Cape, 2000.

McMahon, Jennifer L., and B. Steve Csaki, eds. *The Philosophy of the Western.* Lexington: University Press of Kentucky, 2010.

McNab, Geoffrey. Rev. of *Vera Cruz* (Robert Aldrich, 1954). *Sight and Sound* 11 (8) (2001): 61.

McNeil, Donald. "The Hotel and the City." *Progress in Human Geography* 32 (3) (2008): 383–98.

McWilliams, Carey. *North from Mexico: The Spanish-Speaking People of the United States.* Reprint, New York and London: Greenwood Press, 1990 [1949].

"Meet Jungle Sam." *Life*, March 23, 1953, 79–82.

"Mexican Editor Is Slain by Unidentified Gunmen." *New York Times*, July 28, 1956, 35.

Michel, Manuel, and Neal Oxenhandler. "Mexican Cinema: A Panoramic View." *Film Quarterly* 18 (4) (1965): 46–55.

Miller, Robert Ryal. *Arms across the Border: United States Aid to Juarez during the French Intervention in Mexico.* Philadelphia, PA: American Philosophical Society, 1973.

Millon, Rene. "The Beginnings of Teotihuacan." *American Antiquity* 26 (1) (1960): 1–10.

Mitchell, Lee Clark. *Westerns: Making the Man in Fiction and Film.* Chicago and London: University of Chicago Press, 1996.

Moffitt, Jack. "Hecht-Lancaster, Hill and Aldrich Turn out a Natural." Rev. of *Vera Cruz* (Robert Aldrich, 1954). *The Hollywood Reporter*, December 22, 1954, 3.

———. "Zugsmith Depiction of Dope Ring Dizzy." Rev. of *Touch of Evil* (Orson Welles, 1958). *The Hollywood Reporter*, March 17, 1958, 3.

Montalban, Ricardo with Bob Thomas. *Reflections: A Life in Two Worlds.* Garden City, NY: Doubleday and Co., Inc., 1980.

Moretti, Franco. *Graphs, Maps, Trees.* London and New York: Verso, 2007.

Morkham, Bronwyn, and Russell Staiff. "The Cinematic Tourist: Perception and Subjectivity." In *The Tourist as a Metaphor of the Social World*, edited by Graham M. S. Dann, 297–316. New York: CABI, 2002.

Mulvey, Laura. "Afterthoughts on 'Visual Pleasure and Narrative Cinema' Inspired by King Vidor's *Duel in the Sun* (1946)." In *Visual and Other Pleasures*, by Laura Mulvey, 29–38. Basingstoke: Macmillan, 1989.

———. *Visual and Other Pleasures.* Basingstoke: Macmillan, 1989.

Munn, Mike. "Bridges & Sons." *Photoplay* 30 (5) (1979): 34–5.

Nadel, Alan. *Containment Culture: American Narrative, Postmodernism and the Atomic Age.* Durham, NC, and London: Duke University Press, 1995.

Naremore, James. *The Magic of Orson Welles.* New York: Oxford University Press, 1978.

———. *More than Night: Film Noir in Its Contexts*. Berkley and London: University of California Press, 2008.

Neale, Steve. *Genre and Hollywood*. London: Routledge, 2000.

Negra, Diane. *Off-White Hollywood: American Culture and Ethnic Female Stardom*. London and New York: Routledge, 2001.

Nericcio, William Anthony. *Tex[t]-Mex: Seductive Hallucinations of the "Mexican" in America*. Austin: University of Texas Press, 2007.

Nevins, Joseph. *Operation Gatekeeper and Beyond: The War on "Illegals" and the Remaking of the U.S.-Mexico Boundary*. 2nd ed. New York and London: Routledge, 2010.

Newman, Bruce. "Lloyd Bridges: Hollywood Family Man." *TV Guide*, April 11, 1998, 28.

Newton, Linda. *Illegal, Alien, or Immigrant: The Politics of Immigration Reform*. New York: New York University Press, 2008.

Ngai, Mae M. *Impossible Subjects: Illegal Aliens and the Making of Modern America*. Princeton, NJ, and Woodstock: Woodstock University Press, 2004.

Nilsen, Sarah. *Projecting America, 1958: Film and Cultural Diplomacy at the Brussels World's Fair*. Jefferson, NC: McFarland and Co., Inc., Publishers, 2011.

Noriega, Chon A., ed. *Chicanos and Film: Representation and Resistance*. Minneapolis: University of Minnesota Press, 1992.

———. *Visible Nations: Latin American Cinema and Video*. Minneapolis: University of Minnesota Press, 2000.

Nott, Robert. *Last of the Cowboy Heroes: The Westerns of Randolph Scott, Joel McCrea, and Andy Murphy*. Foreword by Butt Boetticher. Jefferson, NC: McFarland and Co., Inc., Publishers, 2000.

O'Brien, Thomas F. *Making the Americas: The United States and Latin America from the Age of Revolutions to the Era of Globalization*. Albuquerque: University of New Mexico Press, 2007.

O'Neill, Brian. "The Demands of Authenticity: Addison Durland and Hollywood's Latin Images during World War II." In *Classic Hollywood, Classic Whiteness*, edited by Daniel Bernardi, 52–71. Minneapolis and London: University of Minneapolis Press, 2001.

"Obesity Peril Stressed." *New York Times*, February 27, 1953, 25.

Orozco, José Clemente. *Zapatistas*. Museum of Modern Art, New York, 1931.

Osteen, Mark. "Noir's Cars: Automobility and Amoral Space in American Film Noir." *Journal of Popular Film and Television* 35 (4) (2008): 183–92.

Ovalle, Priscilla Peña. *Dance and the Hollywood Latina: Race, Sex and Stardom*. Piscataway, NJ: Rutgers University Press, 2011.

Painter, David S. *The Cold War: An International History*. London: Routledge, 1999.

Palaversich, Diana. "La Ciudad Que Recorro. Un *Flâneur* en Tijuana." *Literatura Mexicana* 13 (2) (2002): 215–27.

Paredes, Américo. *"With His Pistol in His Hand"*: A Border Ballad and Its Hero. Reprint, Austin: University of Texas Press, 2010 [1958].

Parenti, Christian. *The Soft Cage: Surveillance in America from Slavery to the War on Terror.* New York: Basic Books, 2003.

Pease, Donald. "Borderline Justice/States of Emergency: Orson Welles' Touch of Evil." *The New Centennial Review* 1 (2001): 75–105.

Pells, Richard H. *The Liberal Mind in a Conservative Age: American Intellectuals in the 1940s and 1950s.* 2nd ed. Middletown, CT: Wesleyan University Press, 1989.

People Helping People in the Border Zone. "Community Report: Campaign Documents Systemic Racial Discrimination at Arizona Border Patrol Checkpoint." Accessed February 20, 2015. http://phparivaca.org/?p=567.

"People's Capitalism." *New York Times,* June 11, 1957, 34.

Pérez, Louis A. *Cuba in the American Imagination: Metaphor and the Imperial Ethos.* Chapel Hill: University of North Carolina Press, 2008.

Peters, Jeffrey. *Mapping Discord: Allegorical Cartography in Early Modern French Writing.* Newark: University of Delaware Press, 2004.

Pickles, John. *A History of Spaces: Cartographic Reason, Mapping and the Geo-Coded World.* London: Routledge, 2004.

Pietz, William. "The 'Post-Colonialism' of Cold War Discourse." *Social Text* 19–20 (1988): 55–75.

Pike, Frederick B. *FDR's Good Neighbor Policy: Sixty Years of Generally Gentle Chaos.* Austin: University of Texas Press, 1995.

Piper, Karen. *Cartographic Fictions: Maps, Race and Identity.* New Brunswick, NJ: Rutgers University Press, 2002.

Pomerance, Murray, ed. *Cinema and Modernity.* New Brunswick, NJ: Rutgers University Press, 2006.

Porter, Dennis. "Orientalism and Its Problems." In *Colonial Discourse and Post-Colonial Theory: A Reader,* edited by Patrick Williams and Laura Chrisman, 150–61. New York: Columbia University Press, 1994.

Pratt, Mary Louise. *Imperial Eyes: Travel Writing and Transculturation.* London: Routledge, 1992.

Prentice, Claire. "Armchair Deputies Enlisted to Patrol US-Mexico Border." *BBC News,* December 26, 2009. Accessed July 23, 2013. http://news.bbc.co.uk/1/hi/world/americas/8412603.stm.

Preston, William G. "Pesos Go Farther at Story-Book Acapulco." *New York Times,* November 21, 1948, 15.

Price, John A. *Tijuana: Urbanization in a Border Culture.* Notre Dame and London: University of Notre Dame Press, 1973.

Radosh, Ronald, and Allis Radosh. *Red Star over Hollywood: The Film Colony's Long Romance with the Left.* San Francisco: Encounter Books, 2005.

Rees, Richard. *Shades of Difference: A History of Ethnicity in America.* Lanham, MD, and Plymouth: Rowman and Littlefield Publishers, 2007.

Renda, Mary A. *Taking Tahiti: Military Occupation and the Culture of U.S. Imperialism, 1915–1940*. Chapel Hill: University of North Carolina Press, 2001.

Renehan, Edward. *The Monroe Doctrine: The Cornerstone of American Foreign Policy*. New York: Chelsea House, 2007.

Rev. of *Border Incident* (Anthony Mann, 1949). *Variety*, August 31, 1949, 8.

Rev. of *Border River* (George Sherman, 1954). *The Hollywood Reporter*, January 4, 1954, 3.

Rev. of *Border River* (George Sherman, 1954). *Monthly Film Bulletin* 21 (240) (1954): 55.

Rev. of *Border River* (George Sherman, 1954). *Today's Cinema*, February 1, 1954, 14.

Rev. of *Border River* (George Sherman, 1954). *Variety*, January 6, 1954, 3.

Rev. of *Borderline* (William Seiter, 1950). *Motion Picture Herald Product Digest*, January 14, 1950, 153.

Rev. of *Borderline* (William Seiter, 1950). *Variety*, January 11, 1950, 3.

Rev. of *The Houston Story* (William Castle, 1956). *Monthly Film Bulletin* 23 (264) (1956): 91.

Rev. of *Hurricane Island* (Lew Landers, 1951). *Monthly Film Bulletin* 19 (216) (1952): 51.

Rev. of *Sunny Side of the Street* (Richard Quine, 1951). *Monthly Film Bulletin* 19 (216) (1952): 54.

Rev. of *Sword of Monte Cristo* (Maurice Geraghty, 1951). *Monthly Film Bulletin* 18 (204) (1951): 350.

Rev. of *The Tijuana Story* (Leslie Kardos, 1957). *Kinematograph Weekly*, November 7, 1957, 20, 47.

Rev. of *The Tijuana Story* (Leslie Kardos, 1957). *Monthly Film Bulletin* 24 (276) (1957): 153.

Rev. of *The Tijuana Story* (Leslie Kardos, 1957). *Variety*, October 9, 1957, 6.

Rev. of *Vera Cruz* (Robert Aldrich, 1954). *Monthly Film Bulletin* 22 (252) (1955): 55.

Rev. of *Vera Cruz* (Robert Aldrich, 1954). *Today's Cinema*, February 9, 1955, 9.

Rev. of *Vera Cruz* (Robert Aldrich, 1954). *Variety*, December 22, 1954, 6.

Rev. of *Wetbacks* (Hank McCune, 1956). *Harrison's Reports*, March 3, 1956, 34.

Rev. of *Wetbacks* (Hank McCune, 1956). *Kinematograph Weekly*, January 9, 1958, 29–30.

Rev. of *Wetbacks* (Hank McCune, 1956). *Variety*, March 7, 1956, 6.

Richard, Alfred Charles Jr. *Censorship and Hollywood's Hispanic Image: An Interpretive Filmography, 1936–1955*. Westport, CT: Greenwood Press, 1993.

Rippy, Marguerite. *Orson Welles and the Unfinished RKO Projects: A Postmodern Perspective*. Carbondale: Southern Illinois University Press, 2009.

Rivera, Diego. *Peasants.* Museum of Art, Sao Paolo, 1947.

Rivera, Lysa. "Future Histories and Cyborg Labor: Reading Borderlands Science Fiction after NAFTA." *Science Fiction Studies* 39 (3) (2012): 415–36.

Robbins, William G. *Colony and Empire: The Capitalist Transformation of the American West.* Lawrence: University Press of Kansas, 1994.

Rodriguez, Clara E. *Heroes, Lovers and Others: The Story of Latinos in Hollywood.* Washington, DC: Smithsonian Books, 2004.

Rodriguez, Jaime E., and Kathryn Vincent, eds. *Common Border, Uncommon Paths: Race, Culture, and National Identity in U.S.-Mexican Relations.* Wilmington, DE: Scholarly Resources, Inc., 1997.

Rogers, Will. *Will Rogers Scrapbook.* Edited by Bryan B. Sterling. New York: Grosset and Dunlap, 1976.

Rollins, Brooke. "Some Kind of a Man: Orson Welles as *Touch of Evil*'s Masculine Auteur." *The Velvet Light Trap* 57 (2006): 32–41.

Rollins, Peter C., and John E. O'Connor, eds. *Hollywood's West: The American Frontier in Film, Television and History.* Lexington: University Press of Kentucky, 2005.

———. *Why We Fought: America's Wars in Film and History.* Lexington: The University Press of Kentucky, 2008.

Romero, Fernando. *Hyperborder: The Contemporary U.S.-Mexico Border and Its Future.* New York: Princeton Architectural Press, 2008.

Romero, M. "The Free Zone in Mexico." *The North American Review* 154 (425) (1892): 459–71.

Romero, Mary. "Racial Profiling and Immigration Law Enforcement: Rounding up of Usual Suspects in the Latino Community." *Critical Sociology* 32 (2–3) (2006): 447–73.

Rosales, Francisco Arturo. *Chicano! The History of the Mexican American Civil Rights Movement.* Texas: Arte Público Press, 1997.

Roxborough, Ian. "Mexico." In *Latin America between the Second World War and the Cold War, 1944–1948*, edited by Leslie Bethell and Ian Roxborough, 190–216. Cambridge: Cambridge University Press, 1992.

Rubin, Martin. *Thrillers.* Cambridge: Cambridge University Press, 1999.

Ruoff, Jeffrey. "Introduction: The Filmic Fourth Dimension: Cinema as Audiovisual Vehicle." In *Virtual Voyages: Cinema and Travel*, edited by Jeffrey Ruoff, 1–21. Durham, NC: Duke University Press, 2006.

———, ed. *Virtual Voyages: Cinema and Travel.* Durham, NC: Duke University Press, 2006.

Sackett, Andrew. "Fun in Acapulco? The Politics of Development on the Mexican Riviera." In *Holiday in Mexico: Reflections on Tourism and Tourist Encounters*, edited by Dina Berger and Andrew Grant Wood, 161–82. Durham, NC: Duke University Press, 2010.

Sadowski-Smith, Claudia. *Border Fictions: Globalization, Empire, and Writing at the Boundaries of the United States.* Charlottesville and London: University of Virginia Press, 2008.

Said, Edward. *Culture and Imperialism*. Reprint, London: Vintage, 1994 [1993].

———. *Orientalism*. Reprint, London: Penguin, 2003 [1978].

Sáinz, Eloy Méndez, and Jeff Banister. "Transitional Architecture or Espacios de Paso y Simulacro." *Journal of the Southwest* 45 (1–2) (2003): 165–201.

Samora, Julián, ed. *La Raza: Forgotten Americans*. Notre Dame: University of Notre Dame Press, 1996.

Santos, Fernanda, and Rebekah Zemansky. "Death Rate Climbs as Migrants Take Bigger Risks to Cross Tighter Borders." *New York Times*, May 21, 2013, A14.

Saunders, Frances Stonor. *Who Paid the Piper? The CIA and the Cultural Cold War*. London: Granta, 1999.

Saxon, Wolfgang. "Yvonne De Carlo Dies at 84; Played Lily on 'Munsters.'" *New York Times*, January 11, 2007, B6.

Scaggs, John. *Crime Fiction*. London: Routledge, 2005.

Schatz, Thomas. *Boom and Bust: American Cinema in the 1940s*. Berkley and Los Angeles: University of California Press, 1999.

———. *Hollywood Genres: Formulas, Filmmaking, and the Studio System*. Boston, MA: McGraw-Hill, 1981.

Schreiber, Rebecca M. *Cold War Exiles in Mexico: U.S. Dissidents and the Culture of Resistance*. Minneapolis and London: University of Minnesota Press, 2008.

Schueller, Malini Johar. *U.S. Orientalisms: Race, Nation, and Gender in Literature, 1790–1890*. Ann Arbor: University of Michigan Press, 1998.

Secure Border Intelligence. "Hidden Cameras on the Border." Accessed July 23, 2013. http://secureborderintel.org/.

Seed, David. *American Science Fiction and the Cold War: Literature and Film*. Edinburgh: Edinburgh University Press, 1999.

Sharp, Joanne P. *Geographies of Postcolonialism: Spaces of Power and Representation*. Los Angeles and London: Sage, 2009.

Shaw, Donald, and Charles McKenzie. "American Daily Newspaper Evolution: Past, Present…and Future." In *The Function of Newspapers in Society: A Global Perspective*, edited by Shannon E. Martin and David A. Copeland, 135–54. Westport, CT, and London: Praeger, 2003.

Simmon, Scott. *The Invention of the Western Film: A Cultural History of the Genre's First Half-Century*. Cambridge: Cambridge University Press, 2003.

Slotkin, Richard. *The Fatal Environment: The Myth of the Frontier in the Age of Industrialization, 1800–1890*. Middletown, CT: Wesleyan University Press, 1986.

———. *Gunfighter Nation: The Myth of the Frontier in Twentieth-Century America*. New York: Atheneum, 1992.

———. *Regeneration through Violence: The Mythology of the American Frontier, 1600–1860*. Reprint, Norman: University of Oklahoma Press, 2000 [1973].

Smethurst, Paul. *Travel Writing and the Natural World: 1768–1840*. Basingstoke: Palgrave MacMillan, 2013.

Smith, Henry Nash. *Virgin Land: The American West as Symbol and Myth*. 20th anniversary ed. Cambridge, MA, and London: Harvard University Press, 1970.

Sobchack, Vivian. "*The Grapes of Wrath* (1940): Thematic Emphasis through Visual Style." *American Quarterly* 31 (5) (1979): 596–615.

———. *Screening the Space: The American Science Fiction Film*. New York: Ungar, 1987.

Soja, Edward W. *Postmodern Geographies: The Reassertion of Space in Critical Social Theory*. London: Verso, 1989.

———. *Thirdspace: Journeys to Los Angeles and Other Real-and-Imagined Places*. Cambridge, MA, and Oxford, UK: Blackwell Publishers, 1996.

Spener, David, and Kathleen Staudt, eds. *The U.S.-Mexico Border: Transcending Divisions, Contesting Identities*. Boulder, CO, and London: Lynne Rienner, 1998.

Spicer, Andrew. *Historical Dictionary of Film Noir*. Lanham, MD: Scarecrow Press, 2010.

Stacy, Lee. *Mexico and the United States*. New York: Marshall Cavendish, 2003.

Stanfield, Peter. *Hollywood, Westerns and the 1930s: The Lost Trail*. Exeter: Exeter University Press, 2001.

———. *Horse Opera: The Strange History of the 1930s Singing Cowboy*. Urbana: University of Illinois Press, 2002.

"Stars, Production Bolster Fair Story." Rev. of *Borderline* (William Seiter, 1950). *The Hollywood Reporter*, 11, January 1950, 3.

Staudt, Kathleen, and Irasema Coronado. *Fronteras No Más: Towards Social Justice at the U.S.-Mexico Border*. New York: Palgrave Macmillan, 2002.

Steinbeck, John. *The Grapes of Wrath*. Reprint, London: Penguin, 1992 [1939].

Straw, Will. "Documentary Realism and the Postwar Left." In *"Un-American" Hollywood: Politics and Film in the Blacklist Era*, edited by Frank Krutnik, Steve Neale, Brian Neve, and Peter Stanfield, 130–41. New Brunswick, NJ, and London: Rutgers University Press, 2007.

———. "Urban Confidential: The Lurid City of the 1950s." In *The Cinematic City*, edited by David B. Clarke, 110–28. London: Routledge, 1997.

Sturtevant, Victoria. "Spitfire: Lupe Vélez and the Ambivalent Pleasures of Ethnic Masquerade." *The Velvet Light Trap* 55 (2005): 19–32.

Swanson, Philip, ed. *The Companion to Latin American Studies*. London: Arnold, 2003.

Swindell, Larry. *The Last Hero: A Biography of Gary Cooper*. Garden City, NY: Doubleday and Co., Inc., 1980.

Tatum, Charles M. *Chicano Popular Culture: Que Hable el Pueblo*. Tucson: University of Arizona Press.

"Telegram from the Department of State to the Mission at the United Nations," November 1, 1960. In *United Nations and General International Matters*, edited by John P. Glennon, 430–2. Vol. 2 of *Foreign Relations of the United States, 1958–1960*. Washington, DC: United States Government Printing Office, 1991.

Telles, Edward E., and Vilma Ortiz. *Generations of Exclusion: Mexican Americans, Assimilation, and Race*. New York: Russell Sage Foundation, 2008.

Texas Border Patrol. Blueservo.net Border Surveillance Program. Accessed July 23, 2013. http://www.blueservo.net/; accessed July 17, 2015, http://wayback.archive-it.org/all/20130423005812/http://www.blueservo.com/.

Thomas, Victoria. *Hollywood's Latin Lovers: Latino, Italian and French Men Who Make the Screen Smolder*. Santa Monica, CA: Angel City Press, 1998.

Thompson, Howard. "Orson Welles Is Triple Threat in Thriller." Rev. of *Touch of Evil* (Orson Welles, 1958). *New York Times*, May 22, 1958, 25.

Tompkins, Jane. *West of Everything: The Inner Life of Westerns*. New York and Oxford: Oxford University Press, 1993.

Torpey, John. *The Invention of the Passport: Surveillance, Citizenship and the State*. Cambridge: Cambridge University Press, 2000.

Torrans, Thomas. *The Magic Curtain: The Mexican-American Border in Fiction, Film, and Song*. Fort Worth: Texas Christian University Press, 2002.

Torres, Rebecca, and Janet Henshall Momsen. "Gringolandia: Cancún and the American Tourist." In *Adventures into Mexico: American Tourism beyond the Border*, edited by Nicholas Dagen Bloom, 58–73. Lanham, MD, and Oxford, UK: Rowman and Littlefield Publishers, Inc., 2006.

Touch of Evil press pack. British Film Institute National Archive. 1958.

"Treaty of Guadalupe Hidalgo." In *Treaties and Other International Agreements of the United States of America, 1776–1949*, Vol. 9, edited by Charles Bevans, 791–806. Washington, DC: US Department of State, 1972.

Truett, Samuel. *Fugitive Landscapes: The Forgotten History of the U.S.-Mexico Borderlands*. New Haven, CT, and London: Yale University Press, 2006.

Truett, Samuel, and Elliott Young, eds. *Continental Crossroads: Remapping U.S.-Mexico Borderlands History*. Durham, NC: Duke University Press, 2004.

Truffaut, François. Rev. of *Touch of Evil* (Orson Welles, 1958). Translated by Leonard Mayhew in François Truffaut, *The Films in My Life* (New York: Simon and Schuster, 1978). In *Touch of Evil: Orson Welles, Director*, edited by Terry Comito, 229–32. New Brunswick, NJ: Rutgers, 1985. Originally published in *Arts*, June 4, 1958.

Tuan, Yi-Fu. *Topophilia: A Study of Environmental Perception, Attitudes, and Values*. New York: Columbia University Press, 1990.

Turner, Frederick Jackson. "The Significance of the Frontier in American History." 1893. Reprinted in *The Early Writings of Frederick Jackson Turner*, edited by Everett E. Edwards, 185–229. Madison, University of Wisconsin Press: 1938.

Tzioumakis, Yannis. *American Independent Cinema: An Introduction.* Edinburgh: Edinburgh University Press, 2006.

Urry, John. *Mobilities.* Cambridge, UK: Polity Press, 2007.

———. *Sociology beyond Societies: Mobilities for the Twenty-First Century.* London: Routledge, 2000.

———. *The Tourist Gaze: Leisure and Travel in Contemporary Societies*, 2nd ed. London: Sage, 2002.

Vanderwood, Paul J. "An American Cold Warrior: Viva Zapata!" In *American History/American Film: Interpreting the Hollywood Image*, edited by John E. O'Connor and Martin A. Jackson, 183–202. New York: Frederick Ungar Publishing Co., 1979.

———. *Satan's Playground: Mobsters and Movie Stars at America's Greatest Gaming Resort.* Durham, NC: Duke University Press, 2010.

Vanderwood, Paul J., and Frank N. Samponaro. *Border Fury: A Picture Postcard Record of Mexico's Revolution and U.S. War Preparedness, 1910–1917.* Albuquerque: University of New Mexico Press, 1988.

Vaquera-Vásquez, Santiago. "Postcards from the Border: In Tijuana, Revolución Is an Avenue." In *Tijuana Dreaming: Life and Art at the Global Border*, edited by Josh Kun and Fiamma Montezemolo, 117–35. Durham, NC, and London: Duke University Press, 2012.

Vera Cruz press pack. British Film Institute National Archive. 1954.

Vila, Pablo. *Border Identifications: Narratives of Religion, Gender, and Class on the U.S.-Mexico Border.* Austin: University of Texas Press, 2005.

———. *Crossing Borders, Reinforcing Borders: Social Categories, Metaphors, and Narrative Identities on the U.S.-Mexico Frontier.* Austin: University of Texas Press, 2000.

Vulliamy, Ed. *Amexica: War along the Borderline.* London: Vintage, 2011.

Walker, Janet, ed. *Westerns: Films through History.* New York and London: Routledge, 2001.

Weiler, A. H. Rev. of *Borderline* (William A. Seiter, 1950). *New York Times*, March 6, 1950, 17.

Welchman, John C., ed. *Rethinking Borders.* Basingstoke and London: Macmillan Press, 1996.

Welles, Orson. "Heart of Darkness." Film script, 1939. Accessed July 13, 2015. http://www.scribd.com/doc/200623651/Heart-of-Darkness-by-Orson-Welles.

———. *Hello Americans.* CBS Radio. 1942–3.

Welles, Orson. "Memo to Universal." In *This Is Orson Welles*, by Orson Welles and Peter Bogdanovich. Revised ed. edited by Jonathan Rosenbaum, 491–504. New York: Da Capo Press, 1998.

Welles, Orson, and Peter Bogdanovich. *This Is Orson Welles.* Revised ed. Edited by Jonathan Rosenbaum. New York: Da Capo Press, 1998.

Westad, Odd Arne. "The Cold War and the International History of the Twentieth Century." In *The Cambridge History of the Cold War, Volume 1: Origins,* edited by Melvyn P. Leffler and Odd Arne Westad, 1–19. Cambridge: Cambridge University Press, 2010.

"Wetback Action Planned: Mexican President Asserts New Lands Will Be Cultivated." *New York Times,* September 2, 1953, 18.

"Wetback Bill Approved: House Judiciary Committee Will Report Search Measure." *New York Times,* January 25, 1952, 9.

Wetbacks press pack. British Film Institute National Archive. 1956.

White, Armond. "Role Model: How Burt Lancaster Juggled Art, Conscience and Exuberance." *Film Comment* 36 (3) (2000): 30–2.

The White House Office of the Press Secretary. "Fact Sheet: Immigration Accountability Executive Action," November 20, 2014. Accessed February 20, 2015. http://www.whitehouse.gov/the-press-office/2014/11/20/fact-sheet-immigration-accountability-executive-action.

Whitfield, Stephen J. *The Culture of the Cold War.* Baltimore, MD, and London: John Hopkins University Press, 1996.

Wicking, Christopher, and Barrie Pattison. "Interviews with Anthony Mann." *Screen* 10 (4–5) (1969): 32–54.

Wickramasekara, Piyasiri. "Globalisation, International Labour Migration and the Rights of Migrant Workers." In *Globalisation and Migration: New Issues, New Politics,* edited by Ronaldo Munck, 21–38. London: Routledge, 2013.

Williams, Tony. *Body and Soul: The Cinematic Vision of Robert Aldrich.* Lanham, MD, and Oxford: Scarecrow Press, Inc., 2004.

Wilson, Thomas M., and Hastings Donnan, eds. *Border Identities: Nation and State at International Frontiers.* Cambridge: Cambridge University Press, 1998.

Winston, Robert P., and Nancy Mellerski. *The Public Eye: Ideology and the Police Procedural.* Basingstoke: Macmillan, 1992.

Wojcik, Pamela Robertson. *The Apartment Plot: Urban Living in American Film and Popular Culture, 1945–1975.* Durham, NC: Duke University Press, 2010.

Wojcik, Pamela Robertson, and Arthur Knight, eds. *Soundtrack Available: Essays on Film and Popular Music.* Durham, NC, and London: Duke University Press, 2001.

Wollen, Peter. "Foreign Relations: Welles and *Touch of Evil.*" *Sight and Sound* 6 (10) (1996): 20–3.

Wood, Andrew Grant. "How Would You Like an El Camino? U.S. Perceptions of Mexico in Two Recent Hollywood Films." *Journal of the Southwest* 43 (4) (2001): 755–64.

———, ed. *On the Border: Society and Culture between the United States and Mexico.* Lanham, MD, and Oxford: SR Books, 2004.

Wood, Edward. "Motoring in Mexico: Three-Day Trip from Texas to Mexico City Opens Many New Vistas." *New York Times*, December 4, 1949, 24.

Woods, Randall Bennett. *Quest for Identity: America since 1945*. Cambridge: Cambridge University Press, 2005.

Wright, Melissa W. "Necropolitics, Narcopolitics, and Femicide: Gendered Violence on the Mexico-U.S. Border." *Signs* 36 (3) (2011): 707–31.

Wright, Will. *Six Guns and Society: A Structural Study of the Western*. Berkley and London: University of California Press, 1975.

———. *The Wild West: The Mythical Cowboy and Social Theory*. London: Sage, 2001.

Zeta Semanario. Accessed July 12, 2014. http://zetatijuana.com/.

Zureik, Elia, and Mark B. Salter, eds. *Global Surveillance and Policing: Borders, Security, Identity*. Cullompton: Willan, 2005.

Index

CPSIA information can be obtained at www.ICGtesting.com
Printed in the USA
LVOW03*1627221015

459346LV00011B/166/P